Chinese Legal Family and Chinese Modernization of Rule of Law

Xiaobo Dong · Yafen Li

Chinese Legal Family and Chinese Modernization of Rule of Law

Springer

Xiaobo Dong
School of Foreign Languages and Cultures
Nanjing Normal University
Nanjing, Jiangsu, China

Jilin International Studies University
Changchun, Jilin, China

Yafen Li
School of Foreign Languages and Cultures
Nanjing Normal University
Nanjing, Jiangsu, China

School of Foreign Languages
Jiangsu Second Normal University
Nanjing, Jiangsu, China

ISBN 978-981-96-7528-9 ISBN 978-981-96-7529-6 (eBook)
https://doi.org/10.1007/978-981-96-7529-6

This work was supported by National Social Science Fund of China (20AYY008).

This Springer imprint is published by the registered company Springer Nature Singapore Pte Ltd.
The registered company address is: 152 Beach Road, #21-01/04 Gateway East, Singapore 189721, Singapore

Preface

As China's global influence continues to rise, so does the world's interest in understanding the foundations of its governance and legal traditions. The rule of law in China is not merely a product of contemporary reforms but is deeply rooted in centuries of legal evolution, cultural heritage, and governance wisdom. However, despite the increasing global discourse on China's legal modernization, comprehensive works that explore its historical and cultural underpinnings remain scarce.

This book seeks to fill that gap by offering an in-depth examination of the historical and cultural foundations of the Chinese modernization of rule of law. It presents a nuanced analysis of how traditional Chinese legal thought—shaped by Confucian, Legalist, and other indigenous philosophies—has evolved and integrated with modern legal principles to form a distinctive Chinese approach to governance. In particular, a unique feature of this book is its comprehensive insight into the Chinese Legal Family, an influential yet often overlooked legal tradition that once shaped the legal landscapes of East Asia and is now experiencing a revitalization in the new era. We hope that this work will serve as an essential reference for those seeking to understand China's modernization of rule of law, its historical roots, and its future trajectory. In doing so, it aims to bridge knowledge gaps, foster dialogue, and contribute to a more comprehensive global understanding of China's legal culture and governance philosophy.

During the writing of this book, we have received unselfish assistance and strong support from our research team. They have collected and sorted out so many valuable research materials that laid a solid foundation for this book. Therefore, we'd like to direct our deepest gratitude to Geng Xinyi, Song Yuxin, Sun Hui, Wang Lin, and Yang Yuzhi for their altruistic dedication and close cooperation.

Nanjing, China

Xiaobo Dong
Yafen Li

Competing Interests The authors have no competing interests to declare that are relevant to the content of this manuscript.

Contents

Part IV Conclusion

About the Authors

Xiaobo Dong is a Distinguished Professor of Jilin International Studies University and a Professor at School of Foreign Languages and Cultures of Nanjing Normal University, Deputy Director of the Belt and Road Rule of Law Research Center at Academy of China's Modernization of Rule of Law and Researcher at Jiangsu Academy of Talent Development Strategy. He is also Director and Chief Expert of Jiangsu International Rule of Law Research Center, as well as Chief Expert on major programs of the National Social Science Fund of China. His research interests include history of Sino-west civilization exchanges, legal linguistics, legal translation, language policy and planning, cross-cultural communication, as well as area studies. In recent years, he has published over 300 interdisciplinary academic papers and articles in prominent journals and more than 70 books, including academicmonographs, edited volumes, and translations.

Yafen Li is Ph.D. candidate at the School of Foreign Languages and Cultures at Nanjing Normal University and a lecturer at the School of Foreign Languages at Jiangsu Second Normal University. Her research interests include Sino-west civilization exchanges, legal language and translation, and the translation studies of Chinese legal classics.

Part I
The Chinese Legal Family

As one of the five major legal systems in the world, the Chinese Legal Family (中華法系) is a brilliant gem in the Chinese civilization of the rule of law. By grace of its exceptional and enduring national governance system that has been passed down for thousands of years, the Chinese Legal Family encompasses the institutions, ideologies, and culture of the ancient Chinese legal civilization. It was originated during the Xia, Shang, and Zhou dynasties, developed during the Qin and Han dynasties, reached its pinnacle with the *Tang Lü* (《唐律》) (the *Tang Code*), and continued until the late Qing dynasty. Following this historical trajectory, it has gradually formed its own unique evolutionary patterns and spiritual qualities, showcasing the great creativity and profound legal civilization of the Chinese Nation. What's more, it has also exerted profound impacts on such neighboring countries as Japan, Korea, and Annam (modern-day Vietnam).

Throughout history, the excellent traditional Chinese legal culture and the Chinese Legal Family have played indispensable and important roles, serving as crucial means to maintain social order, guide public behavior, and resolve social disputes. As such, the 20th National Congress of the Communist Party of China emphasized the need to inherit the excellent traditional Chinese legal culture and follow a path of socialist rule of law with Chinese characteristics. Against this backdrop, understanding the Chinese Legal Family and exploring its wisdom for inheritance and innovation is both a timely responsibility and an academic mission.

Chapter 1
Historical Origins of the Chinese Legal Family

The term "legal system", or "legal family", refers to "a unique system formed by combining a nation's inherent laws with certain laws adopted from foreign countries or accumulated over a long period in its own history" (Chen 1980: 6). In 1884, Japanese statesman and jurist *Hozumi Nobushige* released the work "Explanation of Five Major Legal Families" in which he first used the term "legal family (in Japanese, *houzoku*)", dividing the world's legal systems into the "Indian Legal Family, Chinese Legal Family, Muslim Legal Family, British Legal Family, and Roman Legal Family", thereby pioneering the study of legal families (Zhang 2018: 3). Subsequently, Western jurists categorized the world's legal systems from different perspectives. For instance, German scholars Josef Kohler and Leopold Wenger, in their 1914 publication *General Legal History* (in German, *Allgemeine Rechtsgeschichte*), categorized the world's legal families into three types: the law of primitive peoples (*das Recht der Primitiven Völker*), the law of the Oriental peoples (*das Recht der Orientalischen Völker*), and the law of the Greek and Roman peoples (*das Recht der Griechen und Römer Völker*). Another instance is American jurist John Henry Wigmore, who in his 1923 article "The Rise, Disappearance, and Transmigration of the World's Legal System" and his 1928 book *A Panorama of the World's Legal Systems*, listed a total of 16 legal systems that have existed globally from ancient times to the present (Yang 1999: 3).

Once introduced, the term "legal system", or "legal family" gained widespread acceptance among legal scholars worldwide. Western comparative law scholars, in particular, classified global legal systems based on common origins, forms, methods, and legislative techniques, drawing on both historical origins and shared characteristics among legal systems. From this perspective, the classification of a legal system primarily focuses on the external forms and historical connections of laws. Laws that share common characteristics or belong to the same tradition constitute a legal system.

X. Dong and Y. Li, *Chinese Legal Family and Chinese Modernization of Rule of Law*,
https://doi.org/10.1007/978-981-96-7529-6_1

1.1 Understanding the Five Major Legal Systems

Currently, the five major legal systems recognized in China are classified by jurists based on the fundamental characteristics of laws in various countries. These include the Civil Law System, the Common Law System, the Islamic Law System, the Indian Law System, and the Chinese Legal Family. Over the past century, different classification methods such as the "Seven-Category Method", "Sixteen-Category Method", and "Three-Category Method" have emerged, but all recognize the Chinese Legal Family as an independent legal system. In other words, regardless of the classification method, the Chinese Legal Family stands out as an important member due to its profound historical background and unique national characteristics. Its past glory has earned it a distinctive place in the history of world legal systems.

The Civil Law System, also known as the Romano-Germanic Law System, is a continuation of ancient Roman law, exemplified by the *French Civil Code* (the *Napoleonic Code*) and the *German Civil Code* (The *Bürgerliches Gesetzbuc*h, abbreviated *BGB*). It is prevalent in countries on the European continent, so in Chinese it is also known as the "*Da Lu FaXi*" (大陆法系) (the Continental Law System). Alongside the Common Law System, it forms one of the two most significant legal systems in the world today. The origins of the Civil Law System can be traced back to ancient Rome. After a period of decline, Roman law regained prominence on the European continent during the late Middle Ages (approximately the twelfth to the fifteenth centuries). By the eighteenth century, many countries on the European continent had enacted codified laws, attempting to enumerate the regulations for various branches of law, hence the Civil Law System is also referred to as the Codified Law System.

The Common Law System, so named because it was "common" to all the king's courts across England, originated in the practices of the courts of the English kings in the centuries following the Norman Conquest in 1066. The British Empire later spread the English legal system to its colonies, many of which retain the Common Law System Today. In other words, the Common Law System first emerged in England and later spread to many countries and regions that were once British colonies or dependencies, including the United States, Canada, India, Pakistan, Bangladesh, Malaysia, Singapore, South Korea, and certain countries and regions in Africa. The Common Law System relies on tradition, judicial precedent, and customs as the basis for judicial decisions, which is why common law is also called judge-made law, or case law.

The Islamic Law System, also known as the Arab Law System, is a body of laws which developed in medieval Arab countries and other Muslim-majority nations that follow Islam. This system encompasses the *Quran*, Hadith (Prophetic traditions), the Fiqh, and indigenous Arab traditions. Especially, the *Quran* contains numerous legal principles and is the primary source of the Islamic law. The Hadith, which interprets and supplements the *Quran*, is the second most important source of the Islamic law. The Fiqh consists of interpretations and developments of Islamic legal principles from the *Quran* and Hadith by renowned jurists, which is essentially the activity of legal innovation to address territorial expansion and the increasing complexity of social life. Indigenous Arab traditions include ancient Arabian beliefs and practices for resolving civil and commercial disputes, which remain valid only if they are not in conflict with Islamism or have been adapted by Muhammad into the Islamic doctrine.

The Indian Law System encompasses the Indian laws and those influenced by such legal principles in other countries. The Indian law was developed on the foundations of Brahmanical law, with the *Manusmriti* (Laws of Manu) as its most notable representation, and other ancient traditions. The *Manusmriti* is a compilation of ancient Indian religious, philosophical, and legal precepts that aimed to uphold theocratic governance and is imbued with strong religious and caste-based characteristics. This body of law once extended its influence to parts of Central and Southeast Asia, including regions like Ceylon (modern-day Sri Lanka), Siam (modern-day Thailand), Burma (modern-day Myanmar), and the Philippines. While the Indian Law System is now a historical term, traces of these ancient laws still persist in the cultural practices of its people.

1.2 The Chinese Legal Family and Its Development Trajectory

The Chinese Legal Family, to a certain extent, encompasses the systems, thoughts, and culture of all the ancient Chinese laws. In a narrow sense, this legal family refers to the legal system emerged and developed under specific social and historical conditions in ancient China, marked fundamentally by the integration of rites and laws, centered around written penal codes, and exemplified by the *Tang Lü Shu Yi* (《唐律疏議》) (the *Tang Code with Commentaries*). In a large sense, the Chinese Legal Family also includes the legal systems of those East Asian countries that emulated the Chinese law. Originated from the cultural soil of the Chinese nation, the Chinese Legal Family represents the fusion of the wisdom of ancient sages and the culmination of governance experiences. Throughout its long historical trajectory, this legal system played a significant role in maintaining national stability and unity, promoting ethnic solidarity, and disseminating the Chinese civilization.

As the only ancient legal system in the world that remained uninterrupted through changes in dynasties and remained free from the influence of other legal systems, the Chinese Legal Family has persisted for over two thousand years. It "began with the compilation of the *Fa Jing* (《法經》) (the *Canon of Laws*) by Li Kui (李悝) during the Warring States period, then underwent evolutionary development during the Qin, Han, Wei, Jin, Southern and Northern dynasties, and reached a mature stage during the Sui and Tang Dynasties. Subsequently, it was inherited and continued through the Song, Yuan, Ming, and Qing Dynasties" (Qiao 1986: 44).

1.2.1 The Nascent Stage

1. **The theocratic law of the Xia and Shang dynasties**

The Xia and Shang dynasties marked the initial formation and development of ancient China's legal system, characterized by a strong theocratic nature.

Around the twenty-first century BCE, Yu the Great (大禹) of the Xia dynasty replaced the system of abdication practiced by tribal alliance leaders and passed the throne to his son, Xia Qi (夏啓), thus beginning the history of "*Jia Tian Xia*" (家天下) (family-based rule). The establishment of this regime deviated from the previous tradition of tribal alliance leaders appointing the virtuous and capable as successors. To legitimize this family-based rule, the Xia regime proclaimed that they ruled by "*Tian Ming*" (天命) (the mandate of Heaven), invoking the reverence of the common people towards "*Tian*" (天) (Heaven) and "*Shen*" (神) (Divinity). Inheriting this idea, Cheng Tang (成湯), the founder of the Shang dynasty, similarly proclaimed the slogan of "*Tian Fa*" (天罰) (the punishment of Heaven), asserting that they acted on behalf of Heaven to punish the tyrant and launched the war to overthrow the Xia dynasty and establish the Shang. As stated in the chapter "Ode to the Shang" in *Shi Jing* (《詩經》) (the *Book of Songs*): "Heaven commissioned the dark bird, which descended to give birth to the Shang."

The establishment of the Xia and Shang regimes was deeply imbued with theocratic characteristics, which were reflected in their legal systems as the theocratic law. Judicial trials during the Xia and Shang dynasties primarily employed the method of "*Shen Pan*" (神判) (Divine Judgments), a judicial practice rooted in the theocratic ideology. The so-called "Divine Judgments" involved determining guilt and punishment based on the will of the gods. During this period, two primary methods of divine judgments were used: one was divination-based rulings, which involved interpreting the will of the gods through divination using turtle shells; the other was mythical beast rulings, where cases were decided by the legendary creature "*Xie Zhi*" (獬豸), a one-horned goat symbolizing judicial fairness in ancient mythology.

The "Divine Judgments" that emerged during the early stages of the Chinese Legal Family was a product of early human societies. It originated from experiences shaped by tribal customs, religious beliefs and other aspects of life. It represents a reflection of people's understanding of the world and their attempts to address conflicts through judicial practice, making its existence inevitable. Although this mystical form of judicial judgment gradually faded in later developments, we should not judge the ancient people's "ignorance" through a modern lens. In the history of the development of legal systems, the Western practice of "Divine Judgments" also existed for a long period. In the early stages of human history, this was the most effective way to resolve conflicts based on humanity's understanding of the world at the time.

2. **The rites and laws of the Western Zhou**

In the eleventh century BCE, King Wu of Zhou (周武王) overthrew the tyrant King Zhou of the Shang dynasty (商纣王) and established the Zhou dynasty, known in history as the Western Zhou. During the war against Shang, the founders of the Western Zhou clearly recognized the immense power of the common people, and it was their support that led to the ultimate victory. Therefore, the Zhou dynasty urgently needed a new political theory to justify the legitimacy of its rule, so the theory of "*Yi De Pei Tian*" (以德配天) (matching virtue with Heaven) was proposed by the Duke of Zhou (周公) in this context. According to this theory, only those with virtue are qualified to be the representatives of Heaven, and as a ruler, one must constantly cultivate their own virtues, or else they risk being replaced by others who possess more virtues.

This concept has influenced China for thousands of years. Guided by this idea, the Western Zhou developed the legal thought of "*Ming De Shen Fa*" (明德慎罰), which refers to the promotion of virtue and the imposition of penalty with prudence. "*Ming De*" (the promotion of virtue) was a requirement for rulers to respect Heaven and protect their people, ensuring that they implemented benevolent governance according to Heaven's will, while caring for and loving their people. This legal thought was also reflected in the application of criminal laws as "*Shen Fa*" (the imposition of penalty with prudence), which simply means to be cautious with the use of punishments and avoid the unjust killing of innocents. In judicial trials, emphasis on the subjective aspects of the crimes led to the differentiation between intentional crimes and negligent crimes.

Under the guidance of the legal thought of "*Ming De Shen Fa*", the Western Zhou gradually established a legal system that integrated "*Li*" (禮) (rites) and "*Fa*" (法) (laws), with *Li* becoming an important source of law during this period. As one of the key manifestations of law in the Western Zhou, *Li* held a core position in the legal system. When measured against modern legal systems, *Li* could be seen as equivalent to today's constitution, serving as the "mother law" with the highest level of authority. The formulation of other laws could not contradict *Li*. The core ideas of "*Zhou Li*" (周禮) (the rites of Zhou), namely "*Qin Qin*" (親親) (proximity to kin) and "*Zun Zun*" (尊尊) (respect for superiors), were employed to maintain the hierarchical social order and promote social harmony and stability. The concept of *Qin Qin* reflects the importance of familial relationships, emphasizing closeness to one's kin and the maintenance of ethical and moral order within the family, rooted in the patriarchal and kinship-based hierarchy. The concept of *Zun Zun* required respect and absolute obedience to those deserving respect, such as rulers by their subjects, superiors by their subordinates, and the noble by the common people, thus preserving the hierarchical structure of society. At its core, *Qin Qin* was centered on "*Xiao*" (孝) (filial piety), while *Zun Zun* was grounded in "*Zhong*" (忠) (loyalty). These principles ensured the efficacy of *Zhou Li* by safeguarding patriarchal and monarchical authority. When a conflict arose between the two, "*Zhong Jun*" (忠君) (loyalty to the ruler) took precedence, reflecting the ultimate protection of the ruling class's authority.

1.2.2 The Development Stage

1. **The codified laws of the Spring and Autumn and Warring States periods**

The Spring and Autumn and Warring States periods mark a time of great turbulence in Chinese history, as well as a significant transformation in the history of legal civilization. Prior to this era, ancient Chinese law was characterized by laws without formal codification. During the Spring and Autumn period, written laws and legal codes began to emerge (Chen 2011: 61–62).

During the Spring and Autumn period, the earliest codified laws were created by the State of Chu. Under the reign of King Wen of Chu (楚文王), the "*Pu Qu Fa*" (《仆區法》) (*Law of Puqu*) was enacted. The term "*Puqu*" means concealment, and the law was mainly used to punish the crime of harboring stolen goods. And later, during the reign of King Zhuang of Chu (楚莊王), the "*Mao Men Fa*" (《茆門法》) (*Law of Maomen*) was established, which stipulated that when "*Zhu Hou*" (諸侯) (feudal lords), "*Da Fu*" (大夫) (ministers), and "*Gong Zi*" (公子) (young nobles) entered the court through *Maomen* (the Mao Gate), their carriages were not allowed to enter the palace gates to ensure the safety of "*Tian Zi*" (天子) (the Son of Heaven). Subsequently, the States of Jin and Song also enacted some codified laws. Although these feudal states created written laws, they were not publicly disclosed, and the laws still retained an element of secrecy. It was only in the later part of the Spring and Autumn period that codified laws began to be officially published to the public. In 536 BCE, Zichan (子産) in the State of Zheng inscribed laws on a bronze *ding* (鼎) (a type of vessel) and made them publicly known, marking the first official publication of a codified law in ancient China. Zichan, a nobleman and the prime minister of Zheng, responded to the demands of the emerging landowning class amid the power struggles among various feudal states, and decided to publicly announce the laws to the public. This legal reform motivated the productivity of the emerging landowning class and provided certain protections for the rights of the common people. Thereafter, the populace could foresee the legal consequences of their actions according to the law. In this case, when their property was damaged or their personal safety threatened, they could defend themselves based on the legal code. The spirit of "legalism" began to take root, and the legal system that required all matters to be decided by law gradually replaced the "secrecy-based" legal system. Thus, Zichan can be regarded as the first person in Chinese history to advocate "*Yi Fa Zhi Guo*" (以法治國), which means governing the country by law.

Following Zichan, the minister of Zheng, Deng Xi (鄧析), "privately compiled" a penal code known as the "*Zhu Xing*" (竹刑) (Bamboo Criminal Laws) and inscribed them on bamboo strips. Aside from drafting and announcing the criminal laws, Deng Xi also established a law school where he taught legal knowledge and instructed people on how to litigate. Although Deng Xi was later executed for "illegally creating the Bamboo Criminal Laws", the code gained legal validity after his death because it aligned with the trends of the time. It was subsequently adopted by the rulers. It can be argued that any legal reform must align with the historical trajectory and tendencies of the time to effectively advance social progress.

The publication of codified laws during the Spring and Autumn period had a significant impact on the establishment of "Legalist" thought in the Warring States period, especially evident in the two most representative legal codes of that time: the *Fa Jing* (《法經》) (the *Canon of Laws*) created by Li Kui (李悝) of the State of Wei and the *Qin Lü* (《秦律》) (*Qin Code*) formulated by Shang Yang (商鞅) of the State of Qin. During the reign of Duke Wen of Wei (魏文侯), in order to strengthen the state and military, Li Kui was appointed as prime minister to carry out legal reforms. Li Kui, known as the founder of Legalism, is regarded as the first reformer in Chinese history, with later figures such as Shang Yang and Han Fei (韓非) being greatly influenced by him. Li Kui implemented comprehensive reforms in areas such as the economy, politics, and legal systems, with his legal reforms having the most profound impact on later generations. Li Kui believed that the primary function of the law was to "settle disputes and clarify divisions", such as clearly defining property ownership so that the owners would not have to worry about losing their property without any legal justification. Drawing on the legislative experiences of other states, he created Wei's first codified law, the *Fa Jing*.

The *Fa Jing* itself has been lost to history, and now only fragments of its contents can be found in historical records. According to these records, the *Fa Jing* consisted of six sections: *Dao Fa* (盗法) (Law on theft and robbery), *Zei Fa* (賊法) (Law on treason), *Qiu Fa* (囚法) (Law on prisoner or extent of justice), *Bu Fa* (捕法) (Law of arrest), *Za Fa* (雜法) (Miscellaneous Laws), and *Ju Fa* (具法) (General principles of sentencing). Its primary focus was to punish thieves and maintain the personal and property safety of the emerging landowning class. Although the legislative structure of the *Fa Jing* was relatively simple, it already contained some basic elements of modern criminal law, such as a "general provisions" section that defined crimes and punishments, and "specific provisions" for different types of offenses. In addition to substantive laws, it also included elements of procedural law. This codified legal system had a profound impact on the development of later legal codes and pioneered a distinctive legislative model that became a hallmark of the Chinese Legal Family.

In the various legal reform movements of the Warring States period, the reforms of Shang Yang in the State of Qin were implemented relatively late, but they achieved the greatest success. According to historical records, Shang Yang's reforms were carried out in two phases and lasted a total of 18 years. The State of Qin, through these reforms, became the most powerful state among the Seven Warring States.

Shang Yang was deeply influenced by the ideas in Li Kui's *Fa Jing*, but his reforms were not simply a replication of its contents. During Zichan's time, laws were often inscribed on bronze vessels, and the legal system was more of a tool for class suppression, focusing primarily on the punitive aspect of the law. After Li Kui's reforms, the name of law changed from "*Xing*" (刑) to "*Fa*" (法) and the focus shifted from punishment to law itself, highlighting the fairness and justice of legal principles. Shang Yang, however, reformed the system into "*Lü*" (律), emphasizing consistency and uniformity in their application. This transformation laid the foundation for the legal structure that would dominate China for thousands of years, where most dynasties adopted unified legal codes known as *Lü*. Beyond these formal changes, Shang

Yang's reforms also introduced new offenses, such as punishment for witchcraft, including the act of abandoning ash in the streets as a crime.

2. **The harsh legal system of the Qin dynasty**

In the legal reforms of the Warring States period, the reforms in the State of Qin came relatively late, but they achieved the greatest success. Shang Yang's reforms rapidly strengthened the power of Qin. After Ying Zheng (嬴政) ascended the throne, he waged large-scale wars and gradually conquered the other six states. In 221 BCE, he unified China, establishing the first centralized imperial state, and became the first emperor in Chinese history, Emperor Qin Shi Huang (秦始皇).

After unifying the country, Emperor Qin continued to apply Legalist principles to govern the state, ruling based on law. The concept of "all matters decided by law" (事皆决于法) emphasized the crucial role of law in both national governance and regulating the lives of the people. The Qin legal system, as the unified law code in China's first centralized state, played a significant role in the development of the Chinese Legal Family. However, it is important to recognize that in order to maintain and consolidate its centralized rule, the Qin dynasty advocated for a regime of harsh punishments, establishing an extensive, complex, and brutal penal system. The harshness of the Qin legal system was evident in its complex and brutal methods of executing the death penalty. In addition, the Qin penal system also imposed harsh forms of "*Tu Xing*" (徒刑) or "*Lao Yi Xing*" (劳役刑), which referred to penal servitude. This punishment provided much of the manpower used during the Qin dynasty to construct the Great Wall, palaces, and tombs. The strictness of Qin law was also reflected in the regulations regarding certain crimes, particularly those related to the consolidation of imperial power and state security.

It should be noted that the harsh punishments of the Qin Dynasty were still based on the principle of "punishment according to the law". Emperor Qin Shi Huang advocated that everything must be done in accordance with the law. The Qin penal system also reflected the concept of "rule of law", which remains valuable even within modern legal frameworks. For example, Qin law stipulated that individuals who voluntarily surrendered or took steps to mitigate the harm caused by their crimes would receive reduced or waived penalties. This principle of sentencing is still visible in modern Chinese criminal law. These legal provisions not only had a profound impact on later legal systems, but even today, these laws, infused with the spirit of the rule of law, continue to shine.

3. **The benevolent governance in the Han dynasty**

Under the influence of Qin's harsh legal system and years of warfare, Liu Bang (劉邦), upon establishing the Han Dynasty, implemented a policy of "*Wu Wei Er Zhi*" (無爲而治) (non-intervention governance) and focused on recuperation and restoration. Beyond the objective social conditions, Liu Bang and his ruling group's grassroots background enabled them to empathize with the sentiments of ordinary people: hatred of brutal rule and longing for a just society. This understanding laid a foundation for the non-intervention governance. Consequently, the Han Dynasty removed some of the most brutal provisions of Qin's legal code.

After Liu Bang occupied the Guanzhong region, he made the famous "*Yue Fa San Zhang*" (約法三章) (Three Articles of Law) with the local elders, which was primarily a temporary measure to win popular support. Once he had unified the country, he instructed Xiao He (蕭何) to draft a formal legal code. Xiao He revised the Qin legal system and created the Han Dynasty's legal framework, known as the *Jiu Zhang Lü* (《九章律》) (the *Nine Chapters Law*), which comprised nine categories of laws. When Emperor Wu of Han (漢武帝) ascended the throne, the Han Dynasty had already achieved significant socio-economic development through the recuperative efforts of Emperor Gaozu (漢高祖, i.e. 劉邦) and the "*Wen Jing zhi Zhi*" (文景之治), a prosperous time under the reign of Emperor Wen (漢文帝) and Emperor Jing (漢景帝). Recognizing the need for active governance, Emperor Wu shifted away from the earlier non-intervention governance and embraced Confucian ideology to guide social management. Following Dong Zhongshu (董仲舒)'s proposal, the policy of "*Ba Chu Bai Jia, Du Zun Ru Shu*" (罷黜百家,獨尊儒術) (Rejecting the Hundred Schools and Exclusively Respecting Confucianism) was adopted. From that point until the fall of the Qing Dynasty, Confucianism dominated as the official national ideology. This shift significantly influenced the Han Dynasty's legal system, as Confucian principles became deeply embedded in its laws, marking the beginning of the Confucianization of Chinese legal institutions.

In governing the state, Confucianism advocated for rulers to implement "*Ren Zheng*" (仁政) (benevolent governance), emphasizing kindness and leniency toward the people rather than relying on harsh punishments to enforce obedience—a philosophy fundamentally different from the Legalist thoughts, which were advocated in the Qin Dynasty. To integrate Confucian ideals into the legal system, Dong Zhongshu proposed interpreting current laws through the lens of Confucian principles, particularly as found in the *Chun Qiu* (《春秋》) (the *Spring and Autumn Annals*), a classic Confucian text. This practice, known as "*Chun Qiu Jue Yu*" (春秋決獄) (judging cases by the *Chun Qiu)*, involved using the principles and precedents recorded in *Chun Qiu* as the basis for judicial decisions. Moreover, Dong Zhongshu deemed the *Gongyang Zhuan* (《公羊傳》) (the *Gongyang Commentary*), which he believed accurately reflected Confucius' teachings, as an authoritative guide in judicial practice.

Another manifestation of Confucian influence in the judicial practice of the Han Dynasty was the implementation of seasonal timing for executions. Dong Zhongshu argued that spring and summer represent the seasons of growth and vitality, while autumn and winter signify the seasons of decline and withering. He proposed that the administration of capital punishment should align with the natural rhythm of the seasons. Executing death sentences during autumn and winter, when nature undergoes its austere phase, would reflect the ruler's *Ren Zheng* and ensure peace and long-term stability for the empire. Consequently, except for crimes of extreme treason or grave immorality, most executions were postponed until the period between *Li Qiu* (立秋) (the beginning of autumn) and *Dong Zhi* (冬至) (the winter solstice). This restriction on the timing of executions not only curbed the excessive use of capital punishment but also embodied Confucian ideals of "*Shen Fa*" (慎罰) (the imposition of penalty with prudence). This practice significantly influenced later legal systems. For instance, the *Tang Lü* (《唐律》) (the *Tang Code*) explicitly prohibited executions after *Li Chun* (立春) (the start of spring), and the "*Hui Shen*" (會審) (joint trial) system during the Ming and Qing dynasties—where death sentences were reviewed and deliberated—traced its origins to this concept. The integration of execution timing with the cycles of nature and Confucian ethical reasoning is a distinctive feature of the development of the Chinese Legal Family, showcasing its unique synthesis of moral philosophy and legal practice.

Under the influence of the Confucian ideal of *Ren Zheng*, the Han Dynasty also established the judicial systems of "*Yi Yu Zou Yan*" (疑獄奏讞) and "*Lu Qiu*" (錄囚). *Yi Yu Zou Yan*, or the reporting and adjudication of complex cases, was essentially a hierarchical system for handling difficult legal disputes. When encountering a case that could not be resolved, judicial officials were required to report it step by step up the chain of command. Skipping levels in the reporting process was strictly prohibited. If the case remained unresolved even by the highest judicial authority, it would be submitted to the emperor for a final decision. *Lu Qiu* or the reviewing of prisoners, on the other hand, served as a supervisory mechanism in which higher judicial authorities reviewed the work of lower courts. Senior officials would personally interrogate detained suspects and record their findings to ensure that the trials conducted by subordinate officials were legal, accurate, and free from errors or wrongful convictions. In essence, *Yi Yu Zou Yan* functioned as a reporting system, while *Lu Qiu* acted as a supervisory system. Together, they aimed to prevent miscarriages of justice and wrongful convictions by combining upward reporting with downward supervision. These measures helped ensure consistency in judicial practices across the empire and contributed to maintaining fairness, justice, and the authority of the judiciary. These systems exemplify the Han Dynasty's judicial implementation of the principle of "*Ming De Shen Fa*" (明德慎罰) (the promotion of virtue and the imposition of penalty with prudence), a central tenet of Confucian governance.

1.2.3 The Maturation Stage

1. **The Tang Lü Shu Yi**

The laws of the Tang Dynasty, although revised based on the legal framework of the Sui Dynasty, embodied a vastly different spirit. While the Sui laws were harsh and severe, the Tang laws were more lenient and humane, reflecting the open-minded social atmosphere and flourishing economy and culture of the Tang era. Building on the legislative experience of previous dynasties, Tang lawmakers continuously revised the legal code and, during the reign of Emperor Gaozong (唐高宗), promulgated the *Yong Hui Lü* (《永徽律》) (the *Yonghui Code*), accompanied by interpretative "*Shu Yi*" (疏議) (commentaries) appended to the legal text. The commentaries were granted the same authority as the laws themselves, forming the *Tang Lü Shu Yi* (《唐律疏議》) (the *Tang Code with Commentaries*). As an outstanding achievement of Tang legislation, *Tang Lü Shu Yi* stands as a representative legal text of the Chinese Legal Family. It not only served as the model for subsequent dynasties' legal systems but was also adopted by neighboring countries such as Japan and Korea at that time.

To gain a comprehensive understanding of *Tang Lü Shu Yi*, it is necessary to explore the sources of the guiding philosophy behind Tang Dynasty's legislation. The founder of the Tang Dynasty, Li Yuan (李淵), was originally a general of the Sui Dynasty and witnessed the rise and fall of the Sui Empire. Reflecting on the swift collapse of the previous dynasty, the rulers of the Tang Dynasty recognized the critical role of law in governance. Not only must ordinary citizens respect and obey the law, but government officials must also act in accordance with legal provisions and cannot exercise power beyond the scope of the law. Furthermore, to maintain social order and stability, moral education must also play a key role in governance. Therefore, *Tang Lü Shu Yi* clearly states the fundamental principle of governance: "virtue and rites are the foundation for governance, while punishment serves as its support" (德禮爲政教之本,刑罰爲政教之用). In other words, ruling a nation requires both moral governance and legal governance—moral governance is the foundation, while legal governance is the tool. The people must be educated, while the subjects must also be punished when necessary.

After Emperor Wu of the Han Dynasty elevated Confucianism as the national ideology, the Han rulers began to combine Confucian principles with legal governance, interpreting the laws of the time through Confucian thought. By the time of "*Sheng Tang*" (盛唐) (Golden Age of the Tang dynasty), the integration of rites and laws emerged, with the formalization of ritual norms through legal codification. Confucian "moral governance" required rulers to practice benevolent rule, to consider the welfare of the people, reduce taxes, moderate punishments, and ensure that the people could live in peace, without fear of arbitrary taxation or concerns about the safety of their property and personal well-being. "*Li*" (禮) (rites), on the other hand, emphasized that each social class should fulfill its proper role and adhere to their respective duties, regulating and restraining their lives and work according to Confucian *Li*. This principle of governance was the fundamental approach of the Tang rulers in national governance.

Tang Lü Shu Yi consists of 20 chapters and 502 articles. It begins with general provisions known as "*Ming Li*" (明例), which are akin to the general principles section in modern criminal law, outlining general rules for defining crimes, sentencing, and the legislative definitions of specialized legal terms. Following this, the specific provisions on substantive crimes are detailed, and finally, there are procedural regulations. Through legal codification, *Tang Lü Shu Yi* formally legalized Confucian *Li*. This differs from the Han Dynasty's approach, where Confucian *Li* was used to explain laws—while such interpretations were legally significant, *Li* remained secondary in terms of form. In the Tang Dynasty, however, the laws and the rites were treated as having equal legal standing, meaning that failing to adhere to the rites was regarded as a violation of the law. The Confucian *Li* emphasizes the maintenance of hierarchical and familial relationships. In ancient times, these hierarchical relationships were concentrated in the authority of the ruler, father, husband, and family head. Any challenge to the emperor's dignity or the disruption of the respected person's status within the family or clan was considered a violation of Confucian *Li*, and a violation of *Li* was equivalent to breaking the law. Using a breach of *Li* as the basis for criminal responsibility and imposing different punishments according to one's rank and status is a key feature of the Chinese Legal Family during its maturation stage.

In *Tang Lü Shu Yi*, the legal codification of *Li* is reflected in several institutional designs, including "*Shi E*" (十惡) (the Ten Abominations), "*Ba Yi*" (八議) (the Eight Deliberations), the system of "*Guan Dang*" (官當) (Rank-for-Punishment Commutation), and the use of "*Wu Fu*" (五服) (the Five Degrees of Mourning Attire) to determine punishments. The ten most serious crimes in *Tang Lü Shu Yi* are defined as *Shi E*, with the code explicitly prescribing severe punishments. Moreover, the crimes listed as *Shi E* are not subject to pardon, which corresponds to the well-known saying, "*Shi E Bu She*" (十惡不赦), meaning the ten abominations are unforgivable. Regardless of the social status, there is generally no possibility of leniency for the offender of *Shi E*. But for crimes other than the *Shi E*, the punishment may vary depending on the perpetrator's status. This reflects the Confucian principle of respecting hierarchy and ranks, and is an embodiment of *Li* in legal practice. The *Ba Yi* system is one such example, which refers to the special treatment given to eight kinds of individuals of special status when they are suspected of committing a crime. In addition to *Ba Yi*, the Tang law also continued the *Guan Dang* system, which was created during the Northern and Southern dynasties. The *Tang Lü Shu Yi* provides very detailed provisions on this system. As an extension of *Ba Yi*, the *Guan Dang* system also reflects the Confucian belief in distinctions of rank and status. In simple terms, it allows an official to substitute for punishment, but this cannot be applied to the death penalty. Only punishments below the level of "*Liu Xing*" (流刑) (banishment) can be commuted. Lastly, the use of *Wu Fu* to determine punishments reflects the respect for hierarchical social structures within common people. In other words, punishment is determined based on the closeness of kinship and status as represented by the five degrees of mourning attire, essentially upholding the family hierarchy.

In terms of the penal system, the Tang dynasty continued to use the "*Wu Xing*" (五刑) (Five Punishments) system established in the Sui dynasty's *Kaihuang Lü* (《開皇律》) (the *Kaihuang Code*), but with some new improvements. The *Wu Xing* prescribed in the Tang law were classified into twenty levels based on severity: five levels for "*Chi Xing*" (笞刑) (light-stick beating), five levels for "*Zhang Xing*" (杖刑) (heavy-stick beating), five levels for "*Tu Xing*" (徒刑) (penal servitude), three levels for "*Liu Xing*" (流刑) (banishment), and two levels for "*Si Xing*" (死刑) (death penalty). The lightest punishment, *Chi Xing*, involved striking the criminal's buttocks or legs with legal-specification bamboo sticks, divided into five levels ranging from 10 to 50 strikes, with an additional 10 strikes for each level, typically used for minor offenses or negligence. *Zhang Xing*, which involved striking the criminal's buttocks, legs, or back with a legal-specification "*Chang Xing Zhang*" (常行杖) (a standard rod), divided into five levels ranging from 50 to 100 strikes, with an additional 10 strikes for each level, slightly harsher than *Chi Xing*. *Tu Xing* deprived the criminal of personal freedom for a fixed term, forcing them to wear shackles while working. The term ranged from 1 to 3 years, divided into five levels, each increasing by six months, serving both a humiliating and enslaving function. *Liu Xing* involved sending the criminal to a distant border region for penal servitude while shackled for one year, with no permission to return to their hometown. The exile distance ranged from 2000 to 3000 *li* (里) (a unit of distance: 1 *li* is approximately 0.5 km), divided into three levels, each increasing by 500 *li*, a punishment only less severe than the death penalty. *Si Xing* deprived the criminal of their life and was the most severe punishment. It was divided into two levels: "*Zhan*" (斬) (decapitation) and "*Jiao*" (絞) (strangulation), with *Jiao* being slightly lighter due to the preservation of the body. One distinctive feature of *Tang Lü Shu Yi*'s regulation on *Wu Xing* was the use of Confucian texts to explain the rationale behind these punishments. For example, when regulating *Liu Xing*, the code referenced a passage from the *Shang Shu* (《尚書》) (the *Book of Documents*), which explained that those whom the authorities are reluctant to execute should be pardoned and banished to distant places. The *Wu Xing* system established by *Tang Lü Shu Yi* became a template for the penal system of the Chinese Legal Family, continuing to be used until the end of the Qing Dynasty.

2. ***Jiao Zi* banks and free trade in the Song dynasty**

The Song dynasty witnessed a period of commercial prosperity in imperial China. The rapid development of private landownership and the tenancy system created favorable conditions for the circulation and exchange of goods. To promote economic growth, the Song rulers adjusted their economic policies, placing emphasis on commercial development while also strengthening legal protections for merchants. As a result, civil and commercial legislation reached an unprecedented level.

The prosperity of the commodity economy led to the emergence of large cities, where commercial trade flourished on an unprecedented scale. Transactions often reached millions in monetary value, posing a challenge to the traditional currency system. In Chengdu, a thriving city at the time, financial institutions specializing in cash deposit services emerged. Merchants entrusted their cash to these institutions, which recorded the deposit amount on paper rolls made from mulberry bark and issued them to depositors in exchange for a custody fee. These temporary deposit slips, known as "*Jiao Zi*" (交子), became the earliest form of paper money in China. The name *Jiao Zi* derived from the Sichuan dialect, meaning "voucher" or "ticket". The institutions managing these deposits, known as *Jiao Zi* banks, were the earliest financial institutions in Chinese history.

Although *Jiao Zi* was recognized by local governments, the central government did not prohibit private issuance of *Jiao Zi* until 1023. That year, the government established an official agency in Chengdu to exclusively issue state-sanctioned *Jiao Zi*. From then on, the central government formally recognized *Jiao Zi* as legal currency, setting regulations on its circulation period, issuance limits, denominations, circulation areas, and exchange rates with iron coins. Additionally, banks were required to maintain a certain amount of statutory reserves, and anyone caught forging *Jiao Zi* would be punished according to the law.

The prosperity of commerce in the Song dynasty and the corresponding legislative developments were not limited to the issuance of *Jiao Zi*. The government also enacted other special laws to build what could be called an "industrial and commercial kingdom" in the Song dynasty. These legislative measures primarily focused on market regulation, the circulation of goods, and taxation of merchants. The flourishing commercial economy was also linked to advancements in civil law. Song dynasty laws saw significant improvements in areas such as land ownership, sales contracts, and property inheritance. However, it is important to note that even during the height of commercial prosperity in the Song dynasty, the legislative framework followed a system of "*Zhu Fa He Ti*" (諸法合體) (a unified legal system), meaning there was no dedicated civil code or independent commercial law. Instead, laws related to civil and commercial matters remained embedded within the criminal code. This was a defining characteristic of the Chinese Legal Family, and it was not until the late Qing legal reforms—when the Chinese Legal Family began to decline—that this legislative model started to change.

1.2.4 The Decline Stage

1. **Laws in the Ming dynasty**

The *Da Ming Lü* (大明律) (the *Great Ming Code*) was the fundamental and most important legal code of the Ming dynasty. After Zhu Yuanzhang (朱元璋) was crowned King of Wu, he ordered the *Zuo Cheng Xiang* (左丞相) (Left Prime Minister), Li Shanchang (李善長), to draft the laws. After 30 years of revisions, the final version was promulgated nationwide. Zhu Yuanzhang devoted immense effort to the *Da Ming Lü*, personally reviewing and approving nearly every provision, making it the ultimate legal embodiment of his governance. Upon its enactment, Zhu Yuanzhang mandated that his descendants adhere strictly to the code, and any officials who proposed amendments would be punished for the crime of "*Bian Luan Zu Zhi*" (變亂祖制) (disrupting the ancestral system). The *Da Ming Lü* represented a departure from the outdated legislative customs of the Yuan dynasty and reestablished the legislative tradition of the Chinese Legal Family, while also introducing new refinements and modifications. Compared to the legal codes of the Tang and Song dynasties, it was more concise and straightforward, consisting of seven sections, 30 volumes, and 460 articles, making it the most succinct legal code in Chinese history.

In the third revision of the *Da Ming Lü*, the central government abolished the *Zhong Shu Sheng* (中書省) (the Grand Council) and the position of *Zai Xiang* (宰相) (Prime Minister), consolidating nearly all governmental power in the hands of Zhu Yuanzhang. He personally took control of the six ministries— *Li* (吏) (Personnel), *Hu* (戶) (Revenue), *Li* (禮) (Rites), *Bing* (兵) (Military), *Xing* (刑) (Justice), and *Gong* (工) (Works)—strengthening centralization. This shift in the legal framework was reflected in the *Da Ming Lü*, which broke away from the previous tradition of dividing legal topics into separate chapters. Instead, it organized the code according to the six ministries, marking a significant change in the history of Chinese legal codes and demonstrating Zhu Yuanzhang's use of legislation to reinforce imperial authority.

To maintain absolute imperial authority, Zhu Yuanzhang advocated governing through severe laws, and the *Da Ming Lü* intensified punishments for crimes that threatened imperial rule. To combat corruption, he personally oversaw the creation of the *Ming Da Gao* (《明大诰》) (the *Great Ming Pronouncements*), which imposed exceptionally brutal penalties. However, Zhu Yuanzhang recognized that relying solely on harsh punishments could not eradicate crime. He warned his successors that while he had no choice but to impose severe penalties to restore order in times of chaos, punishments should be moderated in times of peace.

In the Ming dynasty, the maintenance of imperial authority was not only reflected in the penal system but also in the emperor's use of secret agencies to interfere in judicial affairs. The emergence of the *Chang Wei* (廠衛) (Secret Police) was an inevitable consequence of the extreme centralization of imperial power. The *Chang Wei* was a collective term for the Ming dynasty's secret police agencies, including the *Jin Yi Wei* (錦衣衛) (Embroidered Uniform Guard), the *Dong Chang* (東廠) (Eastern Depot), the *Xi Chang* (西廠) (Western Depot), and the *Nei Xing Chang* (內行廠) (Palace Depot). These agencies strengthened imperial rule and played a role in curbing official corruption. However, their arbitrary interference in judicial matters disrupted the legal order of the state, ultimately undermining imperial stability and diminishing the well-being of the people.

It is important to note that the emperor's *Chang Wei* agencies only intervened in specific cases, while ordinary cases were still handled by the state's judicial institutions. In the Ming dynasty, the central judicial system consisted of the *Da Li Si* (大理寺) (Court of Judicial Review), the *Xing Bu* (刑部) (Ministry of Justice), and the *Du Cha Yuan* (都察院) (Court of Censors), collectively known as the "*San Fa Si*" (三法司) (Three Judicial Offices). The highest judicial authority was *Xing Bu*, while *Da Li Si* was responsible for case reevaluation. *Xing Bu* not only oversaw criminal and civil cases across the provinces but also handled the revision of laws and the execution of punishments. *Du Cha Yuan*, as the central supervisory agency, had certain judicial powers. In cases of significant or complex cases, all three institutions would jointly review the matter in a process known as "*San Si Hui Shen*" (三司會審) (Three-Judicial-Office Joint Trial).

Like the Tang and Song dynasties, the Ming dynasty upheld Confucian ideals of rites-based governance, emphasizing the integration of *Li* (禮) (rites) and *Fa* (法) (laws). While strict law enforcement was maintained, the educative function of *Li* was also valued. Additionally, Zhu Yuanzhang not only prioritized legislative work but also emphasized the promotion of laws, insisting that laws should be understandable to the common people. He believed that the legal codes of previous dynasties were overly complex, hindering effective enforcement, and advocated for laws that were concise and easy to implement. After the promulgation of the *Da Ming Lü*, he worried that the people might not fully comprehend its provisions. To address this, he ordered officials to select legal statutes relevant to everyday affairs, provide detailed explanations, and distribute them across the empire, requiring the populace to study and understand them.

2. **Laws in the Qing dynasty**

The Qing dynasty was the last feudal, centralized monarchy in China, and its legal system, while inheriting many elements from previous dynasties, also achieved several new accomplishments. For example: it abolished some of the cruel punishments from the Ming dynasty and prohibited the emperor from interfering with the judiciary through secret agencies. It also established a more complete legal system, consisting of laws covering criminal, civil, administrative, and litigation matters. Besides, it further regulated the death penalty review process. In areas with multi-ethnic populations, the Qing granted certain degrees of autonomy to ethnic minority regions and established corresponding legal norms. These legal achievements reflected the legislative guiding principles of the Manchu rulers and were an extension of their governance philosophy into the legal system.

When the Manchu entered the Great Wall and unified the Central Plains, they focused on absorbing and applying Confucian thought. They proposed the legislative idea of "*Can Han Zhuo Jin*" (参漢酌金), which meant drawing from the advanced legal systems of the Han people while retaining certain old systems and customs of the *Hou Jin* (後金) (Later Jin). Any aspect of the Han legal system that was beneficial to governance and appropriate for the times was adopted. This inclusiveness and absorption of advanced culture was also a key reason why the Qing dynasty was able to rule for many years.

The legal system of the Qing Dynasty had its advanced aspects, but it also inevitably carried a certain degree of narrowness and drawbacks. At the same time, as a highly developed centralized monarchy, its legal system—especially the criminal law system—was inevitably designed to serve the maintenance of imperial power. The *Da Qing Lü Li* (《大清律例》) (the *Great Qing Legal Code*), as the fundamental law for Qing's criminal legal system, treated Manchu and Han people differently in its application. The Manchu people enjoyed certain privileges in the application of punishments, such as the possibility of a having their crime downgraded to a lesser offense or the option of changing the type of punishment.

Strengthening centralized rule through harsh laws and severe punishments was a major feature of the Qing Dynasty's criminal legal system. On the one hand, the Qing rulers revered Confucian ideals to reinforce imperial power. On the other hand, they harshly suppressed intellectuals who were perceived as a threat to Manchu rule, aiming to eliminate heretical thoughts, engaging in large-scale "*Wen Zi Yu*" (文字獄) (literary inquisition) and imposing ideological and cultural despotism. In addition, the Qing rulers also used criminal legislation to suppress religious organizations that were seen as a threat to their rule. The *Da Qing Lü Li* stipulated that leaders of organizations like the "*Bai Lian Jiao*" (白蓮教) (White Lotus Societies) would be sentenced to "*Jiao Jian Hou*" (絞監候) (strangulation pending further review). Other participants would be subjected to 100 heavy-stick beatings and banished to distant regions up to 3000 *li* (approximately 1500 km) away.

One new development in Qing's criminal legal system was the establishment of crimes related to the trafficking and consumption of opium. In the seventh year of the Yongzheng (雍正) reign (1729), the Qing government issued the first opium ban, which is also considered the world's first anti-drug law. The ban clearly stipulated that those involved in the trafficking of opium would have their goods confiscated, be branded with a wooden collar for one month, and banished to the frontier for forced labor. Those who privately opened opium dens and lured respectable young men into smoking opium were to be punished according to the law against heretical cults, with a sentence of *Jiao Jian Hou*. Other participants would receive 100 heavy-stick beatings and be banished to distant regions up to 3000 *li* (approximately 1500 km) away. The crime of trafficking and consuming opium became a new category of offense and became a major target of severe punishment in the later years of the Qing dynasty.

Everything that reaches its peak eventually declines. As the Qing Dynasty fell, the traditional Chinese Legal System completed its historical mission and gradually faded away. The Qing legal reforms began with constitutional changes, aiming to implement constitutional governance. Naturally, this passive transformation ended in failure, but it ushered in significant changes in China's legal system. By drawing on Western legal systems, China began revising its traditional laws, resulting in a near-complete transformation of its legal structure and marking the beginning of the modernization of Chinese law.

1.2.5 Modern and Contemporary Transformation

1. **Late Qing period**

After the Opium War of 1840, patriots and visionaries sought a path to strengthen and rejuvenate China. Many recognized that the fundamental issue lay in the political system, and called for political reforms. Under the pressures of both internal and external crises, Empress Dowager Cixi (慈禧) sent five ministers abroad for a fact-finding mission. They ultimately proposed adopting a constitutional monarchy—a system that could preserve the imperial throne, alleviate foreign threats, and quell internal unrest.

The Qing Dynasty's preparation for constitutional reform was a gradual process, spanning three stages over roughly five years. While the content of the constitutional reforms gradually deepened, each step was a reactive, rather than proactive, change. As a result, the historical mission that could have been completed through reform was ultimately carried out through revolution. The process of modernizing China's legal system unfolded as a passive, painful, and exceedingly slow one.

The first stage was the promulgation of the *Qin Ding Xian Fa Da Gang* (《欽定憲法大綱》) (*Outline of the Constitution Compiled by Imperial Order*) in August 1908, which was the first constitutional document in Chinese history. This outline was drafted by the *Xian Zheng Bian Cha Guan* (憲政編查館) (Commission for Studying Constitutional Government), a special institution responsible for constitutional affairs at the time, and approved by the emperor. However, it was not passed by the national assembly and thus did not have constitutional authority. Nevertheless, it marked the true beginning of constitutional reform.

The second stage involved the establishment of the *Zi Yi Ju* (諮議局) (Provincial Consultative Bureau) and the *Zi Zheng Yuan* (資政院) (Government Advisory Council). These two institutions were modeled after the Western parliamentary system by the Qing government. The *Zi Yi Ju* was akin to a provincial assembly, while the *Zi Zheng Yuan* resembled a national assembly. However, the Qing rulers imposed various restrictions on the *Zi Yi Ju* to prevent their power from being undermined. For example, they imposed strict limitations on electoral eligibility, with only 0.4% of the national population eligible to vote, effectively excluding the majority of the populace from the electoral process. Additionally, they limited the powers of the elected officials, granting them only the right to deliberate while keeping decisive authority in the hands of local Qing officials. The *Zi Zheng Yuan* served as a transitional body toward a national legislature, with its authority mainly limited to revising laws and voting on the national budget, but all actions required imperial approval to take effect.

The promulgation of the *Xian Fa Zhong Da Xin Tiao Shi Jiu Tiao* (憲法重大信條十九條) (*Nineteen Major Articles of Good Faith on the Constitution*) marked the third stage. This was a reluctant choice made by the Qing government in the face of various challenges after the *Wuchang Qi Yi* (武昌起義) (Wuchang Uprising). However, this constitutional document ultimately failed to save the Qing government's fate. The reason the Qing government pursued constitutional reform was not out of a genuine desire to preserve the nation's survival, limit imperial power, or carry out political reforms, but rather as a desperate attempt to buy time. In the end, they were unwilling to relinquish the power in their hands.

The constitutional reforms of the late Qing period opened the path to the modernization of China's legal system. Meanwhile, other branches of law were being revised either before or after the constitutional reforms. The entire legal system underwent a complete overhaul, with the separation of criminal and civil law, the "debate between rites and laws" in criminal law reform, the establishment of commercial and administrative laws, the promulgation of litigation law, and judicial reforms. All of these had a profound impact on the traditional Chinese legal system. The Consular Jurisdiction, while introducing Western judicial concepts, further undermined China's judicial sovereignty. This duality may be an unavoidable aspect of the modernization of China's legal system.

After the Opium War, China's judicial sovereignty was gradually infringed upon, with Consular Jurisdiction being established in the 1843 *Five Ports Trade Regulations* between China and Britain. Subsequently, 20 countries gained consular jurisdiction in China. To intervene in all types of cases involving their nationals, the foreign powers also introduced the practices of "*Guan Shen*" (觀審) and "*Hui Shen Gong Xie*" (會審公廨). The former refers to the practice where foreign diplomats, consuls, or other representatives were allowed to observe judicial proceedings in China that involved foreigners. As for *Hui Shen Gong Xie*, this term refers to a joint hearing or joint trial system set up by foreign powers in China where Chinese and foreign officials would sit together to hear cases involving foreigners. Consular jurisdiction was a painful price China paid during its modernization. The Qing government, unwilling to reform constitutionally, also refused to accept Western advanced concepts and systems during the passive reform process. By the time the foreign powers invaded, China had no strength to resist, leading to the cession of ports, the establishment of foreign concessions, and the infringement of judicial sovereignty by foreign powers.

With no hope for reform, patriots pinned their hopes on violent and radical revolution, causing the gradual abandonment of our traditional legal essence. Meanwhile, the modern rule of law concepts were neither properly accepted nor applied. Therefore, in the process of modernization, the conflict between tradition and modernity brought us more pain. Fortunately, we have gradually come to realize that tradition must be reserved, and modernity must progress with the times. While the traditional Chinese Legal Family has gradually faded away in the course of history, the spirit and ideals it left behind must continue to be critically examined and carried forward in the process of legal modernization.

2. **Period after the founding of the People's Republic of China**

The founding of the PRC marked a historic moment. It was not only a change in political power but also a monumental transformation in the realms of law, ideology, and culture. The influence brought by the new legal system had a profound impact on the Chinese Legal Family, with new legal concepts and values playing a core role. China began to build and improve a legal system suited to the socialist framework while inheriting the outstanding elements of traditional Chinese legal culture.

First, the founding of the People's Republic of China signified the success of Marxist jurisprudence in China. Unlike previous legal theories, Marxist jurisprudence emphasized the relationship between political and legal logic and the economic base, positing that politics and law are part of the superstructure, whose content and form are influenced by the economic base. This viewpoint dominated the legal system construction in the early years of the PRC, providing a theoretical foundation for the new legal system.

Second, the transformation of the legal system in the PRC meant a new understanding of the role of law. Before this, the Chinese legal system was largely seen as a tool for regulating social behavior. However, after the establishment of the PRC, law was assigned a more important function: promoting socialist construction and maintaining socialist order. This profound change was not only a transformation of legal systems and concepts but also represented the Chinese nation's inheritance and development of legal traditions, alongside the adoption of foreign legal systems.

1.3 Conclusion

Overall, China has always placed great importance on the construction of its legal culture. "Although Chinese legal culture has encountered numerous setbacks, it has remained unyielding, bravely overcoming difficult times. It has undergone reforms in every dynasty, forming a legal culture system that is rich in content, distinctive in characteristics, and broad in influence. Due to its continuity, uniqueness, and inclusiveness, it has become the most splendid chapter in the history of world legal cultures" (Ma and Liu 2022). The contemporary Chinese law integrates three fundamentally different legal systems—feudal law, semi-feudal law, and socialist law—into a cohesive whole. Through the national and historical bonds, these systems have collectively formed the broader Chinese Legal Family (Yu and Long 2005: 35). From a historical perspective, changes in the nature of society do not necessarily lead to the demise of the Chinese Legal Family. It has continued to evolve throughout history and remains one of the most influential legal systems in the world (Shi 2023: 17).

References

Chen, C. 1980. An Initial Exploration of the Characteristics of the Chinese Legal Family. *Legal Research* 1: 90–99.

Chen, G. 2011. *Outline of the Chinese Legal History*. Beijing: The Commercial Press.

Ma, Z., and Liu, Y. 2022. A Brief Discussion on the Characteristics of China's Outstanding Traditional Rule of Law Culture. *Democracy and Law Times* (8), September 29.

Qiao, W. 1986. Basic Characteristics of the Chinese Legal Family. *Journal of Literature, History, and Philosophy* 2: 44–55.

Shi, W. 2023. On the Great Revitalization of the Chinese Legal Family. *Eastern Jurisprudence* 6: 15–26.

Yang, H. 1999. *The Influence of Chinese Law on East Asian Countries*. China University of Political Science and Law Press.

Yu, R. and Long, D. 2005. The Study of the Chinese Legal Family. *Journal of Shanghai University of Political Science and Law (Law and Governance Series)* 4: 31–38.

Zhang, J. 2018. *Treatise on Chinese Legal System*. Beijing: China University of Political Science and Law Press.

Chapter 2
Formation Conditions of the Chinese Legal Family

The formation and development of the Chinese Legal Family are the result of multiple factors working together. Like other legal systems, the Chinese Legal Family exerted its influence through the dissemination and transplantation of laws, which led to the creation of a legal culture circle after the legal system in its country of origin had reached a certain level of maturity. This dissemination and transplantation were deeply rooted in social, historical, and cultural contexts.

2.1 Historical Preconditions: Chinese Slave Law and Early Feudal Law

The Chinese Legal Family is formed by the feudal laws of China after the Han Dynasty, along with those of Korea, Japan, and Vietnam. Before the Han Dynasty, China had already developed a relatively advanced material civilization, sophisticated intellectual culture, and legal system. However, it was during the Han Dynasty that China's feudal legal system began to exert significant external influence, prompting neighboring countries to start adopting Chinese laws.

When it comes to the origin of the Chinese Legal Family, its historical roots lie in the slave law and early feudal law of pre-imperial China. Slave law was primarily represented by the "*Li*" (禮) (rites) of the Western Zhou period, while early feudal law was mainly embodied in the "*Lü*" (律) (codes). As the two fundamental historical sources of the Chinese Legal Family, they formed its foundation and provided the "genetic code" for its formation and development. While this genetic code did not dictate the specific course of the legal system's evolution, it imposed certain qualitative constraints and possibilities, ultimately shaping the fundamental structure of the Chinese Legal Family.

In pre-imperial China, during the disintegration of the communal system based on "*Shi Zu*" (氏族) (tribal clans), the pre-state tribal clan, which was built upon blood

X. Dong and Y. Li, *Chinese Legal Family and Chinese Modernization of Rule of Law*,
https://doi.org/10.1007/978-981-96-7529-6_2

ties, was transformed into a slavery-based "*Zong Zu*" (宗族) (patriarchal clan). The self-governance regulations among different tribes evolved into "*Zong Fa*" (宗法) (patriarchal clan laws). During the Western Zhou period, Duke of Zhou (周公), following the patriarchal clan system's hierarchical distinctions, such as "*Di*" (嫡) (children of the principal wife or primary lines) and "*Shu*" (庶) (children of concubines or collateral lines), seniority by age, and degrees of kinship, incorporated the institutions of the Xia and Shang dynasties along with the Zhou people's customary laws to establish the legislative principles of "*Qin Qin*" (親親) (proximity to kin) and "*Zun Zun*" (尊尊) (respect for superiors). These principles had a profound and lasting influence on later legal systems. The later dynasties' legal codes such as *Tang Liu Dian* (《唐六典》) (*Six Statues of the Tang Dynasty*), *Yuan Dian Zhang* (《元典章》) (*Statues of the Yuan Dynasty*), *Ming Hui Dian* (《明會典》) (*Collected Statues of the Ming Dynasty*), and *Qing Hui Dian* (《清會典》) (*Collected Statues of the Qing Dynasty*), as well as ancient Korea's *Gyeongguk Daejeon* (《經國大典》) from the Joseon dynasty and Japan's *Taihō Code* (《大寶律令》), were all formulated with reference to the "*Zhou Li*" (周禮) (the rites of Zhou) during their legislative processes.

Early feudal laws in China refer to the Qin laws and the feudal laws that preceded it. The Spring and Autumn and Warring States periods were times of social disintegration, with the collapse of traditional rites and intense struggles between rival states. During this period, two social systems—old and new—alternated, and political conflicts were extraordinarily fierce. The laws enacted in this context were inevitably designed to suppress and prevent resistance and subversive activities from hostile classes, while maintaining the feudal order. As a result, early feudal laws, from the *Fa Jing* (《法經》) (the *Canon of Laws*) by Li Kui (李悝) to the Qin laws, were all penal codes. This legislative model and the structure of legal codification had a profound impact on the Chinese Legal Family, with almost all legal codes in Chinese-Legal-Family countries being penal codes.

2.2 Geographical Conditions: The "Central" Position of China

A legal system is often centered around the country of origin and then spreads and radiates outwards to surrounding areas and countries, thus forming a common legal culture circle. In East Asia, up until the early Qing Dynasty, China's socioeconomic development was superior to that of neighboring countries and regions and China remained the cultural center of East Asia. Its more advanced social institutions and exemplary legal culture served as a reference for other countries to emulate. Additionally, China's geographical setting, characterized by a semi-enclosed temperate continental climate, is bordered by the vast ocean to the east, vast deserts to the north, and the world's tallest mountain range, the Himalayas, to the southwest. This unique environment contributed to the direction in which its legal culture spread: eastward, northeastward, and southeastward.

Geographically speaking, China and Korea are closely connected, with their lands and waters intertwined, and direct land routes linking the two countries. The Shandong Peninsula and Liaodong Peninsula in China, along with the coast of Korea, form an irregular semicircle across the Bohai Sea and the Yellow Sea, with relatively short distances between them, making maritime transportation quite convenient. The Korean Peninsula is surrounded by sea on three sides, with land borders only with China, giving it a relatively closed geographic environment. These geographic conditions are highly favorable for the exchange of legal culture between China and Korea.

China and Japan are separated by a narrow body of water, with a sea crossing between them. During the Paleolithic era, there was a land bridge connecting the Chinese mainland with the Japanese archipelago, but due to changes in geography, Japan eventually became an island nation surrounded by the Pacific Ocean. Among Japan's neighboring countries at that time, China was the only one with a relatively developed legal system. Thus, ancient Japan began to look to China as the primary model for learning legal culture and governance system.

Vietnam is located in the eastern part of the Indochina Peninsula, bordered to the east and south by the Gulf of Tonkin and the South China Sea, while to the north it shares mountains and rivers with China. These neighboring geographic conditions were particularly favorable for the transplantation of China's feudal legal system into ancient Vietnam.

In conclusion, the geographical proximity of China, Japan, Korea, and Vietnam, coupled with their distance from other major legal cultural centers, provided unique "geopolitical" conditions that greatly facilitated the formation of the Chinese Legal Family.

2.3 National and Political Foundations: The East Asian Cultural Community

From a historical perspective, the formation of the Chinese Legal Family had profound national and political foundations within the East Asian cultural sphere.

Firstly, the similarities in national conditions provided the possibility for the formation of the Chinese Legal Family. Ancient East Asian countries shared many common characteristics with China. Economically, they were all in a self-sufficient, feudal small-scale agricultural stage. Politically, they were all primarily governed by centralized, autocratic feudal monarchies. Ideologically, Confucianism and the governance by "*Li*" (禮) (rites) were held in high regard. The convergence of national conditions facilitated smoother exchanges and mutual learning among these countries, effectively eliminating the incompatibility of transplanting Chinese laws. This allowed Chinese legal culture to be absorbed, internalized, and innovatively adapted.

Not only did this enrich the content of the Chinese Legal Family, but it also helped create a diverse yet unified East Asian rule-of-law culture—one that harmonized differences while maintaining unity. Furthermore, it provided a practical foundation for the formation of the East Asian rule-of-law cultural community.

Secondly, the tributary relationship between China and its neighboring countries laid the political foundation for the spread of the Chinese Legal Family. Historically, the countries that were part of the Chinese Legal Family were once tributary states to China. During certain periods, these East Asian countries, as Chinese vassals, received official recognition and titles from the central Chinese dynasties. Japan, for example, sent envoys to offer tribute as early as the Han Dynasty. According to the *Hou Han Shu* (《後漢書》) (*Book of the Later Han*), in the second year of the reign of Emperor Guangwu (漢光武帝) (57 CE), *Wakoku* (倭國) (ancient Japan) sent envoys to pay tribute, and Emperor Guangwu bestowed seals of office upon them, granting them the name "*Wa*" (倭) as a mark of favor. From a historical standpoint, the existence of these tributary relations greatly reduced the resistance to the top-down dissemination of Chinese legal culture. This helped establish a strong political foundation for the formation of the East Asian rule-of-law cultural community.

2.4 Ideological Foundations: Confucianism

During the Spring and Autumn and Warring States periods, there was a flourishing of various schools of thought, with Confucianism being one of the most prominent. During the reign of Emperor Wu of the Han Dynasty (漢武帝), he implemented the policy of "*Ba Chu Bai Jia, Du Zun Ru Shu*" (罷黜百家，獨尊儒術) (Rejecting the Hundred Schools and Exclusively Respecting Confucianism). Confucianism thus became the dominant ideology in society, and Confucian legal thought became the theoretical foundation and guiding ideology for nearly two thousand years of feudal law in China.

Being geographically close to China, ancient Korea was quick to adopt Confucianism as the foundational ideology. Confucian classics were considered essential reading for Korean officials and noble youths. During the Joseon Dynasty, Korea implemented a comprehensive "Confucian political system", where feudal bureaucrats derived all the practical knowledge necessary for governing the country and the moral standards for feudal society from Confucian teachings. Consequently, to become an official, one had to study Confucian classics. Schools established by the feudal state focused entirely on Confucian education (Institute of History, Academy of Sciences of the Democratic People's Republic of Korea 1973: 309). For a society in disarray, the Confucian concepts such as name, status, order, rites and righteousness played a crucial role. The indoctrination of Confucian thought provided the theoretical direction for the development of Korea's feudal legal system, which followed the trajectory of the Chinese Legal Family.

In the late fourth century, a scholar from Baekje (a Korean kingdom located in southwestern Korea from 18 BCE to 660 CE) called Wang Ren (王仁) brought the *Lun Yu* (《論語》) (*Analects*) and *Qian Zi Wen* (《千字文》) (*Thousand Character Classic*) to Japan, presenting them to Emperor Ōjin as textbooks for the crown prince. In the mid-sixth century, Baekje sent "*Wu Jing Bo Shi*" (五經博士) (Scholars of Five Classics) such as Duan Yang'er (段揚爾) and Han An'mao (漢安茂) to Japan with Confucian classics, including the *Li Ji* (《禮記》) (*Book of Rites*), *Yue Jing* (《樂經》) (*Classic of Music*), *Lun Yu*, and *Xiao Jing* (《孝經》) (*Classic of Filial Piety*). In 604 CE, Prince Shōtoku of Japan, who was instrumental in the country's political reforms, established the *Seventeen-Article Constitution*, which was guided by Confucian principles. Many of its articles reflected Confucian maxims, such as "Harmony is held supreme" (以和爲貴) and "Rites serve as the foundation" (以禮爲本). During the Ritsuryō system era, the *Taihō Code* stipulated that Confucianism should be made an important subject, requiring the *Lun Yu* and *Qian Zi Wen* to be taught in national schools. In some cases, corporal punishment was used to force students to accept Confucian teachings. For a long period, Confucian classics were the only textbooks. In 757 CE, Empress Kōken issued a decree mandating that every household in Japan own a copy of the *Xiao Jing*. Examination questions for selecting officials were almost entirely based on Confucian content. According to the *Nihonkoku Genzaisho Mokuroku* (《日本国見在書目録》) (*Catalog of Extant Books in Japan*) from the ninth century, Japan at that time had a collection of 1,568 types of Chinese books, totaling 16,725 volumes. This indicates that half of China's classical literature had already been transmitted to Japan by that time. The Japanese government's endorsement of Confucianism and the subtle influence of Confucian thoughts provided the ideological foundation and public support for the large-scale transplantation of China's feudal law system into Japan.

Vietnam was another tributary state of China in ancient times, and the influence of Confucian thought there was even more direct. After gaining independence, Vietnam also adopted Confucianism as the theoretical foundation for governance. The rulers regarded Confucianism as the guiding principle for state-building and governance, establishing various political and social systems based on its teachings. Unlike its neighboring countries, such as Thailand and Cambodia, which became predominantly Buddhist nations, Vietnam's deep integration of Confucianism can be directly linked to the widespread adoption of Confucian thought in the country.

In conclusion, Confucianism made a strong initial impact and spread widely. Most rulers were influenced and shaped by Confucian teachings, which laid the necessary ideological foundation for the Confucianization of the laws in East Asian countries. This, in turn, contributed to the development of a shared legal philosophy centered around the idea of "*De Zhu Xing Fu*" (德主刑輔) (Virtue as the primary principle and punishment as a secondary means).

2.5 Talent Foundation: Immigration and Study Abroad

The formation and development of a legal system is a process of transmitting, processing, organizing, and receiving legal information. In this process, the spread and transplantation of laws did not occur spontaneously; rather, it was carried out consciously under the guidance of a group of skilled legal professionals. This required a group of individuals who were not only familiar with their own country's conditions but also well-versed in the legal systems of the "mother country"—in this case, China. These talented individuals served as intermediaries, facilitating the exchange and dissemination of legal knowledge.

In ancient East Asia, these legal professionals were primarily provided through immigration and study abroad. In other words, official exchanges and learning, primarily led by governments, greatly promoted the development of the Chinese Legal Family. As the mother country of the Chinese Legal Family, China's legal institutions and culture were undoubtedly more advanced and superior compared to those of other contemporary East Asian countries. This led many countries to send envoys and students to China to study its legal system and culture. Government-led official exchanges and learning, in both scale and formality, far exceeded private, informal exchanges. This accelerated the spread and promotion of Chinese legal culture throughout East Asia, ensuring the stable, rapid, and high-quality development of the East Asian rule-of-law cultural community.

In ancient times, some of the Chinese immigrants who migrated to Korea, along with the ancient Korean noble youths who studied in China, brought advanced Chinese production techniques and legal culture to Korea. They became the key theoretical figures and practical implementers of the transplantation of China's feudal law system. Although the *Han Shu* (《漢書》) (*Book of Han*), in its section of "Geography Records", mentions that "Jizi (箕子) (a Chinese sage who is said to have ruled Gija Joseon in the eleventh century BCE) left for Korea and taught its people rites, morality, farming, and sericulture", this claim has not been conclusively proven. However, it is undeniable that during the Warring States period, many people from the Chinese states of Yan (燕國) and Qi (齊國), which were neighboring Korea, migrated in large numbers to Korea. In the early Western Han period, more than a thousand people, including the Yan native Wei Man (衛滿), also migrated to Korea. Emperor Wu of Han (漢武帝) even sent people to reprimand the King Ugeo (衛右渠) (the grandson of Wei Man) of Wiman Joseon, on the grounds that he had "induced an increasing number of Han fugitives" (from *Records of the Grand Historian* 《史記》). Korea also sent large numbers of students to China for study. Throughout the Tang, Song, Yuan, and Ming dynasties, many Korean noble youths studied in China. During the Tang dynasty, the largest group of foreign students in China came from Silla (a Korean kingdom that existed between 57 BCE–935 CE), numbering as many as 260. During the Five Dynasties and Song periods, the Goryeo dynasty (a Korean state that existed during 918–1270 and 1356–1392) also sent students to China for further education. These students often lived in China for extended periods, becoming well-versed in Chinese culture and law. Some even rose to positions of power in China, such as Kim Won-ul (金文蔚), a Silla student who had studied in Tang China. He eventually rose to the position of "*Gong Bu Yuan Wai Lang*" (工部員外郎) (Assistant Director in the Ministry of Works) and was even appointed as a "*Ce Ming Shi*" (冊命使) (Imperial Envoy) to Silla by the Tang Dynasty, akin to a modern-day diplomatic personnel.

In Japanese historical records, "*Shinkan Kikajin*" (秦漢歸化人) referred to early Chinese migrants who settled in ancient Japan during the Qin and Han dynasties. They were among the pioneers and foundational figures in the exchange of legal and cultural knowledge between China and Japan. In the first century BCE, there were over a hundred tribes spread across the Japanese archipelago, and more than thirty of these tribes had sent envoys to the Lelang commandery (樂浪郡), which was under the control of the Han Dynasty on the Korean Peninsula. These individuals, who spoke Chinese and used Chinese characters, were likely Chinese immigrants or people who had been exposed to Chinese culture. Japanese scholars point out that these "immigrants" had a decisive influence on the native population. "Later on the Japanese archipelago, the absorption of Chinese culture, the interactions with China and the Korean Peninsula, and the tribute-paying to the Chinese emperors, were all carried out by these immigrants and the countries established by them" (Yamanaka 1994: 16). "The ancient Japanese absorption of Chinese and Korean culture was entirely the work of these immigrants. Their deep attachment to their homeland, China and Korea, drove them to fully devote themselves to the task of absorbing the culture of their motherland" (Yamanaka 1994: 43). According to historical records compiled by the Japanese imperial government, the surnames of *Kikajin* made up about 30% of all Japanese surnames. During the Eastern Jin and Northern and Southern dynasties, many Chinese people, including intellectuals, migrated to Japan via Korea. Some of these immigrants even held positions in the *Yamato* court, managing records and drafting diplomatic documents. "Chinese legal texts had already been transmitted to Japan as early as the fifth century" (Zhu 1992: 175).

Between 608 and 614, Japan sent students and scholarly monks to China for study, and many members of the *Kentōshi* (遣唐使) (Japanese missions to Tang China) were sent for educational purposes. Upon returning to Japan, these scholars actively "promoted Confucian political thought, introduced the Sui and Tang political systems, and pushed for political reforms" (Wang 1990: 212). These students brought back numerous Confucian classics and legal texts. For instance, Kibi no Makibi (吉備真備) brought the *Tang Li* (《唐禮》) (*Rites of Tang*) and other books back to Japan in 734. After their return, these scholars actively spread Chinese legal culture and, leveraging their advantageous positions in policy-making, worked to encourage the highest authorities to adopt Chinese laws. Having conducted comparative studies of their own country's laws and Chinese laws, they were well-equipped to transplant Chinese legal concepts into Japan. Some of ancient Japan's laws were direct copies of Chinese laws by these returning scholars, while some legal codes were entirely compiled by them. Certain scholars participated directly in drafting, creating, revising, and implementing laws. For example: Takamuko no Kuromaro (高向玄理), who studied in China for 32 years, returned to Japan and was awarded the title *Kuni no Hakase* (國博士) (National Scholar), advising the emperor and playing a key role in the *Taika* Reforms. He also compiled the *Ōmi Code* (《近江令》); Iki no Hakatoko (伊吉博德) and other students who had studied in China were responsible for compiling the *Taihō Code* (《大寶律令》); and in the eighth century, Kibi no Makibi, who had studied in Tang China for 20 years, also revised the legal texts in Japan.

The ancestors of the Vietnamese people were part of the Luoyue (雒越), or in Vietnamese Lạc Việt, branch of the Baiyue (百越) people. Vietnamese scholars acknowledge that "the Lạc Việt people of northern Vietnam were originally migrants from the Luoyue people in Fujian" (Đào 1976: 130). During the Qin Dynasty, Emperor Qin Shi Huang (秦始皇) resettled large numbers of people to the Baiyue region, some of whom then migrated to Vietnam. Even before and after Vietnam's independence, there were continuous migrations from China to Vietnam. Among these immigrants, some were familiar with Chinese feudal laws and played an important role in spreading and transplanting China's feudal law system. Additionally, before Vietnam's independence, many noble youths studied in China's capital cities, and after independence, there were also many students from Vietnam who went to China to study. Over the course of Vietnam's history, successive dynasties modeled their legal systems after Chinese legal codes. Several scholars who had studied in China played prominent roles in the creation and revision of these laws, and some even directly participated in drafting the laws. It is worth noting that throughout Vietnam's history, nine dynasties were founded by individuals of Chinese descent. The founders of these dynasties were either Chinese immigrants or descendants of Chinese immigrants. For example: Đinh Bộ Lĩnh, founder of the Đinh Dynasty, was possibly a "*Yan Huang Zi Sun*" (炎黃子孫) (descendant of Chinese lineage), as his descendants preserved a family genealogy written in Classical Chinese and claimed descent from the Emperor Yandi (炎帝); Lê Hoàn, founder of the Early Lê dynasty, was from present-day Guangxi; Lý Thái Tổ, founder of the Lý dynasty, was of Fujian descent; and Hồ Quý Ly, founder of the Hồ dynasty, was a descendant of people from Zhejiang. As Chinese immigrants or descendants, these rulers' legal thinking was undoubtedly shaped by Chinese feudal legal traditions.

2.6 Medium of Transmission: The Chinese Language

In the early stages, Korea, Japan, and Vietnam did not have their own written scripts and relied heavily on *Han Zi* (漢字) (Chinese characters). Later, while these countries created their own writing systems based on *Han Zi*, *Han Zi* remained the dominant writing system for a long period.

Japan began to develop its indigenous writing systems in the fifth century with the emergence of "*Kana*". In the seventh century, *Man'yōgana* was developed, which used Chinese characters to represent the Japanese language. In the ninth century, two types of *Kana*—"*Hiragana*" and "*Katakana*"—were developed by Kibi no Makibi and Kōbō Daishi (a famous Japanese scholar and Buddhism monk). In Korea, it was not until 1443 that *Hunminjeongeum* (《訓民正音》) (*The Proper Sounds for the Instruction of the People*) was published, introducing the Korean script *Hangul*. In 1446, King Sejong the Great issued a decree, officially recognizing *Hangul* as the official writing system. As for Vietnam, it used *Han Zi* for a long time, and the government formally decreed *Han Zi* as the official script and all government documents were written in Classical Chinese. It was only in the thirteenth-fourteenth centuries that *Chữ Nôm*, a system of writing based on Chinese characters, was created but failed to gain widespread use. Until the seventeenth century, Latin script (via missionary influence) replaced Chinese-based scripts in Vietnam. In this context, Chinese characters played an essential role as the medium for transmitting Chinese legal culture across East Asia. They served as the bridge for the spread of Chinese feudal law and other cultural elements, enabling countries like Japan, Korea, and Vietnam to adopt and adapt Chinese legal texts, codes, and governance structures.

First, Chinese characters were used across the countries of the Chinese Legal Family, effectively eliminating the language barrier for people in Korea, Japan, and Vietnam when learning about China's feudal laws. This facilitated direct access for students, intellectuals, and ruling elites from these countries to study and research Chinese feudal laws. It also helped the general public in these countries understand Chinese legal principles and texts.

Second, under the historical condition that these countries lacked their own writing systems, the widespread use of Chinese characters served as a prerequisite for the formation of the Chinese Legal Family's emphasis on codified laws as the primary legal source. Without a writing system, codified laws would have been impossible. In the context of the Chinese Legal Family, Chinese characters were employed in all of these neighboring countries to articulate laws and to record judicial decisions. For instance, Japan's earliest codified law, the *Seventeen-Article Constitution*, was written in Classical Chinese (Takeuchi et al. 1988: 14). Similarly, legal documents such as the *Kōnin Kyakushiki* (《弘仁格式》), the *Jōgan Kyakushiki* (《貞観格式》), and the *Engi Kyakushiki* (《延喜格式》) were all compiled in Chinese characters.

Third, the Chinese language not only accelerated the legal and cultural exchange in ancient East Asia but also prevented "distortions" in the transplantation of laws. If the recipient country had a different written language from the mother country, inaccuracies in translation or the lack of equivalent legal terminology in the recipient's language could affect the success of legal transplantation. In this sense, the Chinese language served as a medium of transmission, much like how English played a crucial role in the dissemination of the Common Law System, providing the necessary linguistic conditions for the accurate and efficient dissemination of the mother country's legal culture.

2.7 Conclusion

In conclusion, the Chinese Legal Family formed and continuously developed under specific historical conditions, and for a long period, it served as the "parent legal system" for the East Asian countries. The spirit of the Chinese Legal Family became a common legal ideology shared by those East Asian countries, and its influence extended to Southeast Asia and other regions. Liang Qichao (梁啓超), in his essay "On the Evolution and Gains/Losses in the Compilation of China's Codified Laws", pointed out, "Thus, countries like Goryeo (ancient Korea), Japan, and Annam (ancient Vietnam) all inherited our legal system in that era" (Liang 2000: 147). The legal historian Yang Honglie further argued:

> If we compare the histories of various legal systems, the Chinese Legal Family has endured for thousands of years, outlasting even the oldest systems like those of Egypt and Mesopotamia. Its influence on East Asian countries such as Korea, Japan, Ryukyu, Annam, and the Western Regions cannot be compared to the limited scope of influence that ancient Egyptian or Mesopotamian law had. Therefore, it can be said that the Chinese Legal Family is one of the greatest legal systems in the world—who would argue otherwise? (Yang 1999: 4)

The long history and wide geographical reach of the Chinese Legal Family are inextricably linked to the profound reasons discussed earlier. The legal systems of Korea, Japan, and Vietnam were not just influenced by China, but they were actively shaped by the Chinese Legal Family, creating a East Asian rule-of-law cultural community.

References

Institute of History, Academy of Sciences of the Democratic People's Republic of Korea. 1973. *A General History of Korea: Vol. 1, Part 2*. Jilin: Jilin People's Publishing House.

Liang, Q. 2000. *Liang Qichao's Collected Works on Jurisprudence*. Edited by Fan, Z. Beijing: China University of Political Science and Law Press.

Takeuchi, R., et al. 1988. *Dictionary of Japanese History*. Translated by Shen R., et al. Tianjin: Tianjin People's Publishing House.

Wang, J. 1990. *Confucianism and Japanese Culture*. Hangzhou: Zhejiang People's Publishing House.

Yamanaka, Y. 1994. *Fifteen Hundred Years of Ancient Japanese History in the Eyes of a Lawyer*. Translated by Cao, Z. Beijing: China Social Science Press.

Yang, H. 1999. *The Influence of Chinese Law on East Asian Countries*. Beijing: China University of Political Science and Law Press.

Zhu, J. 1992. *Introduction to Comparative Law*. Beijing: China Procuratorial Press.

Đào, D. 1976. *Ancient History of Vietnam, Part I*. Beijing: The Commercial Press.

Chapter 3
Distinctive Features of the Chinese Legal Family

Benefiting from China's long-standing and profound legal civilization, traditional Chinese legal culture has gradually developed its unique spirit and institutional characteristics through a long process of evolution. This has given rise to a distinct legal system, known as the "Chinese Legal Family" (中華法系), which sets itself apart from other legal traditions. As a shining gem of Chinese rule-of-law civilization, the Chinese Legal Family is an essential part of human legal history, demonstrating the remarkable creativity of the Chinese nation and the profound heritage of Chinese legal culture. President Xi Jinping has insightfully pointed out: "Our ancient legal system contains a wealth of wisdom and resources, and the Chinese Legal Family stands out among the world's major legal systems" (Xi 2020: 110–111). He further emphasized, "Since ancient times, our country has developed a unique Chinese Legal Family in the history of world legal systems, accumulating a profound legal culture" (Xi 2021).

3.1 Originality in Creation

China, with its 5000-year-long history, is a quintessentially original civilization. The ever-evolving and richly diverse Chinese national culture has become the spiritual lifeline of the nation, and among its most original contributions is the Chinese Legal Family (Gu 2023).

The origins and development of the Chinese Legal Family are closely intertwined with China's long history. According to historical research, the practice of customary laws in China can be traced back to as early as the twenty-first century BCE during the Xia (夏) Dynasty. The Shang (商) Dynasty further developed a legal system based on slavery, and by the Western Zhou (西周) period, a more structured legal system had emerged. However, in line with China's ancient tradition of codified laws and statutory legal systems, the Chinese Legal Family in its true sense "sprouted during

X. Dong and Y. Li, *Chinese Legal Family and Chinese Modernization of Rule of Law*,
https://doi.org/10.1007/978-981-96-7529-6_3

the legal reforms of the Qin (秦) and Han (漢) dynasties, matured through the cultural legacies of the Tang (唐) and Song (宋) dynasties, and unfolded in the grand historical scroll of Chinese civilization, vividly narrating the legal stories of a great Eastern country while embodying the profound jurisprudential and doctrinal wisdom of the Chinese nation" (Zhang 2023: 4).

The unique historical evolution of the Chinese nation has shaped its distinct legal traditions and practices, creating a legal system that differs from others around the world and has remained uninterrupted despite dynastic changes. Moreover, the development of China's ancient economy played a significant role in ensuring the uniqueness and originality of its legal culture. The self-sufficient economic model allowed the Chinese Legal Family to remain uninfluenced by others, making it the only ancient legal system that did not incorporate elements from other legal cultures. As an indigenous legal system deeply rooted in Chinese culture, the Chinese legal system has been profoundly shaped by traditional sociopolitical conditions, including "an agrarian-based economic structure, stable kinship and geographic bonds, an autocratic political system, the ideological dominance of Confucianism, and a unified multi-ethnic state framework" (Zhang 2010: 3). Throughout its emergence, development, and maturation, the Chinese Legal Family has consistently exhibited a distinctive originality and regional specificity.

3.1.1 The Agrarian-Based Economic Structure

The agrarian-based economic structure had a profound impact on China's ancient legal system and judicial practices. In ancient Chinese legislation, the protection and management of agricultural production were always key priorities. The unearthed bamboo texts recording Qin (秦) laws from the fourth century BCE contain specific laws on agricultural management, such as the "*Tian Lü*" (田律) (Field Laws), "*Cang Lü*" (倉律) (Granary Laws), and "*Jiu Yuan Lü*" (廄苑律) (Stable and Pen Laws). From the Sui (隋) and Tang dynasties onward, various agricultural laws and regulations were enacted, including the *Jun Tian Ling* (《均田令》) (*Equal-Field System Decree*), *Nong Sang Ke Ling* (《農桑課令》) (*Agriculture and Sericulture Mandatory Decree*), *Ken Huang Ling* (《墾荒令》) (*Land Reclamation Decree*), *Zhong Zhi Nong Sang Fa Du* (《種植農桑法度》) (*Laws on the Cultivation of Crops and Sericulture*), *Nong Sang Tiao Hua* (《農桑條畫》) (*Directives on Agriculture and Sericulture*), and *Tui Guang Nong Lin Jian Ming Zhang Cheng* (《推廣農林簡明章程》) (*the Concise Regulations on the Promotion of Agriculture and Forestry*). These laws demonstrate how legal measures were employed to ensure the continuation of agricultural production, rendering agriculture an essential component of legislation.

Furthermore, the calendar system, which was closely linked to agricultural production, was already established as early as the Xia Dynasty. Ancient Chinese calendrical science not only emerged early but was also highly advanced, holding a leading position in the history of global astronomy and calendrical systems. This was closely tied to China's early agricultural development and its national reliance on farming as the foundation of the state. As a result, throughout history, the unauthorized creation of calendars that deviated from the official imperial calendar was met with severe punishment.

In the judicial system, the prioritization of agriculture has been evident since the Zhou Dynasty, particularly through the emphasis on the farming season. During the spring and summer seasons, judicial authorities would not accept lawsuits except for criminal cases. The *Da Qing Lü Li* (《大清律例》) (the *Great Qing Legal Code*) contained specific provisions regarding *Wu Xian* (務限) (Suspension of Civil Cases During Agricultural Seasons):

> Every year, from the first day of the fourth month to the thirtieth day of the seventh month, which is the peak of agricultural activity... all minor cases related to households, marriage, land, etc., shall not be accepted. Only after the first day of the eighth month may such cases be heard and adjudicated. (From the *Da Qing Lü Li* 《大清律例》)

3.1.2 Stable Kinship and Geographic Bonds

In ancient times, China transitioned from "*Jia Tian Xia*" (家天下) (family-based rule) to a state rule, and as a result, clan-based kinship had a strong influence on many aspects of society and the state. During the Western Zhou period, the patriarchal clan system was closely integrated with politics. The formation of the state, its political structure, and state activities were all based on the dual principles of kinship and politics. After entering the feudal society, although the patriarchal clan system was no longer directly manifested as a political system, its principles, spirit, and rules were widely ingrained in every family in society. With Confucianism being recognized as the ruling ideology, the ethical relationships advocated by Confucianism further endowed the patriarchal clan system with new authority. The concept of respecting ancestors and honoring the clan was not only the spiritual force that maintained the clan, but also the moral pillar supporting the society.

In China's feudal law system, ethical laws that regulate the rights and duties between family members, centered around patriarchy, hold an important position. The essence of these laws is to strengthen the authority of the patriarch, which in turn consolidates the imperial power. The family-centered ethical laws of ancient China possess a high degree of stability, a characteristic not found in other legal systems. Moreover, since the Tang and Song Dynasties, larger families have often formulated family laws and clan regulations, which became the behavioral guidelines for clan members. The purpose and content of these family laws and regulations primarily involve filial piety, respect for elders, sibling harmony, peaceful coexistence, adherence to national laws, and payment of taxes and duties. Therefore, the state recognized the legitimacy of family laws and clan regulations, which served as a supplementary form of national laws.

In addition to kinship, the concept of stability and reluctance to move, which arose from the feudal self-sufficient smallholder peasant economy, formed a necessary condition for agricultural reproduction and national security. This idea evolved into the harmonious rural society's geographical bonds. From a political governance perspective, achieving an orderly and harmonious society naturally requires the harmonious coexistence of the common people in their daily lives. Under the influence of stable kinship and geographical bonds, "*Tiao Chu Xi Song*" (調處息訟) (mediation to settle disputes and lawsuits) became prevalent in ancient judicial practices. Such mediation was applied to civil cases as early as the Qin and Han dynasties and became institutionalized by the Tang dynasty, when out-of-court reconciliation flourished as a socially sanctioned norm. Due to the positive social effects of mediation, it was advocated by the highest rulers. For instance, in the Qing dynasty, from the *Sheng Yu Liu Tiao* (《聖谕六條》) (*Six Instructions of the Sacred Edicts*) issued by the Shunzhi Emperor (順治帝), to the *Sheng Yu Shi Liu Tiao* (《聖谕十六條》) (*Sixteen Instructions of the Sacred Edict*) by the Kangxi Emperor (康熙帝), and to the *Sheng Yu Guang Xun* (《聖谕廣訓》) (*Expanded Instructions of the Sacred Edict*) by the Yongzheng Emperor (雍正帝), all included content on "harmonizing the local community to resolve disputes and suppress litigation".

3.1.3 The Autocratic Political System

The Chinese Legal Family was nurtured, developed, and grew under the backdrop of absolute monarchy, thus serving the political system of autocratic centralization of power. Since 221 BCE, when the Qin Dynasty unified the six states and established a centralized feudal autocratic state, the political system of autocracy has continuously strengthened along an ascending spiral trajectory. Under the legal framework of the Chinese Legal Family, imperial power was supreme, overriding the law, which became a common characteristic in all states within the Chinese Legal Family.

Since the unification of China by the Qin Dynasty, legislative power has been highly centralized in the hands of the emperor. Under the emperor's absolute authority, his commands were codified as "*Zhi*" (制) (edicts) and his decrees as "*Zhao*" (诏) (imperial proclamations), rendering his words tantamount to law. No state organs held independent legislative power or specialized legislative functions, as all legal authority emanated directly from the throne. The compilation of legal codes was always overseen by officials appointed or selected by the emperor. As a result, all major legislative enactments throughout the imperial era were promulgated under the designation of "*Qin Ding*" (欽定) (imperially authorized). To lend an air of sanctity to imperial legislation, legal codes often proclaimed that the laws were the will of the "sage" or were "ordained by Heaven". As laws were essential tools for maintaining order, governing the people, and punishing crime, emperors who were capable or active in governance often attached great importance to, and sometimes personally presided over, the process of lawmaking.

To ensure the impartiality of officials in administering justice, supervisory agencies focused on judicial oversight. As early as the Qin Dynasty, after the unification of China, specialized judicial inspectors, known as "*Jun Yu Shi*" (郡禦史) (Commandery Censors), were established to oversee the administration of justice at the *Jun* (郡) (Commandery) level. During the Tang Dynasty, the "*Yu Shi Tai*" (禦史台) (Censorate) was responsible for monitoring officials, acting as the emperor's eyes and ears. When inspectors toured local regions, they prioritized reviewing and correcting criminal cases—larger issues were reported to the emperor for a decision, while smaller cases were directly reviewed and settled. Judicial oversight remained a central element in the supervisory regulations from the Tang through to the Qing Dynasty. However, judicial oversight in the imperial era functioned as a mechanism within the autocratic system and was often constrained by the emperor's will, limiting its ability to have a fully independent and proactive effect.

3.1.4 The Ideological Dominance of Confucianism

During the Spring and Autumn and Warring States periods, there was a flourishing of various schools of thought, and multiple theories coexisted. However, during the reign of Emperor Wu of the Han Dynasty (漢武帝), the policy of "*Ba Chu Bai Jia, Du Zun Ru Shu*" (罷黜百家，獨尊儒術) (Rejecting the Hundred Schools and Exclusively Respecting Confucianism) was implemented, which led Confucianism to dominate the intellectual and political landscape. Under the influence of Confucian culture, the Chinese Legal Family developed the following characteristics:

First, the "*San Gang Liu Ji*" (三綱六紀) (Three Fundamental Bonds and Six Guiding Principles) were codified into law. The "*San Gang*" (三綱) (Three Fundamental Bonds) are: The ruler is the guide for his ministers, the father is the guide for his children, and the husband is the guide for his wife. The "*Liu Ji*" (六紀) (Six Guiding Principles) defined hierarchical duties among: paternal uncles, brothers, clan members, maternal uncles, teachers and elders, and friends. These norms not only encompassed the core social relationships of imperial China but also formalized the protocols and rites governing interpersonal conducts. In ancient Chinese legal codes, the *San Gang Liu Ji* were enshrined as foundational tenets, epitomizing the Confucianization of the Chinese Legal Family.

Second, the Chinese Legal Family embodied the the human-centered philosophy of "*Tian Xia Gui Ren*" (天下歸仁) (all under Heaven returns to benevolence). This ancient Chinese humanism represented a highly rational mode of thinking, manifesting in law as a strong emphasis on humanistic care and concern.

1. **Virtue as the Primary Principle, with Punishment as the Auxiliary, and Clear Laws as Moral Instruction.** "*Ming De Shen Fa*" (明德慎罰) (the promotion of virtue and the imposition of penalty with prudence) was the foundational concept of governance in the Western Zhou Dynasty. Because "Heaven's mandate is not constant", and "only virtue is the foundation", the promotion of virtue, respect for virtue, and reverence for virtue were emphasized. As for "the imposition of penalty with prudence", it aimed at cherishing human life, ensuring that punishments were just and appropriate. This concept was developed over several generations of Confucian thought and, by the Han Dynasty, formed a complete guiding

legal philosophy: "*De Zhu Xing Fu, Ming Xing Bi Jiao*" (德主刑輔，明刑弼教) (Virtue as the primary principle, with punishment as the auxiliary, and clear laws as moral instruction), which was highly endorsed by successive rulers. The reason for this lies in using virtue to guide the people, aligning their thoughts and behaviors with a moral governance model, thus preventing crime. At the same time, it highlights the potential educational role of the law itself, the so-called "clear laws as moral instruction".

2. **The Law Brings About Harmony, Balancing Leniency and Severity.** In Confucian classics, harmony is the highest moral standard. Achieving the state of harmony produces the mysterious effect of "Heaven and Earth taking their positions, and all things being nourished". In the administration of justice, harmony refers to fair and accurate law enforcement, with the appropriate balance of leniency and severity according to the law. The goal of achieving harmony through law is not only to ensure judicial fairness and a balanced approach, but also to foster interpersonal and social harmony, and even harmony between humanity and nature. Confucian thought, through the concept of "*Tian Ren He De*" (天人合德) (the unity of Heaven and humanity in virtue), further elaborates the ethical and moral foundation for harmony between humans and the natural world. The autumn and winter executions practiced after the Han Dynasty were aimed at aligning judicial actions with the principles of "*Yin Yang*" (陰陽) (a concept describing the dualistic nature of the universe and how opposite forces or qualities are interconnected and interdependent), the "*Wu Xing*" (五行) (Five Elements of metal, wood, water, fire and earth), and the natural cycle, thus achieving harmony with nature.
3. **Cautious Punishment, Mercy in Sentencing, and a Deep Respect for Human Life.** Throughout Chinese history, enlightened rulers have often emphasized reducing the death penalty and cherishing human life. In the early Tang Dynasty, although the *Zhen Guan Lü* (《貞觀律》) (*Zhenguan Code*) was based on the *Sui Lü* (《隋律》) (*Sui Code*), it reduced the number of capital crimes by 92 and introduced a procedure for reviewing death sentences, with penalties for unauthorized executions. Due to these measures, including valuing human life, cautious punishment, and reliance on legal principles, the early Tang period experienced a flourishing era known as the "*Zhen Guan zhi Zhi*" (貞觀之治) (Zhenguan Prosperity). After the Tang Dynasty, the Song, Yuan, Ming, and Qing Dynasties essentially followed the Tang system. In the Qing Dynasty, the system of *Qiu Shen Hui Shen* (秋審會審) (an autumn joint-trial system) was implemented before carrying out the death penalty, which helped protect lives and correct miscarriages of justice.
4. **Care for the Elderly and the Young, and Leniency towards the Disabled.** The vision of a harmonious society described in *Li Ji* (《禮記》) (the *Book of Rites*)—"to ensure that the elderly are able to die in peace, the strong are employed, the young are nurtured to maturity, and the widowed, the orphaned, and the childless are all properly provided for"—is also reflected in the Chinese Legal Family. Since the Han Dynasty, laws provided special care for vulnerable groups such as the widowed, the orphaned, the elderly, the sick, and the disabled. Such

laws not only emerged early but also passed down through successive dynasties, demonstrating continuity and consistency. This is rare in the world's legal history of the same period and highlights the civilizational characteristics of the Chinese Legal Family. In ancient Chinese laws, the provisions of "*Cun Liu Yang Qin*" (存留養親) (sparing a convict to care for aging parents) and "*Mian Si Cheng Si*" (免死承祀) (exempting from death penalty to preserve ancestral rites) most vividly embodied the Confucian ethos of familial duty and humanitarian principles. The concept of "*Liu Yang Cheng Si*" (留養承祀) (spared for filial care and lineage preservation) stipulated that if a condemned criminal was the family's only son, or if his elderly or infirm parents had no other means of support, the death penalty could be commuted. The convict would instead return home to care for his parents, thereby preventing the extinction of the family line and ensuring the continuity of ancestral worship.

3.1.5 The Unified Multi-Ethnic State Framework

Since the Qin and Han dynasties, China has formed a unified multi-ethnic state. The "*Zhong Hua Min Zu*" (中華民族) (Chinese nation), as a whole, not only shares a common cultural origin but has also undergone varying degrees of communication and integration throughout its long development. It is this transcendent national spirit, beyond a single ethnic group, that has created the vibrant and colorful Chinese civilization, condensing into the profound "Chinese soul". Similarly, the Chinese Legal Family, like the history of the Chinese nation, has evolved through the convergence of numerous tributaries, just like the surging Yangtze River formed by many tributary streams flowing together.

Historical records indicate that in ancient times, the *Miao* (苗) people, who were outside the *Huaxia* (華夏) ethnic group (a historical concept representing the Chinese nation), had already begun to establish laws. Later, Huang Di (黃帝) (the Yellow Emperor, ancestor of the Huaxia people and initiator of the Chinese culture) defeated their tribe and imposed their penal system. From then on, the Miao people's penal code developed into the *Wu Xing* (五刑) (Five Punishments) of the slavery-based legal system, which was used throughout the Xia, Shang, and Zhou dynasties, and continued to be in effect during the early Han dynasty. During the Northern and Southern dynasties, various ethnic minorities established their own regimes across the vast Central Plains. In response to the governance needs of these large regions, and in accordance with their own ethnic customs, they formulated laws with different scopes of application, which enriched the content of Chinese legal culture and even created legal models directly drawn upon by the Sui and Tang dynasties.

The rulers of the Tang Dynasty held an inclusive attitude towards the laws and customs of ethnic minorities, thus pioneering the concept that, within a unified multi-ethnic state, different ethnic groups could apply their own laws under specific conditions. This regulation also indirectly reflects the development of laws in various ethnic groups, as well as the historical fact that these laws evolved through mutual interaction. During the Song Dynasty, the Khitan (契丹), Tangut (黨項), and Jurchen (女真) peoples rose to power and respectively established the states of Liao (遼), Western Xia (西夏), and Jin (金). These states created legal systems that both incorporated the traditional legal culture of the Central Plains and reflected the distinctive characteristics of each ethnic group.

During the Yuan Dynasty, under the rule of the Mongols (蒙古), the whole country was once again unified. The territory ruled by the Yuan Dynasty was unprecedentedly vast, rendering the ethnic and creative aspects of its legal system even more prominent. The extant *Da Yuan Tong Zhi Tiao Ge* (《大元通制條格》) (*Great Yuan Comprehensive Statutes*) is both an important legal code in the history of the Chinese nation's legal system and a representative of the height achieved by Mongol legal culture. During the early period of the Qing Dynasty, when the Qing began its rule in the northeast outside the Shanhai Pass (山海關), it adopted the "*Can Han Zhuo Jin*" (參漢酌金) approach to legislation, which meant drawing from the advanced legal systems of the Han people while retaining certain old systems and customs of the *Hou Jin* (後金) (Later Jin). After the Qing entered the Central Plains, the "*Can Han Zhuo Jin*" approach was extended nationwide. With the deepening exchange between Han and Manchu legal cultures, by the fifth year of the Qianlong (乾隆) reign, the revised *Da Qing Lü Li* (《大清律例》) (the *Great Qing Legal Code*), except for certain special provisions confirming the rights of the Manchu people, essentially became the same orthodox feudal legal code as the Tang and Ming laws.

As can be seen from the above, since the Chinese nation entered civilization, numerous ethnic groups, including the Han people, have been nurtured on the Chinese soil. Although these ethnic groups have been in different historical positions at various times, due to differences in culture, economy, and policy development, and their roles in the creation of the Chinese Legal Family have varied, the Chinese Legal Family was nonetheless jointly created by all ethnic groups. It embodies the legal wisdom of all the people, and is the result of the exchange and absorption of legal cultures and legal experiences from various ethnic groups.

In addition to the laws formulated by minority ethnic regimes which enriched the Chinese Legal Family, customary law popular among minority groups is also an integral part of the Chinese legal culture. With a long history, distinct characteristics, and close ties to social life, it serves social needs, possesses a solid grassroots foundation, and holds considerable authority. It plays an effective role in regulating and adjusting relations among different ethnic groups. The existence of such customary laws is both necessary and reasonable, making them an integral part of the Chinese legal culture. Therefore, it is not difficult to understand that the Chinese Legal Family, while centered on the Han nation, was jointly created by all ethnic groups within the Chinese nation.

3.1.6 *Conclusion*

Although originating and developing on native soil, the Chinese Legal Family, while showcasing its originality, also gave rise to a relatively complete legal framework and legal departments. Its level of development was not inferior to any other legal system of its time. For example, the legal culture reflected in the Western Zhou bronzeware is comparable to the *Code of Hammurabi*. Similarly, the Qin bamboo slips discovered in Yunmeng, Hubei, dating from around the third century BCE, present detailed legal codes, diverse legal forms, precise judicial interpretations, scientific judicial appraisals, and strict interrogation procedures. These all exemplify the advanced level of Qin's legal culture, which, compared to the early feudal legal culture of the Frankish-Germanic people in the West, was ahead by nearly a thousand years (Zhang 2007). To this day, many of the original excellent ideas and concepts in the Chinese Legal Family still offer reference value for the global civilization of rule of law.

3.2 Continuity in Evolution

The Chinese Legal Family has a long history, enduring through thousands of years of dynastic changes and social transformations without interruption. Its legal system and codified civilization have been passed down through the generations, maintaining continuity in its evolution.

3.2.1 *Continuity in Time*

The Chinese Legal Family has a long history, refined over thousands of years of social changes and dynastic rise and fall. Rulers of newly established dynasties, in their efforts to create a new governing order, would always draw lessons from the legal systems of their predecessors, making necessary reforms and innovations. Through this process, new legislative and judicial systems emerged (Zhang 2020: 151). Outstanding legal codes throughout history have been the result of incorporating previous legislative achievements and summarizing past judicial experiences. Therefore, Chinese legal culture has been characterized by a continuous vertical transmission, with each generation bringing both inheritance and innovation.

The Chinese Legal Family took shape during the Qin (秦) dynasty and gradually matured during the Sui (隋) and Tang (唐) dynasties, with its structure continuing through the Ming (明) and Qing (清) dynasties. From the Qin dynasty's transformation of "*Fa*" (法) (laws) into "*Lü*" (律) (codes), to the late Qing legal reforms in the early twentieth century, the Chinese Legal Family continued for over two thousand years. If we trace its origins further back to the pre-Qin period, when the foundation of the Chinese Legal Family was laid, and examine the legal principles such as "*Ming*

De Shen Fa" (明德慎罰) (the promotion of virtue and the imposition of penalty with prudence), the penal system like the "*Wu Xing*" (五刑) (Five Punishments) system, and codified laws of that era like the *Fa Jing* (《法經》) (the *Canon of Laws*), along with their modern influences, the continuity of the Chinese Legal Family extends even further.

Comparative law scholar Wigmore (1928: 141) aptly remarked that the Chinese Legal Family "is the only old one that has survived continuously to date—a period of more than 4,000 years; in comparison, the other living systems of today are but children." Throughout thousands of years of history, the Chinese Legal Family has never been interrupted, maintaining its continuity over time. This demonstrates that it has not only undergone continuous refinement throughout history but has also withstood the test of time. This enduring vitality is precisely why the Chinese Legal Family remains relevant and vital today.

3.2.2 Continuity in Contents

Examining the legal documents of successive Chinese dynasties, one can easily observe a strong sense of continuity in many contents.

Ancient records indicate that as early as the Xia Dynasty, a penal system was already in place. According to *Zuo Zhuan* (《左傳》) (*The Commentary of Zuo*), "During the Xia, when rebellions arose, the *Yu Xing* (《禹刑》) (the *Penal Code of Yu*) was established to restore order." The Xia Dynasty's legal philosophy can be summarized as enforcing punishments in accordance with the mandate of Heaven. Building upon this foundation, the Shang Dynasty developed its own categories of crimes, penalties, and judicial litigation system, as evidenced by oracle bone inscriptions unearthed in the early twentieth century. The Western Zhou Dynasty marked the pinnacle of early Chinese legal development, establishing guiding legal principles such as "*Yi De Pei Tian*" (以德配天) (matching virtue with Heaven) and "*Ming De Shen Fa*" (明德慎罰) (the promotion of virtue and the imposition of penalty with prudence). Zhou rulers further proposed that only by "*Bao Xiang Yu Min*" (保享于民) (ensuring the well-being of the people) could they "*Xiang Tian zhi Ming*" (享天之命) (receive the Mandate of Heaven), an idea that predates Rousseau's concepts of "natural rights" and "popular sovereignty" by centuries. The Spring and Autumn and Warring States periods represented a time of great upheaval and transformation in Chinese history, serving as a major turning point in the evolution of legal civilization. Before this period, ancient Chinese law was characterized by laws without formal codification. During the Spring and Autumn period, written laws and legal codes began to emerge (Chen 2011: 61–62). As early as the Spring and Autumn period, Zichan (子産) in the State of Zheng inscribed laws on a bronze *ding* (鼎) (a type of vessel) and displayed it in a prominent urban location for public awareness. Later, the minister of Zheng, Deng Xi (鄧析), transcribed Zichan's penal codes onto bamboo slips to facilitate wider dissemination, marking the initial emergence of codified law. During the Warring States period, Li Kui (李悝) of Wei compiled the *Fa Jing* (《法

經》) (the *Canon of Laws*), which consisted of six sections: *Dao Fa* (盜法) (Law on theft and robbery), *Zei Fa* (賊法) (Law on treason), *Qiu Fa* (囚法) (Law on prisoner or extent of justice), *Bu Fa* (捕法) (Law of arrest), *Za Fa* (雜法) (Miscellaneous Laws), and *Ju Fa* (具法) (General principles of sentencing). This became China's first written code. Drawing on this foundation, Shang Yang (商鞅) of Qin transformed laws into statutes and established the *Qin Lü* (《秦律》) (*Qin Code*) with six sections. The Han Dynasty later built upon the Qin's legal framework, with Chancellor Xiao He (蕭何) compiling the *Jiu Zhang Lü* (《九章律》) (the *Nine Chapters Law*). From this point onward, the comprehensive system of codified laws in ancient China was firmly established.

Since the "First Emperor of All Time", Qin Shi Huang (秦始皇), unified the six states and established a centralized, unified, multi-ethnic empire, China has maintained this centralized political system and its fundamental legal framework for over two millennia. By codifying these institutions into systematic legal codes, China not only upheld national unity but also ensured the continuity of its legal tradition. As one scholar noted, "Due to the stability and continuity of the power structure, many features of Qin and Han laws were inherited by later generations and had a profound influence" (Wang 2021: 187). The Three Kingdoms period, Wei, Jin, Northern and Southern dynasties marked the second great period of turmoil in Chinese history. However, despite this instability, the legal system saw significant development, laying a crucial foundation for the legal maturity of the Sui and Tang Dynasties. In the first year of the *Kai Huan*g (開皇) era, Emperor Wen of Sui (隋文帝) ordered Gao Jiong (高熲) to draft a new legal code, the *Kai Huang Lü* (《開皇律》) (*Kaihuang Code*). This code refined and expanded upon the legislative experiences of previous dynasties in both structure and content. The golden age of the Chinese Legal Family was in the Tang Dynasty. The *Wu De Lü* (《武德律》) (*Wude Code*) was initially modeled after the Sui's *Kai Huang Lü*, followed by the *Zhen Guan Lü* (《貞觀律》) (*Zhenguan Code*), which was a revision of the *Wu De Lü*. Later, during Emperor Gaozong's (唐高宗) *Yong Hui* (永徽) era, the *Yong Hui Lü* (《永徽律》) (*Yonghui Code*) was compiled based on its predecessors. With the addition of interpretative "*Shu Yi*" (疏議) (commentaries), authored by Zhangsun Wuji (長孫無忌) and others, these works together formed the *Tang Lü Shu Yi* (《唐律疏議》) (the *Tang Code with Commentaries*), which became the model legal code of ancient China and the hallmark of the Chinese Legal Family. Discussing the evolution of legal codes, late Qing jurist Shen Jiaben (沈家本) remarked, "Scholars universally regard the *Tang Code* as the most refined, and after the Song Dynasty, all subsequent codes followed its principles—though there were occasional modifications, the fundamental structure remained rooted in the *Tang Code*" (Shen 2011). Since its formulation, the *Tang Code* was widely regarded by successive rulers and legislators as a model for emulation. Subsequent dynasties, such as the Song dynasty's *Song Xing Tong* (《宋刑統》) (the *Song Penal Code*), Yuan dynasty's *Da Yuan Tong Zhi* (《大元通制》) (the *Great Yuan General Statutes*) and *Yuan Dian Zhang* (《元典章》) (*Statues of the Yuan Dynasty*), Ming's *Da Ming Lü* (《大明律》) (the *Great Ming Code*), and Qing's *Da Qing Lü Li* (《大清律例》) (the *Great Qing Legal Code*), all based their legal compilations on the *Tang Code*. Nevertheless, it is undeniable that "the brilliant and flourishing legal culture of the Tang dynasty was not the sole achievement of that period but rather the culmination of legal wisdom and practices accumulated over various periods and among different ethnic groups across China since the Xia, Shang, and Zhou Dynasties (He and Zhang 2022: 5).

Of course, continuity does not mean mere copying; rather, successive dynasties made corresponding adjustments and adaptations to the legal codes based on their own governance needs. As one perspective puts it, "The development of Chinese legal culture is rooted in reality, passed down through generations, and continuously reformed... This process is continuous yet also innovative, shaped by the characteristics of each era, making it neither conservative nor unchanging" (Zhang 2020: 152).

3.2.3 Continuity in Thought

Legal codes serve as the carriers of the Chinese Legal Family, while legal thought forms its core—the two are inseparable and mutually reinforcing. The continuity of the Chinese Legal Family is reflected not only in the continuous transmission of its legal codes but also in the enduring legal principles and philosophies behind them. For example, despite dynastic changes and institutional transformations, many legal codes across different periods consistently embodied legal concepts such as "*Yi Min Wei Ben*" (以民爲本) (the people-centered thought), "*Li Fa Bing Yong*" (禮法並用) (the integration of rites and laws), "*Ming De Shen Fa*" (明德慎罰) (the promotion of virtue and the imposition of penalty with prudence), and "*Jin Lao Xu You*" (矜老恤幼) (compassion for the elderly and the young).

The continuity and rationality of legal thought throughout history have shaped the distinctive spirits of the Chinese Legal Family, ensuring that many of its institutional elements remain relevant and vital even today.

Looking back at the thousands of years of evolution of the Chinese Legal Family, its development has never been interrupted. Instead, it has continuously expanded and enriched itself through its historical continuity, ultimately becoming a valuable legal and cultural treasure of global significance.

3.3 Far-Reaching Influence

Although the Chinese Legal Family originated in China, its influence extended beyond its borders, flourishing for over millennia and retaining its appeal even today. Thus, its distinctiveness is also reflected in the profound and far-reaching impact it has had.

3.3.1 Influence in the Horizontal Dimension

In the horizontal dimension, the influence of the Chinese Legal Family extends beyond national borders. A legal tradition cannot be considered a true "legal system"—nor can it embody the characteristics of a "legal community"—if it exists solely in its country of origin without member states. Historically, many East Asian countries actively adopted and incorporated Chinese legal principles, facilitating the rapid development of their own legal systems. As a result, they naturally became member states of the Chinese Legal Family.

Before Western powers forced open China's doors with gunboats, imperial China was the sole cultural source of East Asia. "The East Asian rule-of-law cultural community, centered on China, thrived and stood as a formidable counterpart to the Roman legal tradition that dominated the West" (Dong and Zhang 2021). Liang Qichao (梁启超), in his essay "On the Evolution and Gains/Losses in the Compilation of China's Codified Laws", observed that "Thus, countries like Goryeo (ancient Korea), Japan, and Annam (ancient Vietnam) all inherited our legal system in that era" (Liang 2000: 147). The legal historian Yang Honglie further argued, "The influence of the Chinese Legal Family on East Asian countries such as Korea, Japan, Ryukyu, Annam, and the Western Regions cannot be compared to the limited scope of influence that ancient Egyptian or Mesopotamian law had" (Yang 1999: 4).

Given the sophistication of the Chinese Legal Family and the national strength of imperial China, East Asian countries were naturally integrated as member states into the Chinese Legal Family, with its legal system becoming the unquestioned model for their own legislative frameworks. The *Tang Lü Shu Yi* (《唐律疏議》) (the *Tang Code with Commentaries*), as the pinnacle of the Chinese Legal Family, also served as the parent code for many East Asian nations. Just as "Roman law represents ancient slavery-based civilization" and "the *Napoleonic Code* represents modern capitalist civilization", the *Tang Lü Shu Yi* stands as another milestone in the history of human civilization of rule of law, and was described by Scholar Li Guangcan as "a representation of ancient feudal civilization" (Cao 1989).

Due to similarities in national conditions, tributary political relations, and the formal, government-led exchanges that facilitated legal learning (Dong 2021), Japan, Korea, Vietnam, and other East Asian nations became integral parts of the Chinese Legal Family. While the degree of adoption and the scope of influence varied, their legal systems shared a core legal philosophy that had been upheld by the Chinese Legal Family for thousands of years. For example, Japan's *Ōmi Code*, *Taihō Code*, and *Yōrō Code*, Korea's *Goryeo Code*, and Vietnam's *National Penal Code* (*Quốc Triều Hình Luật)* and *Hồng Đức Code* all took the *Tang Code with Commentaries* as their blueprint, serving as clear evidence of the Chinese Legal Family's comprehensive influence over its neighboring countries.

3.3.2 Influence in the Vertical Dimension

In the vertical dimension, the influence of the Chinese Legal Family transcends time and space. Since modern times, it has faced intense challenges from Western legal cultures, leading to the near disintegration of its legal system and the temporary silence of its legal civilization. However, its jurisprudential foundations remain deeply embedded in history, continuing to shape China's contemporary legal philosophy, legal institutions, and legal practices.

At the conceptual level, modern legal principles in China align closely with traditional legal philosophies of the Chinese Legal Family. The contemporary people-oriented development concept corresponds to the ancient people-centered thought. The principle of governing the country according to law resonates with the traditional notion that "law is the foundation of governance" (from *Xunzi* 《荀子》). Likewise, the pursuit of good laws for good governance echoes the classical belief that "establishing just laws brings order to a nation, and establishing just laws across the world brings order to all under Heaven" (from *Treatise on the Duke of Zhou* 《周公論》).

At the institutional level, there is a clear continuity between China's modern legal system and its historical legal tradition. For instance, the provisions in China's criminal law that exempt minors and the elderly from criminal responsibility or grant them leniency are directly connected to the ancient legal principle of "*Lao Xiao Fei Ji*" (老小廢疾), which granted exemptions or reduced punishments for the elderly, young, and disabled. The modern death penalty review system can be traced back to historical legal practices such as "*Si Qiu Fu Zou Bao Jue*" (死囚覆奏報決), which required final approval for capital punishment. Similarly, contemporary laws on joint criminal liability align with the ancient legal doctrine that stated "in cases of collective crime, the mastermind bears the primary responsibility, while accomplices receive a reduced sentence by one degree" (諸共犯罪者，以造意爲首，隨從者減一等).

At the practical level, approaches such as "dispute source management" and "mediation first" embody the traditional wisdom of "*Tian Xia Wu Song*" (天下無訟) (a society without litigation) and "*Yi He Wei Gui*" (以和爲貴) (harmony is held supreme). Even modern initiatives like the "*He Hu Zhang Zhi*" (河湖长制) (River and Lake Chief System) bear similarities to historical practices, such as the appointment of "*Zhen Zhang*" (圳長) (Ditch Chiefs), "*Yan Zhang*" (堰長) (Weir Chiefs), "*Qu Zhang*" (渠長) (Canal Chiefs), "*He Zhang*" (河長) (River Chiefs), and "*Hu Zhang*" (湖長) (Lake Chiefs), which were used in ancient China to manage water resources and maintain local governance.

3.4 Uniqueness in Core Values

"If the fundamental characteristics of ancient Chinese legal institutions in a formal sense reflect the uniqueness of traditional Chinese legal culture to some extent, then what truly establishes the distinct position of the traditional Chinese Legal Family in the global legal landscape is its underlying spirit and substantive value orientation" (Xia 1997: 57). The originality of the Chinese Legal Family in its creation and its continuity throughout its evolution have shaped its unique core values. Enriched by the intellectual ferment of the Hundred Schools of Thought, particularly the influence of Confucianism, the Chinese Legal Family developed independently, fostering many outstanding legal ideas and principles.

In other civilizations, law was often regarded as a divine gift, carrying strong religious and theological connotations. In contrast, Chinese legal culture originated from an imitation of the "*Tian Dao*" (天道) (natural order), embodying a rational approach to legal thought. Since Emperor Wu of Han's (漢武帝) policy of "*Ba Chu Bai Jia, Du Zun Ru Shu*" (罷黜百家，獨尊儒術) (Rejecting the Hundred Schools and Exclusively Respecting Confucianism), Confucianism has left an indelible mark on traditional Chinese legal culture and its legal system. As the highest ideal of Confucianism, "*He*" (和) (harmony) became the ultimate value pursued in traditional Chinese legal culture. Joseph Needham once observed that the ancient Chinese sought order and harmony throughout the entire natural world and regarded this as the ideal for all human relationships (Needham 1986).

Regarding the jurisprudential essence and political wisdom embedded in the Chinese Legal Family, President Xi Jinping has provided a profound summary from six perspectives, which align with the classical teachings of ancient Chinese thinkers.

3.4.1 The Governance Strategy of Integrating Rites and Law

"*Li*" (禮) (rites) was a unique socio-cultural phenomenon in ancient China, encompassing a vast range of principles and playing a profound role in regulating society. Meanwhile, "*Xing*" (刑) (punishment) was not limited to criminal penalties but, in a broader sense, served as a general term for "*Fa*" (法) (law). Over the course of Chinese history, the deep integration of rites and law gradually took shape and eventually reached a state of refinement. This integration became a defining characteristic of China's legal tradition, ensuring social order while maintaining moral governance.

On the one hand, *Li* occupied a fundamental position in the Chinese Legal Family. The emphasis on *Li* or ritual governance within the Chinese Legal Family was pervasive, manifesting directly in both legal institutions and judicial practices. Some scholars have even argued that "in the past, the component of ritual governance in Chinese law accounted for nearly one hundred percent" (Fan and You 2009: 73). This influence extended to the judicial realm as well. The impact of *Li* on the Chinese Legal Family can be summarized by the principles of "*Na Li Ru Lü*" (納禮入律)

(incorporating rites into law) and "*Chu Li Ru Xing*" (出禮入刑) (breaching rites inviting legal punishment). During the Western Han dynasty, Emperor Wu rejected the hundred schools and exclusively respected Confucianism, initiating the gradual integration of *Li* into legal codes. Later, the Cao Wei (曹魏) dynasty's *Xin Lü* (《新律》) (*New Code*) formally established the "*Ba Yi*" (八議) (Eight Deliberations) system, the Western Jin (西晉) dynasty's *Tai Shi Lü* (《泰始律》) (*Taishi Code*) implemented the use of "*Wu Fu*" (五服) (the Five Degrees of Mourning Attire) to determine punishments, and this integration of rites into laws and punishments continued to develop through the Qi (齊) and Sui dynasties, ultimately reaching full institutional realization during the Tang dynasty.

On the other hand, *Fa* also played a crucial role in ancient state governance. While the principle of *Chu Li Ru Xing* emphasizes the influence of *Li* on laws and punishments, it does not mean that laws and punishments could be replaced, and imperial China did not neglect the importance of law in governance. Meanwhile, the principle of "*Long Li Zhong Fa*" (隆禮重法) (promoting rites while valuing the law) emphasizes that law is an essential tool for state governance. As early as the Spring and Autumn and Warring States periods, the Legalist school advocated that rulers should base governance on the law and link the strength or weakness of the state to the enforcement of the law. For example, Shang Yang (商鞅) argued: "A wise ruler is cautious with laws. Words that do not conform to the law should not be heard; actions that do not conform to the law should not be promoted; matters that do not conform to the law should not be carried out… Therefore, a well-governed state will have vast territory, a strong army, and a respected ruler. This is the peak of governance. A ruler cannot overlook this." Han Feizi (韓非子) also emphasized: "When the law is upheld, governance prevails; when the law is abandoned, chaos ensues." In conclusion, *Long Li Zhong Fa* highlights the importance of integrating both rites and law in governance, without neglecting either aspect.

Although the roles of *Li* and *Xing* in state governance differ, both ultimately converge in the actual practice of governance. *Li* places greater emphasis on regulating the ideal conduct of individuals, primarily through moral education. This encourages the people to voluntarily learn, understand, and follow the rites, thereby preventing unlawful or criminal behavior. On the other hand, *Xing* focuses more on punishing individuals for their actions that have already violated the law. *Li*, *Fa* and *Xing* each constrain and guide human behavior from different perspectives, contributing to the overall governance of the state.

3.4.2 The People-Centered Thought

"In the vast history of Chinese legal civilization, the people-centered thought is the essence of Chinese legal culture and a valuable experience in governance" (Zhang 2022: 123). The ultimate purpose of governance lies in "*Qin Min*" (親民) (drawing close to the people), "*Yang Min*" (養民) (providing for their welfare), and "*Bao Min*" (保民) (safeguarding their well-being).

The people-centered thought emerged as early as the Spring and Autumn and Warring States periods. As recorded in *Shang Shu* (《尚書》) (the *Book of Documents*), "The people should be drawn close, not suppressed. The people are the foundation of a state, and a state can enjoy peace only when the foundation is firm." Public sentiment was regarded as a key factor in a state's rise and fall, and governance was expected to align with the people's will: "Governance thrives when it aligns with the people's will; it falters when it defies their aspirations" (from *Guanzi* 《管子》).

The people-centered thought carries rich connotations, and practicing this principle requires a multidimensional approach. It involves understanding the people's conditions—"If laws are established without examining the people's circumstances, they will not be effective" (from *Book of the Lord Shang* 《商君書》); aligning governance with the people's will—"The sage king first followed the people's will, and thus achieved great success. Many in ancient times have won the people's hearts through virtue and established great achievements" (from *Master Lü's Spring and Autumn Annals* 《呂氏春秋》); ensuring the people's welfare and prosperity—"Governance has its constants, and benefiting the people is fundamental" (from *Huainanzi* 《淮南子》); and educating and guiding the people—"A wise ruler nurtures the people, cares for their hardships, teaches and instructs them, carefully prevents minor transgressions before they grow into major evils" (from *Book of the Later Han* 《後漢書》).

It is important to note that the ancient people-centered thought bore strong imprints of maintaining feudal absolute monarchy. It was a top-down approach, heavily reliant on enlightened rulers and virtuous ministers, and thus had certain historical limitations (Zhang 2022: 140). However, it is equally undeniable that the idea of "*Min Wei Bang Ben*" (民惟邦本) (the people as the foundation of a state) gave rise to numerous commendable institutions and norms, fostering praiseworthy traditions and cultural values that had a lasting impact on later generations. Rooted in this people-centered thought, "In some respects, the law of imperial China was more humane and intelligent than its Western counterpart" (Bodde and Morris 1967: 41).

3.4.3 The Value Pursuit of Harmony and no Litigation

Lawsuits are an important means for human societies to resolve conflicts and disputes, punish unlawful behavior, restore social harmony and stability, and uphold fairness and justice. From a practical perspective, the Chinese Legal Family also values and leverages the active role of litigation in governance, focusing on the selection of judicial personnel, regulating relevant litigation procedures, and establishing a comprehensive judicial system. However, from an idealistic perspective, traditional Chinese legal culture advocates for "*Tian Xia Wu Song, Yi He Wei Gui*" (天下無訟、以和爲貴) (A society without litigation, where harmony is held supreme), and promotes a social environment based on interpersonal harmony. The best way to prevent disputes is to encourage people to settle their differences. In this way, a harmonious, dispute-free, and orderly society governed by rites and righteousness can be achieved, thus attaining peace and the ideal of a society without litigation. The pursuit of harmony and no litigation has become fundamental values in traditional Chinese legal culture.

The value pursuit of harmony and no litigation is closely related to the characteristics of traditional Chinese society. Chinese society is fundamentally rural; the local population typically lives within a close-knit community. When conflicts or disputes arise among the people, the common practice is for local elders or other informal authorities to mediate. Even if the parties involved enter into litigation, mediation is usually the preferred option, as it is the least costly for all involved. This is not only due to the high costs of litigation but also because of the complex web of familial, regional, and social connections between the parties. Once a dispute is brought to the government, it can disrupt the stability and harmony of clan structures and grassroots social order.

The concept of "a society without litigation" does not mean that traditional society lacked a system or mechanisms to safeguard litigation, but rather refers to the political vision and ideal of order in imperial China that sought to minimize lawsuits. Ancient works such as the "*Xi Song Ge*" (《息訟歌》) (*Song of Settling Lawsuits*) expressed a call for reducing litigation among the people. This ideal is also reflected in the "*Jiao Min Bang Wen*" (《教民榜文》) (*Placard for Instructing the People*) issued by Emperor Taizu of the Ming Dynasty (明太祖), which stated: "For disputes regarding marriage, land, or fighting among the people, no small matter should be brought to the officials immediately. It must first be settled by the local elders and community leaders. If not, the accuser shall first be punished with sixty strokes of the rod, and only then will the case be sent back to the community leaders for resolution."

The call for "*Wu Song*" (無訟) (no litigation) and "*Xi Song*" (息訟) (settling lawsuits) arises not only from the limited social and individual resources available but also from a deeper political and cultural context. Regarding the former, in a context where resources were overall scarce, litigation meant the consumption of a significant amount of human and material resources, and the pressures of finding legal advisors, evidence, and so on, were far greater than they are today. For officials, ancient local government officials often had to handle multiple responsibilities, including administration, taxation, public security, and justice. The "*Xing Song*" (興訟) (surge in litigation) would easily overwhelm grassroots administrative units such as county magistrates, burdened by the escalating demands of adjudicating disputes and rendering judgments. From a political and cultural perspective, imperial China placed great emphasis on social harmony and stability, believing that the prosperity of the state was built upon good social order and the well-being of the people. Good social order depended on reducing conflicts and disputes, regulating interpersonal relationships through ritual education, and resolving disputes in a relatively harmonious way when they did arise. Institutions like the "*Shen Ming Ting*" (申明亭), pavilions established during the Ming and Qing Dynasties and used to publicly display the wrongdoings of local offenders by posting notices and moral teachings, were intended to warn the community, discourage bad behavior, and promote a sense of moral responsibility, contributing to social harmony. Behind the ideal of "*Tian Xia Wu Song*" lies the important traditional legal principle of "*Yi He Wei Gui*".

The value pursuit of "*Tian Xia Wu Song, Yi He Wei Gui*" in the Chinese Legal Family is not about forcing people to end disputes, but rather about gently persuading and guiding the parties involved, awakening their inner moral conscience, and helping them genuinely feel the fairness and justice inherent in the process. In this way, they can calmly accept mediation or reconciliation. This principle was also reflected in the handling of criminal cases by the "*Shi Da Fu*" (士大夫) (scholar-officials), who often applied it in specific legal proceedings.

3.4.4 The Principle of "De Zhu Xing Fu"

It is widely recognized by scholars that "*De Zhu Xing Fu*" (德主刑輔) (Virtue as the primary principle and punishment as a secondary means) is an important characteristic of the Chinese Legal Family. This characteristic reflects the emphasis of the Chinese Legal Family, rooted in the agrarian-based society, on morality and ethical order (Ma 2014). "*De*" (德) (virtue) and "*Xing*" (刑) (punishment) represent two distinct social control systems in imperial China. *De* is centered on moral norms, while *Xing* is concerned with punishment and sanctions. In the Chinese Legal Family, the former holds the primary position, while the latter serves as a complement and support to the former.

As early as the pre-Qin period, philosophers and politicians recognized that punishment was a means to assist in moral education, as seen in the saying, "Clarify the five punishments to assist the five teachings" (from *Book of Documents* 《尚書》). On this basis, Confucius further clarified the different roles of virtue, rites, governance, and punishment in national governance, stating that virtue and rites are the foundation, while punishments are a tool: "If you govern the people through administrative decrees and regulate them through punishments, they may avoid wrongdoing but will lack a sense of shame. If you guide them through virtue and unify them through rites, they will cultivate a sense of shame and self-discipline" (from *Analects* 《論語》). In the Han Dynasty, Dong Zhongshu (董仲舒) combined the theory of the operation of Heaven-earth (天地) and Yin-Yang (陰陽) to form the concept of "*De Zhu Xing Fu*", which was promoted by the imperial court.

By the Tang Dynasty, the concept of "*De Zhu Xing Fu*" directly became the fundamental principle of state legislation. The *Tang Lü Shu Yi* (《唐律疏議》) (the *Tang Code with Commentaries*) emphasizes at the outset that the code and its commentaries were formulated based on the idea of "*De Zhu Xing Fu*". It states, "Virtue and rites are the foundation for governance, while punishment serves as its support. Together, they are as interdependent and mutually sustaining as the cycles of day and night or the complementary phases of spring and autumn". Subsequent dynasties followed this as the basic principle of legislation, emphasizing virtue as the foundation and punishment as the final tool.

The concept of "*De Zhu Xing Fu*" was also implemented in specific judicial rulings. In imperial China, judicial officials often cited legal provisions in their judgments, initially using punishment to deter the parties involved. However, the ultimate aim was still to educate the people, guiding them to understand the principles of rites, righteousness, and morality. For example, when descendants were found to be disrespectful to their parents and ancestors, judicial officials would explicitly order them to recite the "*Xiao Jing*" (《孝經》) (*Classic of Filial Piety*) in the judgment. The act of reading the "*Xiao Jing*" itself served as a form of punishment, thereby achieving the goal of moral education and restoration of family harmony.

This political view, where *De* and *Xing* complement each other while *De* remains the foundation, gave rise to the legal philosophy of "*Shen Xing*" (慎刑) (the imposition of punishment with prudence) within the Chinese Legal Family. Of course, in specific circumstances, such as during social unrest, rampant violence, or when the people are unsettled, the government must give priority to the law, imposing severe punishments and harsh laws.

3.4.5 The Concept of Equality Before the Law

The current criminal law in China stipulates the principles of legality and proportionality in sentencing. However, similar legal theories and legislative proposals were already proposed by ancient Chinese sages.

On one hand, imperial China had the practice of "*Yuan Fa Duan Zui*" (援法斷罪) (judging crimes based on the law). The section of "Records of Criminal Laws" in *Jin Shu* (《晉書》) (*Book of Jin*) records:

> In judicial conviction, all judgments must be based on the explicit provisions of legal statutes. If there is no specific provision applicable, judgment shall be rendered in accordance with the General Principles of the Code. Where neither specific provisions nor the General Principles contain relevant stipulations, such cases shall not be subject to punishment.

Similarly, the *Tang Lü Shu Yi* (《唐律疏議》) (the *Tang Code with Commentaries*) states: "All judicial convictions must cite the authoritative texts of statutes, ordinances, regulations, and precedents. Those who violate this rule shall be punished with thirty blows of the bamboo rod."

On the other hand, imperial China also embraced the concept of "*Fa Dang Qi Zui*" (罰當其罪) (punishment should fit the crime). This idea is reflected in the principle that criminal punishment should be proportionate to the crime committed: "When the punishment fits the crime, it commands authority; when it does not, it invites contempt" and "Punishment must never exceed the gravity of the crime" (from *Xunzi* 《荀子》). Furthermore, "the greater the crime, the heavier the punishment; the lesser the crime, the lighter the punishment" (from *Book of Han* 《漢書》). It is also evident in the principle that criminal punishment should not be influenced by factors such as status, which are unrelated to the crime: "A sage ruler governs the state through uniform rewards, uniform punishments, and uniform education… By 'uniform punishments', it means there shall be no hierarchical distinctions in legal sanctions" (from *Book of Rites* 《禮記》). Additionally, "The law does not favor the noble, just as a plumb line does not bend to follow crooked wood. When the law is applied, the wise cannot evade it with rhetoric, nor can the brave defy it through force. Punishments spare no high officials, and rewards leave no commoners unrecognized" (from *Rites of Zhou* 《周禮》).

Although the ancient Chinese practice of "*Yuan Fa Duan Zui*" does not fully align with the modern principle of legality in sentencing, and "*Fa Dang Qi Zui*" may not have always been perfectly applied, in the historical context of the time, these concepts undoubtedly reflected a notion of legal equality and proportionality. They highlighted the civilized and advanced nature of the Chinese Legal Family.

3.4.6 The Humanitarian Principle of Leniency

"Old people are able to die in peace", "children are nurtured to maturity", and "the widowed, the orphaned, the childless, the disabled, and the ill are all properly provided for" (from *Book of Rites* 《禮記》) are ideals that continue to resonate in the Chinese nation's dream of a harmonious society. The widowed, the orphaned, the childless, the elderly, children, women and the disabled are vulnerable groups within society, and providing them with special care and protection reflects the principle of "*Ren Zheng*" (仁政) (benevolent governance). In imperial China, the protection of these special groups was primarily embodied in two aspects: "*Xu Xing*" (恤刑) (lenient punishment) and social welfare.

Regarding "*Xu Xing*", the concept of "*San She*" (三赦) (three pardons) was already present in the Western Zhou (西周) period. These were categorized as: "the first pardon is for the young and weak, the second pardon for the elderly and senile, and the third pardon for the mentally impaired or foolish" (from *Rites of Zhou* 《周禮》). The *Tang Lü* (《唐律》) (the *Tang Code*) made extensive provisions regarding lenient punishment, based on factors such as age (three different groups of "seventy and above, fifteen and below", "eighty and above, ten and below", "ninety and above, seven and below"), degree of disability ("disability", "severe chronic illness"), and type of crime ("crimes punishable by banishment or lesser penalties", "treason, rebellion, and capital murder", and "theft and assault"). These provisions allowed for a gradient and typified approach to lenient punishment, which was largely followed in later dynasties. The *Tang Lü* also established specific regulations regarding the punishment of pregnant women and penalties for those who did not follow these provisions.

Regarding social welfare, in ancient times, special protection was provided to the vulnerable groups such as the widowed, the orphaned and the childless through measures like the provision of relief supplies and adoption or placement.

3.4.7 Conclusion

The six aspects mentioned above reflect the unique core values of the Chinese Legal Family, highlighting its legal essence and political wisdom. First, these core values maintained the stability of ancient social order. Throughout history, the Chinese Legal Family proposed numerous principles and methods to maintain social order, involving dimensions like patriarchal clan laws, ritual governance, and the kingly way, incorporating values such as the people-centered thought, benevolence, fairness, and harmony, which laid a solid foundation for the stability of ancient Chinese society.

Second, these core values nurtured the distinctiveness of the Chinese Legal Family. Under the guidance of these classical Chinese legal principles, the Chinese legal system was conceived, established, and developed, and has been accepted and emulated by different dynasties and countries.

Third, the core values of the Chinese Legal Family contributed to the shaping of Chinese culture. It was under the influence of Chinese legal principles that concepts such as benevolence, the people-centered thought, harmony, and lenient punishment gradually formed, enabling Chinese culture to thrive and Chinese civilization to shine brightly.

Lastly, the influence of the core values of the Chinese Legal Family transcends time and space. Even today, many of these principles continue to profoundly influence China's legal system, and they will likely maintain their impact in the future.

3.5 Superiority in Codification

The "Code" is the institutional manifestation of the Chinese Legal Family, and codification is a major feature of this system. As a country with a long history of writing and as the birthplace of *Han Zi* (漢字) (Chinese characters), our ancestors had long learned to use writing to express laws, transform laws into culture, and codify written laws. Over time, they gradually developed a legal culture and tradition of codification, characterized by "having codes and records" and "systematically compiling laws and regulations". The distinctive features and advantages of ancient Chinese codification are mainly reflected in the following four aspects.

3.5.1 Maintaining National Unity, Social Stability, and Peace of the People Through the "Code"

First, over the course of more than five thousand years of civilization, China gradually formed a comprehensive set of national systems and governance frameworks, including the imperial court system, the system of shared governance between the ruler and ministers, the commandery-county system, land distribution system, taxation system, monopoly on salt and iron, imperial examination system, supervisory system, and military system. Since the Qin Dynasty ended the "*Fen Feng Zhi*" (分封制) (Enfeoffment System) and implemented the "*Jun Xian Zhi*" (郡縣制) (Commandery-County System), standardizing weights and measures, unifying track gauges for carts, establishing a uniform writing script, and consolidating administrative codes, China has maintained a centralized authoritarian system and fundamental legal framework for over two millennia. This political structure and legal institution have effectively safeguarded national unity, facilitated ethnic integration, and driven social development throughout history. The codification of laws served to institutionalize these norms into an authoritative legal system, thereby better preserving territorial integrity and centralized governance.

Second, the codification of laws, on one hand, clearly defined the boundaries of what is allowed and what is prohibited, and along with ethical and moral norms centered around *Li* (禮) (Rites), it formed the behavioral standards in imperial China. These standards guided the actions of the people and prevented arbitrary violations of rules. On the other hand, codified laws set out a series of punitive measures after violations, serving to punish and deter unlawful actions while monopolizing the power of punishment within the state, thus preventing social conflicts from escalating due to private vengeance. In this regard, the codification of laws promoted social stability.

Lastly, in the context of ancient societies with relatively low productivity, the codification of laws also effectively protected people's peace of mind through means such as safeguarding property rights, protecting vulnerable groups, maintaining the family hierarchy, and shaping cultural identity.

3.5.2 Adapting to Reforms and New Policies Through the "Code"

Throughout China's history, various reforms have been accompanied by the process of codifying laws, from the reforms of Shang Yang (商鞅) during the Warring States period, to Wang Anshi's (王安石) reforms in the Song Dynasty, and Zhang Juzheng's (張居正) reforms during the Ming Dynasty. Notably, the famous political and legal reformer Li Kui (李悝) in the Warring States period compiled the *Fa Jing* (《法經》) (the *Canon of Laws*), and Shang Yang used these texts as a foundation to formulate the *Qin Lü* (《秦律》) (*Qin Code*), all with the aim of promoting reforms and implementing new policies.

The theoretical logic behind using a "legal code" to support "reforms" and "new policies" lies in the fact that any reform or new policy often involves a process of breaking the old and establishing the new. Whether it is the profound social changes stemming from "breaking the old", or the accompanying policies and institutional tools needed for "establishing the new", these all require clarification through the form of a legal code to prevent potential confusion or disorder during the process. Moreover, a systematic and complete new legal code often helps to further consolidate and expand the outcomes of the reforms, laying the foundation for the emergence of a prosperous era and accumulating strength for long-term stability. As President Xi Jinping pointed out:

> Emperor Taizong of Tang (唐太宗) emphasized the importance of upholding the law for governance, and the *Zhen Guan Lü* (《貞觀律》) (*Zhenguan Code*) contributed to the flourishing era known as the "*Zhen Guan zhi Zhi*" (貞觀之治) (Zhenguan Prosperity); the *Tang Lü* (《唐律》) (the *Tang Code*) revised from the *Zhen Guan Lü* laid the legal foundation for the flourishing of the Tang Dynasty. (Xi 2020: 226)

3.5.3 Achieving Legal Unification Through the "Code"

From the perspective of the "evolution" of law, if the codification of customary law marks the first breakthrough in the "history of evolution", then the codification of written law represents the second leap in this evolutionary process. Codification is not merely a simple listing or crude "binding" of existing norms; rather, it involves integrative innovation on the basis of these norms, using a unified format, systematic content, cohesive mechanisms, and harmonious intentions.

From a historical perspective, the legal system of the feudal society, which aimed to maintain imperial authority and the interests of the ruling class, inevitably prioritized criminal punishment as a key aspect of legislation. "Focusing on punishment" was its essential characteristic. However, with the increasing complexity of economic, familial, and social relations, there arose a need for comprehensive regulations covering various aspects such as people's livelihoods, property, marriage, inheritance, and litigation. The Chinese Legal Family successfully fulfilled this mission, responding to the changing demands of the times. It evolved from the "*Zhu Fa He Yi*" (諸法合一) (combination of laws) to the "*Zhu Fa He Ti*" (諸法合體) (a unified legal system), eventually leading to the development of comprehensive legal codes. This process resulted in the formation of well-structured, comprehensive, and consistent legal codes.

3.5.4 Showcasing Legal Craftsmanship Through the "Code"

For example, from the *Fa Jing* onward, various representative legal codes adopted the structure of "general principles" and "specific provisions". The definitions and clarifications within these codes were extremely precise, and the legal language was sophisticated yet straightforward, aiming for simplicity and unity. The legal texts strived for "clarity and brevity", ensuring that the established laws and regulations were easily understandable and concise. Besides, the codification culture contains numerous original juridical concepts, such as "*Lü Mu*" (律母) (Statutory

Operators)—grammatical particles within legal provisions that govern logical relationships between clauses, and "*Lü Yan*" (律眼) (Statutory Modifiers)—precision qualifiers that calibrate legal consequences with surgical exactness.

Additionally, during the development of the legal codification, legal interpretative techniques were also highly advanced and provided an effective supplement to the application of the codes. For example, the Qin bamboo texts discovered from the tomb of a Qin administrator at Shuihudi (睡虎地) in Yunmeng County, Hubei, China, offer interpretations of many articles and terms in the *Qin Lü* (《秦律》) (*Qin Code*). By providing explanations, examples, and detailed elaborations, this document helped resolve the tension between the simplicity of the legal text and the complexities of practical application, enriching the study materials for contemporary legal interpretation. Similarly, the *Tang Lü Shu Yi* (《唐律疏議》) (the *Tang Code with Commentaries*) presented highly detailed explanations of the Tang legal provisions in the form of "*Shu Yi*" (疏議) (commentaries), which, even today, remains remarkable. This demonstrates the exquisite legal craftsmanship within the Chinese Legal Family.

3.6 Conclusion

Stepping into the vast realm of classical texts, through the prism of history, we gain a glimpse of the grandeur of the Chinese Legal Family and a deeper understanding of its uniqueness. History is the best teacher; only by learning from history can we pave the way for the future. As President Xi Jinping pointed out:

> "History and reality tell us that only by inheriting the excellent traditional Chinese legal culture, exploring a rule of law path suitable for our own country from the practice of our revolution, construction, and reform, and drawing on the beneficial achievements of foreign legal systems, can we solidify the rule of law foundation in the building of a socialist modernized country in all respects and the great rejuvenation of the Chinese nation." (Xi 2021)

As a result, "we must pay attention to studying our ancient legal traditions and their ups and downs, excavating and inheriting the essence of Chinese legal culture, drawing nourishment from it, and choosing what is good to use" (Xi 2020: 111). On the new journey of advancing the Chinese modernization of rule of law, we should deepen our historical understanding of the Chinese Legal Family, enhance our historical confidence in Chinese legal civilization, further excavate the rich resources of traditional Chinese legal culture, scientifically explain the Chinese Legal Family, and promote the creative transformation and innovative development of Chinese legal civilization. We must strive for the revitalization of the Chinese Legal Family, the progress of Chinese legal civilization, and the great rejuvenation of the Chinese nation.

References

Bodde, D., and Morris, C. 1967. *Law in Imperial China.* Cambridge: Harvard University Press.
Cao, M. 1989. *Annotation on the Tang Code with Commentaries.* Jilin: Jilin People's Publishing House.
Chen, G. 2011. *Outline of the Chinese Legal History.* Beijing: The Commercial Press.
Dong, X. 2021. Translation and Dissemination of Ancient Chinese Legal Classics. *Guang Ming Daily* (11), May 22.
Dong, X., and Zhang, Y. 2021. *Attaching Importance to the Translation of Legal Classics Helps Revitalize the Chinese Legal Family.* February 2. Available at http://sscp.cssn.cn/xkpd/gjskjj/202102/t20210202_5309334.html.
Fan, Z., and You, C. 2009. *Why Rebuild the Chinese Legal Family: Juzheng's Selected Works on Law and Politics.* Beijing: China University of Political Science and Law Press.
Gu, H. 2023. On the Inheritance and Innovation of China's Outstanding Traditional Legal Culture in Xi Jinping's Thought on the Rule of Law—From the Perspective of the 20th CPC National Congress Report on Law-Based Governance. *Journal of Chongqing University (Social Science Edition).* April 6. Available at https://kns.cnki.net/kcms/detail/50.1023.C.20230405.0956.004.html.
He, Q., and Zhang, S. 2022. Superposition of National Wisdom: the Brilliance of Chinese Legal Culture in the Tang Dynasty. *Legal Forum* 1: 5–18.
Liang, Q. 2000. *Liang Qichao's Collected Works on Jurisprudence.* Edited by Fan, Z. Beijing: China University of Political Science and Law Press.
Ma, X. 2014. The Inherent Meaning of the Chinese Legal Family. *China Law Review* 3: 120–130.
Needham, J. 1986. *Needham's Collected Works.* Translated by Chen, Y., et al. Shenyang: Liaoning Science and Technology Publishing House.
Shen, J. 2011. *A Study of Criminal Law Across Dynasties.* Beijing: The Commercial Press.
Wang, Z. 2021. The Political Mechanics of Chinese Law: a Comparative Perspective Based on the Qin and Han Dynasties and Ancient Rome. *Social Sciences in China* 10: 167–187, 208.
Wigmore, J. 1928. *A Panorama of the World's Legal Systems.* St. Paul: West Publishing Company.
Xi, J. 2020. *On Adhering to Comprehensive Law-Based Governance.* Beijing: Central Party Literature Press.
Xi, J. 2021. Resolutely Follow the Path of Socialist Rule of Law with Chinese Characteristics to Provide Strong Legal Guarantees for the Comprehensive Construction of a Socialist Modernized Country. *Qiushi* 5: 4–15.
Xia, J. 1997. The Tradition and Transformation of Chinese Legal Culture. *Nanjing Journal of Social Sciences* 9: 55–61.
Yang, H. 1999. *The Influence of Chinese Law on East Asian Countries.* Beijing: China University of Political Science and Law Press.
Zhang, J. 2007. *Review and Prospect of the Chinese Legal Family.* Beijing: China University of Political Science and Law Press.
Zhang, J. 2010. Interpreting the Indigenous Nature of Chinese Culture. *Tribune of Political Science and Law* 5: 3–10.
Zhang, J. 2020. Carry Forward the Chinese legal Culture and Construct the Chinese Legal Family in the New Era. *Contemporary Law Review* 3: 151–160.
Zhang, J. 2022. On the People-Centered Thought in Ancient China. *China Legal Science* 5: 122–142.
Zhang, W. 2023. The Uniqueness of the Chinese Legal Family and Its Three-Dimensional Structure. *Oriental Law* 6: 4–14.

Part II
Chinese Modernization of Rule of Law

Modernization is a continuous historical stream. In the historical course of global modernization, in consideration of the various factors such as socio-economic conditions, political systems, social structures, cultural traditions, historical foundations, and even geographical environments, different modes of modernization are inevitably shaped. The unique cultural tradition, historical destiny, and national conditions have provoked China to follow a modernization path suitable for its own characteristics.

In 2021, during his speech at the celebration of the 100th anniversary of the founding of the Communist Party of China, President Xi Jinping introduced the concept of "Chinese modernization." The Report of the 20th National Congress of the CPC shed light on Chinese modernization in a systematical and comprehensive way. Subsequently, the modernization concepts in relevant fields have also been proposed, as evidenced by Chinese economic modernization, Chinese modernization of national governance, Chinese educational modernization, and so on. In the field of legal research, the concept "Chinese modernization of rule of law" has emerged as a scientific proposition that permeates the entire legal governance framework and its jurisprudential architecture. It is also a contemporary topic, key area, and hot issue in China's legal research.

Chapter 4
Conceptual Connotations of Chinese Modernization of Rule of Law

The "Chinese modernization of rule of law" is not a simple combination of the concepts of "rule of law" and "modernization", nor a casual application of the popular word "Chinese". Instead, it is produced based on scientific theoretical foundations and profound practical bases.

The Chinese modernization of rule of law is a concentrated manifestation of Chinese modernization in the legal field, and also a process of legal reforms carried out under China's specific national conditions. It represents a legal modernization with distinctive socialist characteristics, reflects the modernization of rule of law in civilized societies, and affirms a new form of human civilization of rule of law. Specifically, the Chinese modernization of rule of law has several inherent characteristics, as outlined below.

4.1 Carrying Profound Historical Depth

President Xi profoundly pointed out: "To follow our own path is the foundation of all the Party's theories and practices, and also the historical conclusion drawn from the Party's century-long struggle" (Xi 2021c: 13). The Resolution of the Sixth Plenary Session of the 19th Central Committee of the CPC regards "adhering to the Chinese path" as one of the valuable historical experiences drawn from the Party's century-long struggle, stressing that "in the history of mankind, no nation or state has ever achieved greatness and rejuvenation by relying on external forces, copying foreign models, or blindly following others" (People's Daily 2021). This important historical experience and scientific assertion can be perfectly applied to the modernization of rule of law.

X. Dong and Y. Li, *Chinese Legal Family and Chinese Modernization of Rule of Law*,
https://doi.org/10.1007/978-981-96-7529-6_4

4.1.1 Grounded in China's National Conditions

Chinese Rule of Law Philosophy stands at the height of world history, "using the telescope of historical rules to carefully observe" (Xi 2017: 442) the development of rule of law in human society. In contemporary China, the CPC remains committed to the national conditions and the requirements of the times, explore its own path of the rule of law, and finally carve out a new path for the Chinese modernization of rule of law. Focusing on China's national conditions and characteristics, Xi Jinping deeply inspects the historical movement trajectory of the national system and legal system. He emphasizes:

> With over 1.4 billion people, China is making a collective leap into modernization, a scale that exceeds the total population of all developed countries combined. This unprecedented challenge is marked by both complexity and difficulty, and the development path and implementation methods will inevitably have their own characteristics. We always approach issues, decision-making, and actions from the perspective of China's national conditions—neither chasing unrealistic ambitions nor sticking rigidly to old ways. We maintain historical patience, adhere to a steady yet progressive approach, and continue to advance step by step. (Xi 2023a: 22)

China has always been one of the world's major countries, and ancient Chinese law also had a broad influence. However, after the Opium War in 1840, China was gradually degraded into a semi-colonial and semi-feudal society, which interrupted the autonomous development of Chinese law. To change the future and destiny of the Chinese nation, countless patriots and intellectuals have been desperately seeking a political and legal development path suited to the country's unique national conditions. They "attempted various institutional models, including constitutional monarchy, parliamentary system, multi-party system, and presidential system, but all ended in failure" (Xi 2020: 262).

History has proven that these systems were unworkable in China and could not provide the institutional guarantees for national prosperity and people's well-being. Ultimately, China chose a new path for the modernization of its legal system. Over the course of the century since the founding of the Communist Party of China, it has adhered to the laws of governance, integrating Marxist rule of law theory with China's specific realities and excellent traditional Chinese legal culture. This has led to unrelenting efforts in building a socialist system and legal system with Chinese characteristics, thereby paving the way for a distinctive path of the Chinese modernization of rule of law.

4.1.2 Carrying Forward China's Outstanding Traditional Legal Culture

It is worth noting that the unique cultural traditions of the Chinese nation dictate that China must follow a path of the Chinese modernization of rule of law that suits its own characteristics. The Chinese nation has a long and unique legal cultural tradition. Over the course of its enduring five-thousand-year civilization, the Chinese people have forged a profound and extensive legal culture that embodies the distinct legal character of the nation. The unique Chinese Legal Family, as the root of Chinese legal culture, contains excellent Chinese legal principles that serve as the valuable source of knowledge and cultural foundation for the Chinese modernization of rule of law.

President Xi Jinping pointed out, "Our ancient legal system contains a wealth of wisdom and resources... We must study the traditions of our ancient legal system, reflect on its successes and failures, extract the essence of Chinese legal culture, and apply what is good" (Xi 2015a). Even today, many of the legal principles embedded in the Chinese Legal Family, such as "the governance strategy of integrating rites and law", "the people-centered thought", "the value pursuit of harmony and no litigation", "the principle of virtue as the primary principle and punishment as a secondary means", "the concept of equality before the law", and "the humanitarian principle of leniency" still hold unique value and modern relevance.

In contemporary China, upholding and expanding the new path of Chinese modernization of rule of law is, to a large extent, a process of creatively transforming and innovatively developing China's outstanding traditional legal culture. This culture represents our deepest soft power in terms of rule of law, and it serves as the cultural foundation on which the Chinese modernization of rule of law is formed and developed. The CPC, through long-term practical exploration, has paved a new path for the Chinese modernization of rule of law. This is by no means accidental, but is determined by our historical heritage and cultural traditions. On the important issue of maintaining and expanding the Chinese modernization of rule of law, we must have confidence, determination, and resolve. "In comparison to Western modernization of rule of law, the continuity of China's profound and vast legal civilization is a defining feature and unique advantage of the Chinese modernization of rule of law" (Zhang 2024: 13).

4.2 Reflecting Distinct Socialist Nature

China's path to the rule of law is by no means a mere replica of the Western capitalist legal system, but rather a path of socialist rule of law with Chinese characteristics. As Xi Jinping pointed out:

> The socialist rule of law path with Chinese characteristics that we must adhere to is essentially the specific manifestation of the socialist path with Chinese characteristics in the field of rule of law; the socialist rule of law theory with Chinese characteristics that we aim to develop is essentially a theoretical achievement of the socialist theory with Chinese characteristics in addressing issues of rule of law; and the socialist rule of law system with Chinese characteristics that we seek to build is essentially the legal expression of the socialist system with Chinese characteristics. (Xi 2021b)

> Specifically, regarding the achievements of our rule of law construction, we can list dozens or even scores of accomplishments. However, they all boil down to the establishment of the path of socialist rule of law with Chinese characteristics. (Xi 2020: 105)

The path of socialist rule of law with Chinese characteristics is the only correct path to the Chinese modernization of rule of law, reflecting its distinct socialist nature.

4.2.1 Leadership of the Communist Party of China

The leadership of the CPC is the defining feature, as well as the greatest strength of Chinese socialism. President Xi Jinping pointed out, "The leadership of the Party is the defining feature of socialism with Chinese characteristics and the fundamental guarantee for socialist rule of law" (Xi 2020: 92). "The leadership of the Party is the soul of the socialist rule of law with Chinese characteristics and the biggest difference between our rule of law and that of Western capitalist countries" (Xi 2015b: 35). Therefore, the leadership of the Party determines the political direction and development path of the modernization of rule of law, as well as its achievements and losses.

The Chinese modernization is a modernization under the leadership of the CPC, and the Chinese modernization of rule of law is inevitably a modernization of rule of law under the leadership of the CPC. The leadership of the CPC is the fundamental guarantee for the modernization of the rule of law in China. A review of history reveals that upholding the leadership of the CPC is the most valuable experience in the construction of the rule of law in China. Over the past century since its founding, the CPC has united and led the people in arduous and magnificent struggles, establishing the People's Republic of China, opening and expanding a new path of Chinese modernization, and writing a splendid chapter of socialism with Chinese characteristics in the new era. Scientific socialism has demonstrated vigorous vitality on the land of China, "and significantly shifted the worldwide historical evolution of and contest between the two different ideologies and social systems of socialism and capitalism in a way that favors socialism" (People's Daily 2021). From the perspective of unifying history and reality, domestic and international contexts, and theory and practice, the CPC has conducted an in-depth review of the historical lessons of the global socialist movement as well as the efforts in the construction of the socialist rule of law since the founding of the PRC. They have made a series of strategic plans for advancing the rule of law under socialism with Chinese characteristics, fully demonstrating the socialist nature of Chinese modernization of rule of law. In the twenty-first-century China, the modernization of socialist rule of law has shown great vitality, making significant historical contributions to the global socialist rule of law modernization in this century, and offering Chinese wisdom to mankind's exploration of building better social systems.

4.2.2 *The System of Socialism with Chinese Characteristics*

The system of socialism with Chinese characteristics is the fundamental cornerstone of the Chinese modernization of rule of law. In contemporary China, to correctly understand the socialist nature of Chinese modernization of rule of law, it is most important to grasp the nature and characteristics of the national political system.

> Since the reform and opening-up, the Party has led the people in adhering to the path of socialist political development with Chinese characteristics and developing socialist democracy, and has achieved substantial progress in this regard. Learning lessons from successes and failures in political development both at home and abroad, the Party has become deeply aware of the following: to have full confidence in the system of socialism with Chinese characteristics, we must first and foremost foster strong confidence in the political system of socialism with Chinese characteristics; to promote socialist democracy and socialist political advancement, we must ensure that the political system of socialism with Chinese characteristics is deeply rooted in China. (People's Daily 2021)

The political system and institutions of a country are the primary decisive factors in its modernization of rule of law. The CPC serves as the core leadership of the cause of socialism with Chinese characteristics. Upholding and improving the leadership of the Party, and strengthening its leadership over the construction of national and legal institutions, constitute the fundamental system within the system of socialism with Chinese characteristics, thus fundamentally determining the basic nature of the new path for the Chinese modernization of rule of law.

The political system and institutions of socialism with Chinese characteristics provide the new path for the Chinese modernization of rule of law with a distinct socialist nature. In terms of economic development, basic socialist economic systems, such as the system of public ownership playing a leading role and all forms of ownership growing side by side, the system of distribution according to work being dominant and a variety of modes of distribution coexisting, and the socialist market economic system, highlight the superiority of the socialist system, thus constituting the economic foundation of China's new path to modernization of the rule of law. In addition, in the process of upholding and developing socialism with Chinese characteristics, promoting common prosperity and fostering social equality and justice embody the essential attributes and fundamental purpose of socialism, reflecting the distinctive direction of China's rule of law modernization. "Bringing prosperity to all is an essential requirement of socialism, as well as an important feature of the Chinese modernization" (Xi 2021a). The socialist nature of Chinese modernization of rule of law inherently requires that the rule of law development in contemporary China consistently focuses on and takes seriously issues of promoting common prosperity and safeguarding social equality and justice. It is imperative to accelerate the establishment of rule of law systems that play a significant role in promoting common prosperity and fostering social equality and justice, thereby laying a solid foundation of rule of law values for upholding and expanding the new path for the Chinese modernization of rule of law.

4.2.3 The People-Oriented Development Concept

China always adheres to the principle that the rule of law construction serves the people, relies on the people, benefits the people, and protects the people. The representation of the people's interests, the reflection of their wishes, the protection of their rights and interests and the improvement of their well-being must be implemented throughout the process of law-based governance in all respects. Realizing, safeguarding and developing the fundamental interests of the overwhelming majority of the people must be rendered our starting point and ultimate goal of the rule of law construction. This is the fundamental political stance and core value of socialist rule of law with Chinese characteristics, and the most essential distinction between the rule of law in China and that in the West.

Putting the people first means upholding the principal position of the people. China's socialist system guarantees the principal position of the people as masters of the country, as well as in the comprehensive promotion of law-based governance, which is the essence and strength of our system. China is a socialist state under the people's democratic dictatorship led by the working class and based on the alliance of workers and farmers. This state system determines that all power in our country belongs to the people. "The people's congress system is a great creation of the Chinese people in the history of human political systems" (Xi 2014a: 4–5). As the organ of state power, the National People's Congress (NPC) occupies a central position in the national institutional system. The state administrative organs, supervisory organs, trial organs, and procuratorial organs are all created by the NPC in accordance with procedures stipulated by the Constitution and laws. Executive power, supervisory power, and judicial power are all derived from the organs of state power, ensuring that all state power ultimately belongs to the people for unified exercise.

Since the 18th National Congress of the Party, the Party Central Committee with Comrade Xi Jinping at its core has put forward the "*Quan Guo Cheng Ren Min Min Zhu*" (全过程人民民主) (whole-process people's democracy) as a key concept on the basis of an increasingly profound understanding of the rules governing the development of democracy. Xi Jinping has eloquently summarized the basic features of whole-process people's democracy:

> Whole-process people's democracy in China is a complete system with supporting mechanisms and procedures, and fully-fledged civil participation...... Our whole-process people's democracy has achieved the integration of process democracy and outcome democracy, procedural democracy and substantive democracy, direct democracy and indirect democracy, as well as the unity between people's democracy and the national will. It is a democracy that extends through the entire chain, covers all dimensions, and encompasses full coverage—the most extensive, authentic, and effective form of socialist democracy. (Xi 2023b: 531–532)

Whole-process people's democracy strongly advances the modernization of democracy, while leading the modernization of rule of law. As a scholar pointed out:

> Democracy is a common value of all humanity and a lofty goal in the modernization of rule of law for human society. We should further promote whole-process people's democracy, firmly

> base the modernization of rule of law on socialist democracy with Chinese characteristics, and rely on whole-process people's democracy to advance the reform of rule of law and ensure that the new path for the modernization of rule of law is stable and sustainable. (Zhang 2022: 28)

4.3 Mirroring Objective Laws of Legal Modernization

According to the basic tenets of the Marxist historical materialism, the historical development of human society is by no means a mere accumulation of a large number of fortuitous events, but a process of regular movement. Similarly, modernization is the historical replacement of traditional ways of life and systems with modern ones. This historical leap has brought about monumental innovations in the value system of human civilization. This process is not only a worldwide phenomenon and historical process, but also a phenomenon with distinct national characteristics. Modernization is therefore an organic integration of universality and particularity. The modernization of the rule of law is a profound revolution in the process of legal development in civilized societies, with its own inherent and intrinsic laws of movement.

4.3.1 From the Perspective of the Historical Trend of Chinese Modernization of Rule of Law

The Chinese modernization of rule of law is the product of certain social and historical conditions, deeply reflecting the basic trend and intrinsic laws of the rule of law modernization in civilized societies. The development of human civilization has objectively shaped different historical forms of legal development, and varying types of legal evolution have very different value objectives. The modernization of the rule of law constitutes both the evolutionary growth and transformative leap of humanity's legal civilization, representing a profound revolution in the development trajectory of legal systems within civilized societies. It vividly portrays the captivating panorama of jurisprudential transformation during the pivotal transition from pre-modern to modern social structures.

In a major developing socialist country in the East like China, characterized by vast territory, large population, multi-ethnic composition and complex national conditions, the modernization of its rule of law demonstrates a process of legal transformation under China's specific national conditions. Chinese modernization of the rule of law is a historic transformation in the evolution of China's legal civilization, reflecting a unique internal logic. In contemporary China, the CPC, from the strategic height of ensuring the long-term stability of the Party and the country, has gained a profound understanding of the critical role of the rule of law in the process of national modernization. By integrating the basic tenets of Marxist rule of law theory with China's specific realities and with the excellent traditional Chinese legal culture, it has independently and successfully pioneered, upheld and expanded a new path of the Chinese modernization of rule of law which is tailored to its national conditions.

4.3.2 *From the Perspective of the Basic Nature of Chinese Modernization of Rule of Law*

To evaluate the modernization level of the rule of law in a society, it is important to scrutinize the jurisprudential attainment index in that country. Any nation that has achieved the modernization of the rule of law inherently manifests as a substantively institutionalized rule-of-law entity.

In contemporary China, the modernization of the rule of law is a multifaceted process that encompasses legal thoughts, legal systems, legal behaviors, legal practices and so on, and thus constitutes an important component in the modernization of the national governance system and governance capacity. Since the 18th CPC National Congress, the CPC Central Committee with Comrade Xi Jinping at its core has positioned the strategic primacy of adhering to comprehensive law-based governance within the panoramic framework of the national modernization in the new era. It has exercised overall leadership on the strategies of the new path of Chinese rule of law modernization and has put forward the major strategic task of upholding and improving the system of socialism with Chinese characteristics, and advancing the modernization of the country's governance system and governance capacity. This profoundly reflects the inevitable need of adhering to and developing socialism with Chinese characteristics. It aims to promote the further maturity of the system of socialism with Chinese characteristics, so as to provide a more complete, stable and effective institutional system to ensure the Party's and the country's long-term stability. This is an extremely ambitious social project, which requires a comprehensive deepening of reforms to advance the modernization of the national governance system and governance capacity in all areas.

Xi Jinping pointed out: "the law is an important tool for governing the country, and the rule of law is an important support for the national governance system and governance capacity" (Xi 2020: 92). Therefore, as an important part of the modernization of national governance, to promote the modernization of the rule of law entails achieving a historic transformation from a traditional national governance system based on "rule by man" to a modern national governance system based on "rule of law". To adhere to the new path of Chinese modernization of rule of law, it is necessary to accelerate the establishment of a socialist rule of law system with Chinese characteristics, and to make efforts to enhance the effectiveness of the rule of law in promoting the modernization of the national governance system and governance capacity. The modernization of the rule of law in China and the construction of a national governance system based on the rule of law is an inherent requirement for deepening the modernization of national governance.

4.3.3 *From the Perspective of the Strategic Direction of Chinese Modernization of Rule of Law*

Looking at the historical process of global modernization of the rule of law, we can see that the modernization of the rule of law is a universal historical process around the world, constituting the main theme of national and legal transformations since the modern era. However, this process exhibits different historical characteristics in different countries, thereby giving rise to different paths of the modernization of rule of law. Thus, the modernization of the rule of law constitutes a dialectical synthesis of pluralism in jurisprudential evolution. The legal development of different nations or states always evolves along specific trajectories under the influence of different conditions. Within the same social formation, the levels of economic, cultural and ideological development differ among countries, as do their state structures and political systems. Each country has its own specific historical development, customs and national traditions, on top of the varying geographic locations, natural conditions, demographic conditions, etc. These complex factors inevitably result in the display of rich and varied historical characteristics during the modernization of rule of law in civilized societies.

Under the influence of factors such as economic development levels, cultural traditions and geographical environments, the development of the rule of law in different regions of contemporary China also exhibits certain disparities. Consequently, the development of the rule of law in China has been marked by a combination of unity and diversity, which reflects the rich and diverse nature of the Chinese modernization of rule of law, as well as profoundly demonstrates the development imbalance inherent in China as a major Eastern country. We must respect this reality by maintaining national legal unity while adapting to local economic conditions. Through legal frameworks, we should drive regional economic and social development, advance the modernization of regional social governance, and combine area-based and cross-regional legal approaches. This helps establish the strategic direction for comprehensively advancing the Chinese modernization of rule of law in the new era.

4.4 Confirming the Inherent Character of Autonomous Development

Generally speaking, the development of the rule of law can be categorized into autonomous development and dependent development, based on whether it aligns with the national conditions of the country. These two different types of rule of law development reflect the varying positions of countries or regions in the global process of rule of law development, which may be asymmetrical or unequal. Autonomous rule of law development refers to a model where a country, based on a deep understanding of its specific realities, independently chooses a path of rule of law development suited to its societal conditions, thereby steadily advancing the modernization of the rule of law. On the other hand, dependent rule of law development occurs when some developing countries, deviated from their own national conditions and needs, adopt and implement rule of law construction schemes in accordance with the legal system models of foreign countries (mainly Western countries). As a result, their own rule of law development becomes dependent on the legal systems of these foreign countries. Obviously, these two distinct modes of rule of law development inevitably lead to two vastly different outcomes.

Under the new era conditions of reconstructing the global order, China's legal practices become increasingly intertwined and interactive with global legal practices. How can China's rule of law reforms and development in contemporary times maintain its independent and autonomous character? This is a major challenge of the times that it must face. Since the beginning of reform and opening up, Deng Xiaoping (邓小平) has repeatedly stressed,

> In the past, when conducting the democratic revolution, it was necessary to adapt to China's situation and follow the path of encircling the cities from the countryside pioneered by Comrade Mao Zedong (毛泽东). Now, in pursuing development, it is also essential to adapt to China's situation and forge a path of modernization with Chinese characteristics. (Deng 1994: 163)

He also pointed out, "Regarding the construction of socialism in China, it cannot be found in Marx's writings, nor in Lenin's writings. Each country has its own circumstances and different experiences, so independent thinking is required. This is true not only for economic issues but also for political issues" (Deng 1994: 261).

China's development of the rule of law is a practice of reform and innovation of its rule of law system, institutions and mechanisms, carried out under specific temporal and spatial conditions, with its unique historical traditions and social conditions. Since the 18th National Congress of the CPC, in the face of the prevailing trend of contemporary globalization and various new situations and problems, Xi Jinping, from the perspective of upholding and developing socialism with Chinese characteristics in the new era, has further pointed out:

> "Independence is an inevitable conclusion drawn by our Party from China's reality, after going through the stages of revolution, development and reform by relying on the strength of the Party and the people. We should always rely on ourselves when seeking our national development and defending our national pride and confidence, and resolutely follow our own road now and in the future as we did in the past." "Adhering to independence means that Chinese affairs must be dealt with and decided by the Chinese people themselves. There is no such thing in the world as a development model that can be applied universally, nor is there any development path that remains carved in stone. The diversity of historical conditions determines the diversity of the development paths chosen by various countries. In the whole history of mankind, no nation or state has ever been able to rise to power and rejuvenate itself by relying solely on external forces or blindly following others; doing so inevitably leads to failure or subservience." (Xi 2014b: 29)

Since the founding of the PRC in 1949, and especially since reform and opening up was launched in 1978, the CPC has adapted Marxist theory on the rule of law to China's specific realities. Adhering to independence, pioneering and striving forward, the Party has autonomously chosen its own path of rule of law development, continuously deepened its understanding of the laws of Communist Party governance, the construction of socialist rule of law and the laws of human social development, and strived to establish a socialist country and legal system with distinctive Chinese characteristics, thus invigorating the cause of socialist rule of law with Chinese characteristics. This has opened up an independent path for the rule of law in China and laid a solid institutional foundation for the "*Zhong Guo zhi Zhi*" (中国之治) (Chinese Governance). The Chinese model of rule of law modernization, gradually shaped in the social and legal transformations in contemporary China, possesses its own unique historical character and distinctive Chinese features. As emphasized by the Party Central Committee, "Independence is the essence of the China's national spirit, and an essential principle for building the Party and the PRC. We must follow our own path—this is the historical conclusion our Party has drawn from its century-long struggle" (People's Daily 2021).

References

Deng, X. 1994. *Selected Works of Deng Xiaoping (Volume II)*. Beijing: People's Publishing House.

People's Daily. 2021. Resolution of the Central Committee of the CPC on the Major Achievements and Historical Experience of the Party's Century-Long Struggle (1). November 17.

Xi, J. 2014a. *Speech at the Celebration of the 60th Anniversary of the Founding of the National People's Congress*. Beijing: People's Publishing House.

Xi, J. 2014b. *Xi Jinping: The Governance of China (Volume I)*. Beijing: Foreign Languages Press.

Xi, J. 2015a. Accelerating the Construction of a Socialist Rule of Law Country. *Qiushi* 1.

Xi, J. 2015b. Speech at the Seminar for Provincial and Ministerial-Level Main Leaders on Studying and Implementing the Spirit of the Fourth Plenary Session of the 18th Party Congress and Comprehensively Advancing the Rule of Law. In *Excerpts from Xi Jinping's Discourses on Comprehensive Law-Based Governance*, edited by Central Compilation and Translation Bureau. Beijing: Central Literature Press.

Xi, J. 2017. *Xi Jinping: The Governance of China (Volume II)*. Beijing: Foreign Languages Press.

Xi, J. 2020. *On Adhering to Comprehensive Law-Based Governance*. Beijing: Central Party Literature Press.

Xi, J. 2021a. Make Solid Progress Towards Common Prosperity. *Qiushi*. October 15. Available at http://www.qstheory.cn/dukan/qs/2021-10/15/c_1127959447.htm.

Xi, J. 2021b. Resolutely Follow the Path of Socialist Rule of Law with Chinese Characteristics to Provide Strong Legal Guarantees for the Comprehensive Construction of a Socialist Modernized Country. *Qiushi* 5: 4-15.

Xi, J. 2021c. *Speech at the Celebration of the 100th Anniversary of the Founding of the Communist Party of China*. Beijing: People's Publishing House.

Xi, J. 2023a. *Selected Readings from the Works of Xi Jinping (Volume I)*. Beijing: People Press.

Xi, J. 2023b. *Selected Readings from the Works of Xi Jinping (Volume II)*. Beijing: People Press.

Zhang, W. 2022. The New Path to the Modernization of Rule of Law in China. *China Legal Science* 1: 5-31.

Zhang, W. 2024. "Common Features" and "Chinese Characteristics" of Modernization of Rule of Law. *Politics and Law* 2: 2-15.

Chapter 5
Basic Characteristics of Chinese Modernization of Rule of Law

In leading the Chinese people in their arduous and great social struggles, the CPC, by adhering to the integration of Marxist theory on the rule of law with China's reality and excellent traditional Chinese legal culture, has pioneered a new path of the modernization of rule of law with distinctive Chinese characteristics.

Xi Jinping pointed out, "the path of rule of law modernization that a country takes and the legal system that it builds are determined by its fundamental national conditions" (Xi 2020a: 110). The conditions or factors of China's socio-economic, political, cultural, historical and geographical environment determine or constrain the basic orientation and trajectory of the Chinese modernization of rule of law. Since the founding of the PRC in 1949, the arduous practice of exploring a new path for the Chinese modernization of rule of law has historically shaped the basic characteristics of the Chinese approach to the rule of law modernization.

5.1 Fundamental Political Safeguard: Strengthening the Party's Leadership

In contemporary China, the Communist Party of China (CPC), as the highest force of political leadership in the country, is in a leading position in the whole country and the entire social life, thus it is a must to uphold and strengthen the Party's leadership over comprehensive law-based governance, which is the fundamental political safeguard for the Chinese modernization of rule of law.

Comrade Xi Jinping pointed out, "the leadership of the Party is the soul of the socialist rule of law with Chinese characteristics and the biggest difference between our rule of law and that of Western capitalist countries" (Xi 2015b: 35). "In upholding the path of socialist rule of law with Chinese characteristics, the most important thing is to uphold the leadership of the Communist Party of China" (Xi 2015a). The purpose of comprehensively deepening reform, building the rule of law in China, and

X. Dong and Y. Li, *Chinese Legal Family and Chinese Modernization of Rule of Law*,
https://doi.org/10.1007/978-981-96-7529-6_5

strengthening the national institution and national governance system is to continuously promote the self-improvement and development of the socialist system with Chinese characteristics. The core of this is to uphold and improve the leadership of the Party. Therefore, the Party's leadership is the most fundamental guarantee for the comprehensive law-based governance and the Chinese modernization of rule of law. It is essential to uphold and strengthen the Party's leadership over comprehensive law-based governance, so as to ensure the correct direction in building the rule of law in China and promoting the Chinese modernization of rule of law.

5.1.1 Strengthening the Party's Leadership is Mandated by the Nature and Mission of Comprehensive Law-Based Governance

In his speech at the first meeting of the Central Committee for Comprehensive Law-Based Governance, Comrade Xi Jinping clearly put forward the scientific proposition of "new concepts, ideas and strategies for comprehensive law-based governance", and summarized its scientific connotations and core essence as "*Shi Ge Jian Chi*" (十个坚持) (Ten Upholds), the first of which is "upholding the Party's leadership". When this speech was published in the 4th issue of *Qiushi* in 2019, the author chose the title of "Strengthening the Party's Leadership Over Comprehensive Law-Based Governance". This fully underscores that strengthening the centralized and unified leadership of the Party is not only the primary guideline of Xi Jinping's speech, but also the general premise of this historic task. It indicates that the Party's leadership plays an overarching, comprehensive and decisive role in the cause of comprehensive law-based governance.

Comrade Xi Jinping has repeatedly pointed out, "advancing comprehensive law-based governance is a systematic project, as well as a broad and profound revolution in the realm of national governance" (Xi 2015a). "Profound revolution" means that many reforms involve tough challenges, which translate to an urgent need for the Party Central Committee to strengthen top-level design and overall coordination. It is also necessary to strengthen the organizational leadership and political guidance by Party committees at all levels in the rule of law work. As for the expression of "systematic project", it implies that comprehensive law-based governance is a complex, long-term and arduous project, which not only involves various fields such as economic, political, cultural, social, ecological civilization construction, national defense and military construction, and Party building, but also encompasses all aspects of reform, development, stability, internal affairs, foreign policy, national defense, and the governance of the Party, the country and the military. Moreover, it also signifies that comprehensive law-based governance is a long-term historical task. Only by fully exerting the Party's leadership role in exercising overall leadership, coordinating the efforts of all, designing the overall plan, and ensuring unified arrangements, can the overall planning of this "systematic project" be accomplished.

This is the only way to effectively promote the Chinese modernization of rule of law, and realize the ultimate goal of advancing comprehensive law-based governance and building the rule of law in China.

5.1.2 *Strengthening the Party's Leadership is a Multidimensional Jurisprudential Paradigm*

The Party's leadership over comprehensive law-based governance, first and foremost, lies in its leadership regarding directions and objectives, the development path, and strategic decision-making. This includes establishing the overarching goals, the general line, and key implementation mechanisms of comprehensive law-based governance, embodied in its strategic planning and top-level design.

Since the 18th National Congress of the CPC, the CPC Central Committee with Comrade Xi Jinping at its core has, at every historical juncture, put forward the basic theory of law-based governance, pointed out the direction for progress, and established the task list, roadmap and timetable. On the 18th CPC National Congress, it was emphasized that the rule of law is the basic way of national governance, made the strategic decision to "advance the comprehensive law-based governance", and proposed the new 16-character policy of "sound lawmaking, strict law enforcement, impartial administration of justice, and the observance of law by all" (科学立法、严格执法、公正司法、全民守法). At the Fourth Plenary Session of the 18th CPC Central Committee, the top-level design, roadmap and blueprint for advancing comprehensive law-based governance were formulated. In 2015, the CPC Central Committee and the State Council issued the implementation outline for building a law-based government. The 19th CPC National Congress put forward the new tasks and requirements for deepening the practice of comprehensive law-based governance in the new era, explicitly setting the goal of basically establishing a law-based country, government, and society by 2035. After the 19th CPC National Congress, the CPC Central Committee issued the plan for building the rule of law in China and the implementation outline for building a law-based society, along with many new initiatives to advance comprehensive law-based governance. The Central Working Conference on Comprehensive Law-Based Governance, held from November 16th to 17th 2020, comprehensively summarized the achievements in rule of law construction since the 18th CPC National Congress, scientifically answered a series of major theoretical and practical questions concerning the construction of the socialist rule of law with Chinese characteristics, and set force new strategic arrangements and requirements for the current and future work on comprehensive law-based governance. The practices since the 18th CPC National Congress have proved that the fundamental reason for the major achievements in China's rule of law construction lies in the fact that it has always adhered to the centralized and unified leadership of the CPC Central Committee with Comrade Xi Jinping at its core and followed the Chinese Rule of Law Philosophy.

5.1.3 Strengthening the Party's Leadership Must Have Concrete Implementation Mechanisms

Comrade Xi Jinping pointed out, "upholding the Party's leadership is not an empty slogan; instead, it requires that the CPC exercises leadership in legislation, ensures law enforcement, supports the judiciary, and takes the lead in observing the law" (Xi 2015a). It is necessary to improve the institutions and working mechanism for the Party's leadership over comprehensive law-based governance, strengthen the Party's organizational leadership over rule of law work, and reinforce the Central Committee's leadership in areas like sound lawmaking, strict law enforcement, impartial administration of justice, the observance of law by all, and rule of law reforms. On the one hand, the Party must fully leverage its role in exercising overall leadership and coordinating the efforts of all, bringing all aspects of law-based governance work under its overall planning, and implementing the Party's leadership throughout the entire process of law-based governance in all respects. On the other hand, efforts must be made to refine the Party's leadership over comprehensive law-based governance by "improving the institutions and working mechanism for the Party's leadership over comprehensive law-based governance" (Xi 2019b), ensuring that the Party consciously operates within the bounds of the Constitution and laws, and continuously enhances its capacity of law-based governance and law-based exercise of state power.

Through leadership in legislation, the Party transforms its views into the will of the state through legal procedures, providing the institutional and legal guarantee for the implementation of the Party's guidelines and policies. By ensuring law enforcement, the Party establishes a law-based administrative system characterized by unified power and responsibility with strong authority and high efficiency, and builds a law-based government that is scientifically structured, with clearly defined powers and responsibilities, strict law enforcement, transparency, fairness, integrity, efficiency, adherence to the law, and honesty, so as to safeguard the authority, dignity and unity of the law. By Supporting the judiciary, the Party ensures that judicial power is exercised independently and impartially in accordance with the law, optimizes the allocation of judicial powers, regulates judicial behavior, ensures the impartial administration of justice, and upholds social equity and justice. By taking the lead in observing the law, the Party sets an example for the public, supervises officials at all levels to act as models of respecting, learning, observing and applying the law, and fosters the favorable social ethos of respecting, learning, observing, applying and protecting the law. By coordinating and advancing major reforms in the field of rule of law, the Party aims to achieve the revolutionary change from the "rule by man" to the "rule of law", from legal systems to the rule of law, and from formal rule of law to good laws and good governance. Strengthening the Party's leadership over comprehensive law-based governance requires the whole Party and the people to strengthen the "*Si Ge Yi Shi*" (四个意识) (Four Consciousnesses), namely enhance political integrity, develop a better understanding of the general picture, follow the core leadership of the Central Committee, and act consistently with its policy; to foster the "*Si Ge Zi Xin*"

(四个自信) (Four-spere Confidence), namely, to have full confidence in the path, theory, system, and culture of socialism with Chinese characteristics; and to firmly adhere to the "*Liang Ge Wei Hu*" (两个维护) (Two Upholds), namely upholding General Secretary Xi Jinping's core position at the CPC Central Committee and in the whole Party, and upholding the Central Committee's authority and its centralized, unified leadership.

5.2 Theoretical Guide: Chinese Rule of Law Philosophy

Chinese Rule of Law Philosophy is profound, rich in content, logically rigorous and systematically complete. Based on the integration of theory and practice, it provides scientific answers to a series of major questions about upholding and expanding a new path for the Chinese modernization of rule of law. It has established an original and innovative Marxist theoretical framework on the rule of law for the twenty-first century, serving as a theoretical guide for advancing the Chinese modernization of rule of law.

5.2.1 Creatively Addresses the Strategic Position of Advancing the Chinese Modernization of Rule of Law

Since the founding of the Communist Party of China in 1921, it has led the Chinese people in a great social revolution of extraordinary hardship and grandeur. In the light of China's national conditions, it has successfully pioneered and expanded the path of rule of law for China. On the path to rule of law modernization, the Party has always adhered to the guidance of Marxist theory on the rule of law, especially its adaptation to China's specific realities and the needs of the times. As a result, Chinese Rule of Law Philosophy was established as the fundamental guiding principle for comprehensive law-based governance and building the rule of law in China.

Chinese Rule of Law Philosophy was created in the great practice of comprehensive law-based governance and promoting the modernization of rule of law. It has scientifically summarized China's historical achievements and rich experiences in building the rule of law, creatively transformed and innovatively developed excellent traditional Chinese legal culture, and critically inherited and selectively drawn upon the fruits of human rule of law civilization. It deeply reveals the internal logic between the "rule of law" and "modernization", as well as the universal laws of the modernization of rule of law. Chinese Rule of Law Philosophy is not only the fundamental guide for building the rule of law in China in the new era, but also steers the development of human rule of law civilization, serving as a beacon for the Chinese modernization of rule of law.

A modernized country is inevitably a rule of law country. Reviewing the historical process of global rule of law modernization, the "rule of law" and "modernization" are inherently linked, mutually dependent and inseparable. The issue of the "rule of law" versus the "rule by man" is a fundamental issue in the history of human political civilization, and also a major challenge that all countries must face in the process of achieving modernization. The modernization of rule of law signifies a historical transformation from the "rule by man" to the "rule of law", reflecting the inherent requirements of national modernization.

The rule of law is an important basis for the national governance system and governance capacity. Consequently, China must adhere to advancing the modernization of national governance system and governance capacity along the track of the rule of law. To promote the Chinese modernization of rule of law, we must closely focus on the strategic goal of modernizing the national governance system and governance capacity, so as to realize the historic transformation from a national governance system based on "rule by man" to one based on "rule of law". It requires firmly adhering to and improving the socialist rule of law system with Chinese characteristics, so as to build a modernized national governance system grounded in the modernization of rule of law.

Contemporary China has entered a new development stage. For this new, the Report of the 19th National Congress of the CPC clearly puts forward the strategic vision of building a modernized socialist country in all aspects and achieving the Second Centenary Goal, as well as a blueprint for building the rule of law in China. This strategic vision provides a roadmap and timetable for the "*Xin Liang Bu Zou*" (新两步走) (new two-step strategic plan) to achieve the Chinese modernization of rule of law in the new era, which marks the beginning of a new journey to accelerate the building of a modernized China governed by the rule of law. The proposition of the new strategic goal of building a modernized socialist country in all respects not only means that the rule of law has become more important in the whole country and the entire social life, but also denotes that its functions have become more comprehensive and its institutions and mechanisms more sound. The Chinese modernization of rule of law has become an integral element of the endeavor to build a modernized socialist country in all respects.

5.2.2 Creatively Reveals the National Conditions for Advancing the Chinese Modernization of Rule of Law

The most fundamental national condition of China is the leadership of the CPC, which is also the defining feature of socialism with Chinese characteristics. As is emphasized by President Xi Jinping (2017: 28), "What is meant by "Chinese characteristics"? This is it. The system led by the CPC is our own; it is not cloned from anywhere, nor is it a mere copy of others". Upholding and improving the system of the Party's leadership and strengthening the Party's leadership over the construction of the national system and legal system are the fundamental political guarantees for advancing the Chinese modernization of rule of law.

The Chinese modernization of rule of law is deeply rooted in the profound historical and cultural traditions of the Chinese nation. During the 18th group study of the Political Bureau of the CPC Central Committee, President Xi Jinping pointed out, "How should we approach our own history? How should we approach our own traditional culture? These are questions that every country must resolve in pursuing modernization". The Chinese nation has a long and unique legal culture tradition. Over the course of more than five thousand years of Chinese civilization, the Chinese nation has forged the Chinese Legal Family that embodies the unique legal character of the nation, as well as a profound and rich legal culture. In contemporary China, upholding and expanding the new path of the Chinese modernization of rule of law is an organic process of inheriting the excellent traditional Chinese legal culture, and a process of the creative transformation and innovative development of this legal culture. The excellent traditional Chinese legal culture is the deepest source of legal cultural soft power, and it serves as the cultural fertile ground for the formation and development of the new path of the Chinese modernization of rule of law.

In the complex and multifaceted process of contemporary globalization, the major challenge that we must face is to maintain the independent character of contemporary China's rule of law development, and forge a new path for the modernization of rule of law with Chinese characteristics. President Xi Jinping has profoundly pointed out,

> There is no such thing in the world as a development model that can be applied universally, nor is there any development path that remains carved in stone. The diversity of historical conditions determines the diversity of the development paths chosen by various countries. (Xi 2014b: 29)

Since the founding of the CPC in 1921, it has united and led the Chinese people to independently and proactively forge ahead, successfully pioneering and expanding an autonomous new path for the Chinese modernization of rule of law. This new path has laid a solid legal foundation for the realization of the "*Zhong Guo Qi Ji*" (中国奇迹) (Chinese Miracle) and "*Zhong Guo zhi Zhi*" (中国之治) (Chinese Governance), demonstrating the unique charm of autonomous rule of law modernization. This has transcended the "Western-centered" model of rule of law modernization. In other words, China has created a new paradigm for the global rule of law modernization, provided a brand-new choice for developing countries to pursue modernization, and contributed a Chinese approach to humanity's quest for better social systems.

5.2.3 *Creatively Analyzes the Intrinsic Motivations for Advancing the Chinese Modernization of Rule of Law*

First, it actively responds to the new demands of the people for the rule of law. In promoting the Chinese modernization of rule of law in the new era, the starting point and ultimate goal is to keep abreast of the new changes in the principal challenge facing the Chinese society, understand the new demands and expectations of the people for the rule of law, and insist on evaluating the results of comprehensive law-based governance by whether the people are satisfied and whether the people have a "sense of gain".

Secondly, it is conducive to the continuous development of whole-process people's democracy. President Xi Jinping has creatively elaborated on the Marxist theories on the state and law, scientifically revealed the rules governing the development of socialist democracy with Chinese characteristics, and proposed the significant concept of the "*Quan Guo Cheng Ren Min Min Zhu*" (全过程人民民主) (whole-process people's democracy). To uphold and expand the new path for the Chinese modernization of rule of law, it is necessary to respond to the new changes in the principal challenge facing the Chinese society. Meanwhile, developing whole-process people's democracy, upholding the people's principal position, and enabling orderly participation by citizens in democratic politics and rule of law construction must be regarded as important principles for promoting the Chinese modernization of rule of law. Through a variety of channels, mechanisms and approaches, efforts should be made to improve institutions of democracy, diversify forms of democracy and expand channels of democracy. This will foster a whole-process people's democracy that is broader, more comprehensive and more sound, thus injecting powerful momentum into opening up new horizons for the Chinese modernization of rule of law.

Thirdly, it helps to unswervingly promote reforms in the field of rule of law. Since the 18th National Congress of the CPC, under the guidance of Chinese Rule of Law Philosophy, reforms in the field of rule of law in the new era have focused on the prominent and key issues that are of great concern to the people and are essential to the overall development of rule of law. By integrating the top-level design with the principle of "wading across the river by feeling for the stones", and by upholding the fundamental value standard of safeguarding social fairness and justice, reforms have been advanced comprehensively with highlighted priorities. As a result, the field of rule of law has undergone historic transformations and achieved historic accomplishments, which have given a strong impetus to the deepening development of the Chinese modernization of rule of law.

5.3 Core Value Orientation: The People-Oriented Development Concept

In order to advance comprehensive law-based governance and build the rule of law in China, it is necessary to uphold the people-oriented development concept in the building of the rule of law, and to effectively safeguard and promote social fairness and justice. This is the basic value orientation of the Chinese modernization of rule of law. In this historical process, it is essential to insist that the rule of law construction serves the people, relies on the people, benefits the people, and protects the people.

5.3.1 *Upholding the Principal Position of the People*

The people are not only the principal subject but also the backbone of building the rule of law in China. In a socialist country where the people are the masters, promoting the rule of law must always keep the "*Ren Min Li Chang*" (人民立场) (people's standpoint) in mind and uphold the people's principal position. This is the primary manifestation of the people-oriented development concept in the Chinese modernization of rule of law.

The so-called "*Ren Min Li Chang*" means that Party members and officials stand firmly on the side of the people, making the people the starting point of their thoughts and actions. No matter what they think, say or do, they must unswervingly represent and safeguard the fundamental interests of the overwhelming majority of the people. China's socialist system ensures the principal position of the people as masters of the country, and also guarantees their principal position in advancing comprehensive law-based governance. This is the our institutional strength, as well as the fundamental difference between the socialist rule of law with Chinese characteristics and the capitalist rule of law.

Therefore, it is necessary to uphold and safeguard the people's principal position in deeply advancing comprehensive law-based governance, to uphold the key principle of the people's principal position in the Constitution, and to uphold the organic unity of Party's leadership, the people's status as masters of the country, and law-based governance of the country. It is essential to give rein to people's democracy, pool together people's wisdom, and reflect the common will of all the people. As the fundamental law, China's Constitution has established the socialist system and the people's congresses system, which, from the perspective of legal institutions, collectively embody the constitutional principle that all state power in China belongs to the people. President Xi Jinping has repeatedly emphasized on several important occasions that unswerving adherence to the national system of people's democratic dictatorship and the political system of people's congress system, as established by the Constitution, is a fundamental requirement for upholding the people's principal position and the constitutional principle that all state power in China belongs to the people, in the process of deeply advancing comprehensive law-based governance in the new era. These important statements have profoundly clarified the supreme principal position of the people in China's socialist system and socialist rule of law.

5.3.2 Protecting the People's Lawful Rights and Interests

An important connotation of the people-oriented development concept in the Chinese modernization of rule of law is to protect the people's lawful rights and interests. The fundamental purpose of promoting comprehensive law-based governance is to safeguard the rights and interests of the people in accordance with the law. The rule of law plays a crucial role in protecting rights, and safeguarding people's rights and interests is an important mission for the socialist rule of law with Chinese characteristics (Yu 2021). Adhering to the people-oriented nature in deeply advancing comprehensive law-based governance means to give full play to the function of the rule of law in protecting rights, so as to better safeguard the lawful rights and interests of the people. It is essential to firmly uphold social fairness and justice as the core value pursued by the rule of law, "striving to make the people feel fairness and justice in every legal system, every law enforcement decision, and every judicial case" (Xi 2019b). In this way, the promotion and realization of social fairness and justice will be implemented throughout the entire process and all aspects of adhering to the comprehensive law-based governance. Social fairness and justice cover the value ideals of socialism, embody the fundamental attributes of the socialist system, and constitutes the ultimate support for the social value system. The rule of law system is the carrier of fairness and justice. "Justice is the lifeline of the rule of law." "Comprehensive law-based governance must closely revolve around safeguarding and promoting social fairness and justice" (Xi 2017a: 101).

In the construction and practice of rule of law, officials at all levels play a crucial role in safeguarding the lawful rights and interests of the people. Officials exercise the Party's governance power as well as the state's legislative, executive, supervisory and judicial powers, and are thus pivotal to the comprehensive law-based governance (Xi 2021a). The Party's efforts to exercise leadership in legislation, ensure law enforcement, support the judiciary, and take the lead in observing the law are mainly manifested and realized through the concrete actions and work of officials at all levels (Xi 2020a: 135). Therefore, since the 18th CPC National Congress, the CPC Central Committee, with Comrade Xi Jinping at its core, has emphasized the need for officials to take the lead in respecting, learning, observing, and applying the law, which is recognized as critical for deeply advancing comprehensive law-based governance and protecting the people's lawful rights and interests. This fully demonstrates the people-oriented nature of Chinese Rule of Law Philosophy, and profoundly elucidates the importance of leading officials upholding the rule of law in protecting the lawful rights and interests of the people.

5.3.3 Relying on the People to Advance the Rule of Law

Relying on the people to promote the rule of law is an important manifestation of the people-oriented development concept in the Chinese modernization of rule of law. The broadest and deepest foundation of comprehensive law-based governance is the people, and it is essential to uphold the principles of serving the people and relying on the people. The cause of socialist rule of law with Chinese characteristics in the new era must rely closely on the collective efforts of the people. Under the centralized and unified leadership of the CPC Central Committee over comprehensive law-based governance, it is urgent to fully stimulate the people's enthusiasm for respecting the rule of law, and give full play to the active role of the people in consciously participating in the development of socialist rule of law.

Under the guidance of Chinese Rule of Law Philosophy, the *Implementation Outline for Building a Law-Based Society (2020–2025)* issued by the CPC Central Committee in December 2020 stresses the need to cultivate the rule of law belief in the whole society, to enhance the pertinence and effectiveness of rule of law publicity and education, and to guide all the people to become devoted advocates, conscientious observers, and resolute defenders of the socialist rule of law, thus rendering the rule of law a social consensus and a basic principle. The *Plan for Building the Rule of Law in China (2020–2025)* issued by the CPC Central Committee in January 2021 emphasized and deployed specific arrangements for closely relying on the people to advance comprehensive law-based governance. These important decisions are of great practical guidance for how to better organize and mobilize the whole people under the new historical conditions, and to unite and focus efforts on advancing the construction of socialist rule of law.

5.3.4 Adhering to the People's Evaluation of the Rule of Law

The criteria for evaluating the rule of law vary depending on the subject of evaluation, and thus possess subjectivity and class bias (Luo 2021: 130). In socialist China, the people are the principal subject of the comprehensive law-based governance and the "examiners" of rule of law, so the effectiveness of rule of law ultimately has to be evaluated by the people (Zhou 2021: 22). Xi Jinping stressed, "the people are the highest arbiters and final judges of our Party's work" (Xi 2014b: 367), and "The fundamental standard for measuring the success or failure of all work is whether the people support it, agree with it, are happy with it, or approve of it" (Wang et al. 2021). This requires, in the deepening of comprehensive law-based governance, to fully respect the people's inner sense of fairness and justice, and to pay close attention to the people's "sense of gain" regarding the rule of law. Whether the rule of law is just or not is not merely about the perception of legal professionals, but more importantly, it is about ensuring that the people feel fairness and justice.

The rule of law is the foundation of good governance, and good laws are the cornerstone of good governance. As the socialist legal system with Chinese characteristics, centered around the Constitution, continues to improve, our country and various aspects of social life have generally achieved the state of "*You Fa Ke Yi*" (有法可依) (where there are laws to follow). Under this legislative context, the focus of the people's attention on legislation is no longer "whether laws can be enacted to ensure that there are laws to follow", but rather "whether good laws can be enacted to achieve good governance". As President Xi pointed out,

> The people's expectations for legislation are no longer about whether there are laws, but whether the laws are good, effective, and capable of solving practical problems. Not every law can govern the country, and not every law can govern the country well. The more we emphasize the rule of law, the more we need to improve the quality of legislation. (Xi 2020a: 20)

The actual effectiveness of rule of law construction depends on whether it has truly brought tangible material benefits to the people, and whether it has genuinely met their various needs for a better life. The real experiences of the people serve as the most convincing measure of evaluation. Therefore, it is essential to understand the degree to which the people recognize the rule of law, and use the people's satisfaction and "sense of gain" as the criteria to assess the success or failure of rule of law development.

5.4 Strategic Objective: Building the Rule of Law in China Characterized by Good Laws and Good Governance

There are various rule of law models in the world. The CPC has systematically examined and deeply reflected on these various models from both ancient and modern times, at home and abroad. Based on this, it has firmly established the concept of "*Liang Fa Shan Zhi*" (良法善治) (good laws and good governance), emphasizing the path of socialist rule of law with Chinese characteristics and building the rule of law in China characterized by good laws and good governance.

In 2014, in the *Decision of the CPC Central Committee on Several Major Issues Concerning the Comprehensive Advancement of Law-Based Governance*, it was emphasized that "law is the crucial instrument for governing the country, and good laws are the prerequisite for good governance". In his explanatory remarks on this *Decision*, Xi Jinping pointed out,

> The people's expectations for legislation are no longer about whether there are laws, but whether the laws are good, effective, and capable of solving practical problems. Not every law can govern the country, and not every law can govern the country well. The more we emphasize the rule of law, the more we need to improve the quality of legislation. (Xi 2020a: 20)

In 2017, the Report of the 19th National Congress of the CPC proposed, "we should promote scientific, democratic and lawful legislation and use good laws to promote development and ensure good governance". In 2018, at the first meeting of the Central Committee for Comprehensive Law-based Governance, Xi Jinping emphasized, "we must ensure that the socialist core values are reflected throughout the processes of legislation, law enforcement, judiciary, and the observation of law, so that the socialist rule of law becomes a system in which good laws ensure good governance" (Xi 2020a: 236).

5.4.1 Good Laws Serving as the Premise

Building the rule of law in China is based on the premise of "*Liang Fa*" (良法) (good laws). As the ancient Greek philosopher Aristotle said: "Law is order; only with good laws can there be good order" (Aristotle 1885: 214). Similarly, the Song dynasty statesman and thinker Wang Anshi (王安石) remarked: "If good laws are established throughout the world, the world will be governed; if good laws are established in one country, the country will be governed" (Wang 1974: 302). President Xi Jinping has profoundly pointed out, "good laws are the prerequisite for good governance" (Xi 2020a: 233). "Not every law can govern the country, and not every law can govern the country well; the more we emphasize the rule of law, the more we need to improve the quality of legislation" (Xi 2020a: 20). "We should promote scientific, democratic and lawful legislation and use good laws to promote development and ensure good governance" (Xi 2020a: 186). "Good laws" are the embodiment of desirable values at the level of legal norms and form the foundation of a sound rule of law order.

"Good laws", in ancient Chinese society, referred to laws that embodied traditional virtues such as benevolence, people-centered governance, integrity, upholding justice, advocating harmony, pursuing universal peace, and integrating reason with human sentiment. In contemporary Chinese society, the term denotes laws that reflect socialist core values, traditional Chinese moral principles and virtues, and common values of humanity, including harmony and order, democracy and freedom, fairness and justice, personal dignity, and property security. In summary, "good laws" are laws that reflect the people's will, respect and protect human rights, effectively constrain public power, uphold fairness and justice, promote harmony and stability, safeguard reform and development, guide social trends, and gain the people's support. They are laws that respect and reflect the objective rules of human nature, humanistic values, natural order, economy, politics, culture, society, and ecology. These laws manifest the people's will, wisdom, and interests, align with the spirit of the Constitution and the principles of rule of law, and maintain the unity of the country's rule of law.

Aside from its substantive content, good laws are also laws that are well-crafted, clear and easy to implement—laws that adhere to the principle of legal authority, where legal provisions are reasonable and enforceable (behavioral norms prescribed by law are feasible, executable, and applicable). Rights, obligations, and responsibilities are balanced, with transparency, unified standards, broad applicability, continuity, and stability. Such laws are not retroactive, and there is consistency and coordination between rules, laws, legal departments, and between substantive and procedural laws—without contradictions, conflicts or confusion. This makes it easier for all people to obey and for state organs to enforce and apply the law.

5.4.2 Good Governance Serving as the Goal

Building the rule of law in China aims to achieve "*Shan Zhi*" (善治) (good governance), which encompasses two dimensions. First, in terms of value, it refers to "virtuous governance" that seeks to "establish effective social governance and sound social order, promote social fairness and justice, ensure the people's contentment in their lives and work, and substantiate their senses of gain, happiness and security with greater fulfillment, stronger safeguards, and more sustainable foundations" (People's Daily 2018). Second, in terms of methodology, it emphasizes "proficient governance" characterized by "collaborative governance" in the public sphere. This includes approaches such as "multi-party co-governance", "consultative co-governance", "co-governance of law and virtue" and "co-governance of law and science".

"*Duo Yuan Gong Zhi*" (多元共治) (multi-party co-governance), also known as multi-stakeholder governance or public governance, emphasizes the "goodness" of governance entities. First, it maximally absorbs public participation by expanding the voice, participation and decision-making rights of citizens and social organizations, further integrating democratic principles and mechanisms into national governance. Second, it maximizes consensus-building, promoting mutual respect and recognition among different political parties, classes, groups, and social sectors through dialogue, communication, and debate. Third, it maximally facilitates the construction of a social governance system led by the Party committee, with government responsibility, democratic consultation, social collaboration, public participation, legal safeguards, and technological support, and forms a social governance community where everyone has responsibilities, everyone fulfills their duties, and everyone shares the benefits. Fourth, it maximally expands the space for self-governance, so that each entity can maintain its individuality, autonomy and independence, stimulating social vitality through self-governance.

"*Xie Shang Gong Zhi*" (协商共治) (consultative co-governance), also known as consultative democracy or democratic governance, emphasizes the "goodness" of governance methods. President Xi Jinping attaches great importance to consultative democracy, stating, "under the system of socialism with Chinese characteristics, everything can be discussed amicably and matters concerning everyone are negotiated by everyone, so as to find the greatest common denominator of the will and demands of the entire society—this is the true essence of people's democracy" (Xi 2019a). "The people exercise their rights through elections and voting, and through the conducting of thorough consultation before major decisions to reach consensus on common issues as much as possible. These two important forms of Chinese socialist democracy together constitute the institutional characteristics and strengths of China's socialist democratic politics" (Xi 2022). Since the 19th CPC National

Congress, the Party has attached greater importance to building the consultative democracy system, giving full play to the important role of the Chinese People's Political Consultative Conference (CPPCC) as an institutional arrangement, important channel and specialized body for socialist consultative democracy. The development of consultative democracy has taken on new features such as diversified channels, enriched content, and multi-level structures. It complements and reinforces the strengths of electoral democracy, together constituting a hallmark of democratic governance with Chinese characteristics.

"*Fa De Gong Zhi*" (法德共治) (co-governance of law and virtue) emphasizes the "goodness" of the governance mechanism. Law is codified morality, while morality is uncodified law; both are indispensable norms in national and social governance. This approach values not only the regulatory function of law but also the educative function of morality, ensuring that the two norms and governance mechanisms complement and enhance each other. This synergy embodies the essence of excellent traditional Chinese legal culture and represents a key advantage of the Chinese modernization. The practical rationality of the co-governance of law and virtue has broken the "moral black box" of legal absolutism, playing a unique role in fostering a good rule of law order and advancing a new rule of law civilization.

"*Fa Ke Gong Zhi*" (法科共治) (co-governance of law and science) emphasizes the "goodness" of governance instruments. In contemporary China, the extensive use of digital technology has made social governance increasingly intelligent, while the formation of a rule of law order has become increasingly dependent on the support and empowerment of digital technology. The co-governance of law and science has thus become an objective principle of national and social governance. Empowering the rule of law with digital capabilities while ensuring that digital operations adhere to legal frameworks has become a widely accepted principle and common practice in modern governance. Take integrity governance as an example. In traditional society, integrity governance relies on law and morality, whereas in a digital society dominated by algorithms and ubiquitous networks, the rapid development of big data storage, processing, and application capabilities—along with the continuous maturity of cloud computing and blockchain technology—has provide powerful technological support for maintaining social integrity and building a credit-based society. Personal statements and behavioral traces completed through electronic means are now recorded, permanently stored, and leave digital footprints, compelling individuals to uphold honesty and integrity, exercise caution in speech and act, and comply with laws and regulations.

The rule of law in China characterized by "good laws and good governance" has achieved the integration of the moral and authoritative aspects of law, unifying the inherent goodness and external binding force of law, as well as combining the institutional advantages of rule of law with the intelligent advantages of technology. It also fosters the complementary relationship between Party governance and public governance, integrating self-governance, rule of law, and rule of virtue, thereby creating a unique and harmonious model of "good governance" in China.

5.5 Pathway Selection: Adhering to Comprehensive Law-Based Governance

Advancing the comprehensive law-based governance is a practical choice for promoting the Chinese modernization of rule of law and the only path to its realization.

"Comprehensive law-based governance is a systematic project, and we must take all factors into consideration, focus on key areas, and formulate integrated plans, pursuing this goal in a more systematic, holistic and coordinated way" (Xi 2020a: 229). "To advance comprehensive law-based governance, we must correctly handle the relationship between politics and the rule of law, reform and the rule of law, law-based governance and moral governance, and law-based governance of the country and rule-based governance of the Party" (Xi 2019b). In this way, we can ensure the correct direction of the Chinese modernization of rule of law and demonstrate the "Chinese logic" for the modernization of rule of law.

5.5.1 Uphold the Organic Unity of the Party's Leadership, the People's Status as Masters of the Country, and the Law-Based Governance

This is a fundamental experience in building the socialist rule of law in China and a key to success in forging a new path toward the Chinese modernization of rule of law. Xi Jinping emphasized:

> In China, the key to developing socialist democratic politics, ensuring that the people are masters of the country, and maintaining both vitality and stability in national political life is to uphold the organic unity of the Party's leadership, the people's status as masters of the country, and the law-based governance. (Xi 2020a: 70)

The Party's leadership is the fundamental guarantee for both the people's status as masters of the country and the law-based governance. The people's status as masters of the country is the defining feature of socialist democratic politics, while law-based governance is the fundamental means by which the Party leads the people in governing the country.

The People's Congress system is the fundamental political institutional arrangement for upholding the unity of the Party's leadership, the people's status as masters of the country, and the law-based governance. To guarantee the people's status as masters of the country, this fundamental political system must be upheld and refined. The People's Congress system helps to exert the Party's core role in exercising overall leadership, coordinating the efforts of all sides, and ensures that the Party's guidelines, policies and decisions are fully implemented and effectively enforced in all aspects of national affairs. The People's Congress is the fundamental means and the highest form for the Chinese people to realize their status as masters of the country.

It is only when the National People's Congress and local People's Congresses at all levels give full play to their roles that the will of the people can be effectively transformed into national laws and regulations through legal procedures, ensuring that national governance always conforms to the people's will and gains their support, and that the people being masters of the country does not become an empty slogan. The People's Congress system provides the political foundation and institutional prerequisites for comprehensive law-based governance. To advance comprehensive law-based governance, we must promote all aspects of the country's undertakings and work in accordance with the Constitution and laws formulated by the People's Congress, ensuring the people's rights to equal participation and equal development, safeguarding social fairness and justice, respecting and protecting human rights, and realizing the rule of law in all national affairs.

In his speech, President Xi Jinping proposed that the Party's leadership and the socialist rule of law are inherently consistent:

> We emphasize the organic unity of upholding the Party's leadership, ensuring the people's status as masters of the country, and advancing law-based governance, with the Party's leadership as the most fundamental principle. Upholding the Party's leadership means supporting the people in being masters of the country and effectively implementing law-based governance as the fundamental strategy by which the Party leads the people in governing the country. (Xi 2020a: 42)

Only by upholding the Party's leadership can the people's status as masters of the country be fully realized, and the institutionalization and legalization of national and social life be advanced in an orderly manner. At the same time, adhering to law-based governance and law-based exercise of state power helps consolidate the Party's governing position, improve its governance methods, enhance its governance capacity and fulfill its governance mission. Under no circumstances should the Party's leadership be set in opposition to the people's status as masters of the country and law-based governance, nor should the latter be used to undermine or negate the former.

5.5.2 Uphold the Organic Unity of Law-Based Governance of the Country and Rule-Based Governance of the Party

Upholding the organic unity of law-based governance of the country and rule-based governance of the Party is a distinctive feature of the new path for the Chinese modernization of rule of law. In China, the CPC is the core leadership of the cause of socialism with Chinese characteristics, the only and long-term ruling party. It holds leadership and governing authority over the state and society, as determined by history, chosen by the people, and established by the Constitution. Given the Party's nature, status and mission, it is essential to uphold the organic unity of law-based governance of the country and rule-based governance of the Party, advancing both in a coordinated manner. This approach ensures that the national legal system and the Party's regulatory system complement, reinforce and safeguard each other, facilitating the mutual transformation of the Party's institutional strengths and the country's institutional strengths into one cohesive force.

From a theoretical perspective, law-based governance of the country and rule-based governance of the Party are inherently and necessarily connected. Governance of the Party and governance of the country are mutually complementary and inseparable, while law-based governance and rule-based governance are highly aligned and are indispensable to each other. As Deng Xiaoping pointed out, "Without Party rules and regulations, it would be difficult to ensure the enforcement of state laws" (Deng 1994: 147). Xi Jinping has similarly emphasized, "to govern the country, the Party must first be well-governed" (Xi 2012). He further stated that "only when rule-based governance of the Party takes root in the hearts of Party members can the law-based governance take root in the hearts of the people" (Xi 2019b).

In the practice of promoting rule of law modernization, we focus on coordinating the law-based governance of the country and rule-based governance of the Party across seven key areas: comprehensively strengthening the Party's overall leadership over legislative work; integrating the Party's regulatory framework into the socialist rule of law system with Chinese characteristics; expanding the "joint legislation" by the Party and the government, as well as jointly issuing guiding and regulatory documents; promoting the unified implementation of the Constitution and the Party Constitution, as well as national laws and Party regulations; establishing and improving coordination mechanisms for integrating law-based governance of the country and rule-based governance of the Party, ensuring their joint planning, deployment, and advancement; vigorously promoting reforms in the Party and state governance systems, including exploring the merger or co-location of Party and government organs with similar functions (Zhang 2021).

5.5.3 Uphold the Integration of Law-Based Governance and Moral Governance

Law and morality are two essential types of social norms, while law-based governance and moral governance are two important governance approaches. In terms of national and social governance, "law is codified morality, while morality is law internalized in the heart; both serve to regulate social behavior and maintain social order" (Xi 2020a: 109). Similarly, "Law is the standard that must always be followed, while morality is the foundation that must never be neglected" (Xi 2020a: 165).

Throughout history, law-based governance and moral governance have both been indispensable and irreplaceable means of national and social governance. "Law brings stability to the nation, while morality nurtures the people's hearts" (Xi 2020a: 165). "Law-based governance serves as a rigid means of maintaining social order, while moral governance is a flexible one. Only by integrating the two can social harmony be effectively preserved and the healthy and coordinated development of society be ensured" (Xi 2007: 206). Looking at China's history, periods marked by a proper balance between rites and law, and an effective integration of morality and law, have often witnessed stable order and sustained development.

On the new path for the Chinese modernization of rule of law, we have drawn on historical lessons and uphold the integration of law-based governance and moral governance. "We closely align legal development with moral development, combine external regulation with self-discipline, and ensure that rule of law and rule of virtue complement and reinforce each other" (Xi 2020a: 20). We adhere to a dual emphasis on both law-based governance and moral governance, ensuring that both are strong and effective. Our goal is to embody moral principles through the rule of law, strengthening the role of law in promoting moral development, while also nurturing the spirit of rule of law through morality, reinforcing the moral foundation for rule of law. In this sense, the new path for the Chinese modernization of rule of law is one where "morality" and "law" advance side by side: without morality, there can be no good law; without law, morality lacks structure. The integration of law and morality reflects the unity of China's rule of law history, contemporary practice and underlying logic.

5.5.4 *Pursue Coordinated Progress in Law-Based Governance, Exercise of State Power, and Government Administration, and Integrate the Construction of a Law-Based Country, Government, and Society*

Xi Jinping has applied the Marxist philosophical concept of systematic thinking as a foundational ideology and working method in the field of rule of law. He put forward the method to "pursue coordinated progress in law-based governance, exercise of state power, and government administration, and integrate the construction of a law-based country, government, and society" (Xi 2020a: 112–113). He further emphasized the need to "focus on coordinated progress and exert efforts in integrated development" (Xi 2020a: 113). The coordinated progress in law-based governance, exercise of state power, and government administration, along with the integrated construction of a law-based country, government, and society, constitutes both the overarching framework for comprehensive law-based governance and the core project for promoting the modernization of rule of law in the new era.

In terms of "coordinated progress", law-based governance, law-based exercise of state power, and law-based administration form an organic whole. "Law-based governance is the fundamental national governance strategy as established by the Constitution. Whether it can be effectively achieved depends on whether the Party adheres to law-based exercise of state power and whether governments at all levels practice law-based administration" (Xi 2020a: 113). As for "integrated construction", "a law-based country, a law-based government, and a law-based society each have distinct focuses while complementing one another. A law-based country is the ultimate goal of the rule of law construction, a law-based government is the primary subject in building a law-based country, and a law-based society serves as its foundation" (Xi 2020a: 229–230).

In general, we should not only advance law-based governance, but also promote law-based exercise of state power and law-based administration. Similarly, we should not only build a law-based country, but also establish a law-based government and a law-based society. Furthermore, we must go beyond developing the rule of law at national level to promote the coordinated development of national, local, regional, social and sectoral rule of law. In addition to developing the legal system, we must also foster a legal culture. Xi Jinping's call for "coordinated progress" and "integrated construction" aims to address key issues in developing the rule of law, such as fragmented efforts, jurisdictional conflicts, and mutual obstruction. By tackling imbalances and inadequacies in developing the rule of law, this approach enhances the systematic, holistic, and coordinated nature of rule of law construction, ensuring balanced and sufficient rule of law progress across regions, localities and sectors.

5.5.5 Uphold the Overall Approach of Building a Socialist Rule of Law System with Chinese Characteristics

Building the socialist rule of law with Chinese characteristics is not only the overarching goal and overall approach of advancing comprehensive law-based governance, but also an important goal and key focus of promoting the Chinese modernization of rule of law.

Following the establishment of the socialist legal system with Chinese characteristics, Xi Jinping, through extensive research and analysis, introduced the original and timely proposition of "building the socialist rule of law with Chinese characteristics", and provided a profound explanation of its scientific connotation and strategic significance. He pointed out,

> Advancing comprehensive law-based governance involves many aspects. In practice, there must be an overall approach that guides and coordinates all efforts. This overall approach is to build a socialist rule of law system with Chinese characteristics. All aspects of law-based governance must be planned and advanced around this central task. (Xi 2020a: 93)

Building this system means:

> Under the leadership of the Communist Party of China, we must uphold the socialist system with Chinese characteristics, implement the theory of socialist rule of law with Chinese characteristics, establish a well-developed system that includes a sound legal framework, an efficient law enforcement system, a rigorous legal supervisory system, a powerful legal guarantee system, and a comprehensive system of intra-Party regulations. (Xi 2020a: 93)

On December 6th, 2021, the Political Bureau of the CPC Central Committee held its 35th collective study session on building a socialist rule of law system with Chinese characteristics. While presiding over the session, Xi Jinping further emphasized that the socialist rule of law system with Chinese characteristics is an integral part of the socialist system with Chinese characteristics. He stressed the need to firmly uphold the defining feature of this system, remained committed to the path of socialist rule of law with Chinese characteristics, and focus on addressing key issues in the field of rule of law to better advance the construction of this system. The establishment of the overarching goal of and overall approach to comprehensive law-based governance, along with the clear characterization of the rule of law system's socialist nature, has provided greater clarity, confidence, and determination for the entire Party and the whole people. This, in turn, ensures a more scientific and orderly progress in building the socialist rule of law in China and advancing the modernization of rule of law and of national governance.

5.5.6 *Uphold Comprehensive Reforms in the Field of Rule of Law as a Powerful Driving Force*

Throughout the history of Chinese political civilization, driving the development of the legal system through reforms has been repeatedly verified and praised. Many outstanding statesmen in ancient China attached great importance to "*Bian Fa*" (變法) (reforms): Shang Yang's reforms helped the state of Qin to unify the other six states, the reforms in the early Han Dynasty led to "*Wen Jing zhi Zhi*" (文景之治) (a prosperous time under the reign of Emperor Wen and Emperor Jing), the reforms in the early Tang Dynasty achieved the "*Zhen Guan zhi Zhi*" (貞觀之治) (a prosperous time under the reign of Emperor Taizong), Wang Anshi's reforms in the Song Dynasty transformed the Song dynasty from poverty and weakness to prosperity, and although the "*Wu Xu Bian Fa*" (戊戌變法) (Hundred Day's Reform) in the late Qing Dynasty failed politically, it promoted ideological enlightenment. In summary, the successive reforms in feudal society provided a powerful driving force for the transformation of the feudal system, alleviated social conflicts to a certain extent, and fostered economic growth and social stability. These are valuable historical experiences. For contemporary China, building the rule of law in China and promoting the modernization of rule of law also requires summarizing and drawing on the historical experience of reforms, applying dialectical thinking to reforms in the field of rule of law, activating the endogenous driving force for the development of rule of law through reform, and accelerating the modernization of rule of law.

The 19th National Congress of the Communist Party of China put forward the scientific judgment that "the principal contradiction facing Chinese society in the new era is the contradiction between the people's ever-growing needs for a better life and unbalanced and inadequate development." The reflection of the changes in the principal contradiction of society in the new era in the field of rule of law is manifested in the people's higher demands for democracy, the rule of law, fairness, justice, security and the environment, as well as their growing expectations for better protection of fundamental and emerging rights such as personal rights, personality rights, property rights, information rights, and digital human rights. However, the quality and development level of the rule of law are not sufficient to fully meet the people's requirements and expectations for a better life. To resolve the main contradictions and pressing issues in the field of rule of law, it is necessary to promote rule of law reforms, and seek development, progress and innovation through reform. In a sense, it can be said that the profound transformation of the principal social contradiction has given rise to the rule of law reforms in the new era.

Since the 18th National Congress of the CPC, the CPC Central Committee, with Comrade Xi Jinping at its core, has vigorously promoted the reforms in the field of rule of law as a component of the broader agenda for comprehensively deepening reforms. More than 200 major reform measures have been launched successively, driving forward sweeping changes in the field of rule of law. These reforms have focused on addressing prominent issues such as defective legislation, non-compliance with laws, lax law enforcement, judicial injustice, lack of supervision, abuse of power, inadequate human rights protections, and insufficient safeguards for property rights. Efforts have been made to reform and improve leadership mechanisms for rule of law affairs, legislative and administrative law enforcement systems, judicial structures, governance mechanisms for political and legal affairs, and legal education systems. Notably, the system of reeducation through labor and the custody and education system have been abolished, while extensive in-depth education in the general knowledge of law, along with the rule of law publicity and education campaigns, has been carried out. Practical experience has demonstrated that reforms in the field of rule of law have significantly advanced the modernization of rule of law, serving as a powerful driving force for building the rule of law in China and promoting the modernization of rule of law.

5.6 Global Positioning: Chinese Modernization of Rule of Law in the Global Context

In contemporary times, the efforts of the CPC to promote the Chinese modernization of rule of law are intrinsically intertwined with the great changes in the global rule of law civilization, historically reshaping the development pattern of global rule of law civilization, and encompassing the basic value elements of a new form of human rule of law civilization. This is the global positioning of the Chinese modernization of rule of law.

5.6.1 Diversity and Interactivity of Human Rule of Law Civilization

The diversity of civilizations is a fundamental characteristic of the world and a source of human progress. The civilization of rule of law is an important component of human civilization, a core element of human political civilization, and a significant marker of the progress of human civilization. It plays a pivotal role in safeguarding and promoting the development of overall social civilization, including both material and spiritual civilization.

1. **The diversity of rule of law civilization is an inherent attribute of human civilization**

The diversity of human civilization determines the diversity of the connotations of the rule of law in human societies.

Since ancient times, China has developed a unique legal tradition—the Chinese Legal Family—within the history of global legal systems, accumulating a profound legal culture. Unlike the civil law system, the common law system, and the Islamic legal system, the Chinese Legal Family emerged under China's specific historical conditions, demonstrating the great creativity of the Chinese nation and the deep foundation of Chinese rule of law civilization. At the same time, it embodies the spirit and wisdom of the Chinese people, containing many valuable ideas and principles worthy of inheritance. On the other hand, the rule of law in Western society originated from the political and legal practices of ancient Greek city-states, particularly in Athens. It was not until the seventeenth and eighteenth centuries, during the rise of capitalist societies, that the legal worldview centered on "rule of law" and "constitutionalism" became prevalent. Concepts such as "rule of law", "equality before the law", "judicial independence", "separation of powers", "freedom and equality", and "natural rights" greatly enriched the Western thought of rule of law. The modernization of the rule of law civilization has been realized through the collision and integration of Eastern and Western legal traditions.

The diverse cultural foundations and unique historical trajectories of human civilizations have led to different paths and approaches in the pursuit of rule of law, resulting in various rule of law models. As Xi Jinping has emphasized, "there are no identical political systems in the world, nor is there a one-size-fits-all model of political institutions for all countries" (Xi 2014a: 16). In modern Britain, the rule of law gradually developed through a prolonged struggle to limit monarchical power. Over time, judicial practices aimed at safeguarding human rights contributed to the formation of the British Constitution, shaping a judiciary-centered model of rule of law development. In France, the rule of law was deeply influenced by the late eighteenth-century Revolution and the ideas of Jean-Jacques Rousseau, leading to a legislative-centered model that emphasizes the role of parliament, as the representative of popular sovereignty, in enacting laws to protect human rights and freedoms. The American rule of law model has blended the historical traditions of the common law system with European Enlightenment ideas. On one hand, it emphasizes a written constitution to safeguard civil liberties and rights, and establishes a system of separation of powers to balance individual freedoms and state authority. On the other hand, it introduced the system of constitutional review, highlighting its critical role in the operation of rule of law (Chen 2019). China's rule of law model, by contrast, has developed along a path suited to its national conditions, drawing from the historical achievements of the Chinese Legal Family while evolving through continuous theoretical exploration and practical innovation by the Communist Party of China. The diversity of political institutions and legal traditions across civilizations, shaped by distinct historical and national contexts, has given rise to different pathways for rule of law development. As a result, unique political and legal systems have emerged, enriching human civilization with their diversity and vibrancy.

2. **The interactivity of rule of law civilization is an important source for promoting the development of human civilization**

The diverse development models of human civilization has converged into the historical torrent of human civilization, and the progress of human civilization draws its continuous and powerful driving force from the diverse development of various civilizations rising and falling, exchanging and interacting. Therefore, Xi Jinping vigorously advocates promoting exchanges and mutual learning among civilizations, pointing out that "civilizations become colorful through exchanges, which in turn promotes mutual learning and their further development" (Xi 2020b: 468). He also emphasized:

> The rule of law is one of the important achievements of human civilization. The essence and gist of the rule of law are of universal significance to the national and social governance of all countries. We must learn from and draw on the outstanding achievements of the global rule of law civilization. (Xi 2015a)

First, human civilizations are not isolated from each other. The diversity of human civilizations determines the inherent necessity of mutual learning among civilizations. Since their birth, various human civilizations have engaged in different forms of interaction and exchange in different life interactions and economic activities. With the rapid development of science and technology, the great improvement of communication methods, and the increasing advancement of economic globalization, exchanges between human civilizations have gradually broken through the boundaries of time and space, broken down spiritual and cultural barriers, and greatly improved in the level, depth, and breadth of exchanges. The exchange and mutual learning of rule of law civilizations make the development process of human rule of law civilization full of vitality. Chinese civilization is an open system formed in the process of continuous collision and interaction with other civilizations, absorbing fresh blood and nutrients directly or indirectly.

> From the 'eastward transmission of Buddhism' and the 'integration of Islam and Confucianism' in history, to the 'eastward spread of Western learning', the New Culture Movement, and the introduction of Marxism and socialist thought into China in modern times, and then to the all-round opening up since the reform and opening-up, Chinese civilization has always remained new through inclusiveness. (Xi 2020b: 471)

Secondly, the diverse human civilizations are equal, and exchanges and mutual learning must be based on the principle of equality. Xi Jinping once mentioned in his speech:

> Every civilization is rooted in its unique cultural environment, condensing the extraordinary wisdom and spiritual pursuit of a country or nation, and has its own value. Humans only differ in skin color and language, and civilizations only differ in their diversity and richness, but there is absolutely no distinction between high and low, superior and inferior... We should

> break down the barriers of cultural exchanges with a broad mind, absorb the nutrients of other civilizations with an inclusive attitude, and promote the common progress of Asian civilizations in exchanges and mutual learning. (Xi 2020b: 468–469)

The development history of human civilization also tells us that although various civilizations have different lengths of history, there is no distinction between high and low, superior and inferior. All civilizations should be equal and should be treated with equal respect. For the sustainable development of rule of law civilization, it is necessary to treat all kinds of human civilizations equally, recognize the reality of the long-term coexistence of different social systems and different legal cultures, adhere to the concept of diversified development, seek common ground while reserving differences, integrate with each other in collision, learn from each other's strengths and make up for weaknesses. This not only conforms to the objective reality of the diversity of human civilization, but also is the inherent law of the sustainable development of human rule of law civilization, and is the only way to promote the continuous optimization of human civilization. Practice has proved that the socialist rule of law civilization with Chinese characteristics has unique advantages and strong vitality. We must unswervingly follow the path of socialist rule of law with Chinese characteristics in building a socialist rule of law country.

Finally, human civilization is inclusive and it is essential to advocate an inclusive attitude, seeking common ground while reserving differences, and adhering to harmony without uniformity.

> There are more than 200 countries and regions, more than 2500 ethnic groups, and more than 7 billion people on this planet. Trying to erase their differences will not work. Such differences should not become an obstacle to communication, let alone a reason for confrontation. The diversity and exchange of different civilizations, social systems, and development paths can provide a powerful impetus for the progress of human society. We should have less arrogance and prejudice, more respect and broad-mindedness, embrace the rich diversity of the world, and strive to seek common ground while reserving differences, learn from each other's strengths and make up for weaknesses, and seek harmonious coexistence and win-win cooperation. (Xi 2020b: 458)

5.6.2 Upholding the Global Governance Concept of Extensive Consultation, Joint Contribution, and Shared Benefits

In today's world, the international landscape is evolving at an accelerated pace. With the rising comprehensive strength of emerging market economies and developing countries, the global governance system established after World War II is increasingly out of sync with profound shifts in international power dynamics. At the same time, new global governance challenges continue to emerge, as humanity faces pressing issues such as climate change, major infectious disease prevention and control, cyberspace governance, and refugee crises. However, the deficiencies of the current global governance system are becoming increasingly evident, making its reform an inevitable trend. Since the 18th National Congress of the Communist Party of China, the CPC Central Committee, with Xi Jinping at its core, has keenly grasped the global trends of the times and the trajectory of human civilization. On this basis, it has creatively proposed the concept of global governance based on "*Gong Shang Gong Jian Gong Xiang*" (共商共建共享) (extensive consultation, joint contribution, and shared benefits), offering Chinese wisdom to the reform of the global governance system and the resolution to global governance challenges.

The global governance concept of extensive consultation, joint contribution, and shared benefits is China's basic philosophy and proposition for actively participating in the reform and construction of the global governance system. It follows the independent foreign policy stance of successive generations of CPC leaders, inherits and develops China's peaceful foreign policy, and upholds the diplomatic concepts of friendly consultation and seeking common ground while reserving differences. It is a governance concept that stands at a historical height, grasps the global trend, and is based on the people.

1. **Extensive consultation as the foundation of global governance**

"*Gong Shang*" (共商) (extensive consultation) refers to the democratization of global governance. In the report of the 19th National Congress of the CPC, President Xi Jinping stated, "China upholds the global governance concept of extensive consultation, joint contribution and shared benefits, advocates the democratization of international relations, and insists on the equality of all countries, regardless of their size, strength, or wealth" (Xi 2017b: 66). This implies that in global governance, all countries—big or small, strong or weak—enjoy equal opportunities, equal rights, and equal application of rules. On the basis of equality, nations should engage in mutual communication and understanding, using extensive consultation to build consensus, which serves as the foundation of global governance.

"Equal opportunities" in global governance means that in addressing common challenges faced by humanity, every sovereign state, as an equal member of the international community, has the right to participate in decision-making, express its concerns and positions, and benefit from governance outcomes on an equal footing. "Equal rights" refers to the entitlement of every sovereign state to the rights granted by international law, while also bearing the corresponding obligations imposed by the international community. "Equal application of rules" signifies opposition to hegemony, nationalism, and pragmatism, as well as the rejection of "double standards". All sovereign states should be held to the same standards and required to abide by international rules without discrimination.

2. **Joint contribution as the path of global governance**

"*Gong Jian*" (共建) (Joint contribution) is the fundamental pathway to achieving global governance, built upon the foundation of extensive consultation and shared consensus. It means that all countries should participate in global development, advance cooperation together, shoulder responsibilities collectively in the governance process, address global challenges jointly, achieve common development, and share the benefits of governance outcomes.

One aspect of joint contribution is the collective response to global challenges. No country can remain unaffected by global governance difficulties, and many challenges cannot be tackled alone. This necessitates adherence to the principle of joint contribution, where nations work together, leverage their respective strengths, and complement one another to achieve mutual benefits and win–win outcomes. However, in the process of joint contribution, it is important to recognize the differences in capacity and development levels between developing and developed countries. While pursuing the same overarching goals, countries should assume common but differentiated responsibilities.

Another aspect of joint contribution is the reform of the global governance system. China's concept of joint contribution advocates for all countries to work together in building an international system centered on the United Nations and an international order based on international law.

3. **Shared benefits as the goal of global governance**

"*Gong Xiang*" (共享) (Shared benefits) is founded on joint contribution, while the ultimate goal of joint contribution is to achieve shared benefits. The primary essence of shared benefits lies in enabling sovereign states to collectively enjoy the fruits of global governance in areas such as the economy, culture, and ecology through coordinated governance efforts.

Xi Jinping has emphasized, "all countries should be participants, contributors, and beneficiaries of global development. It is unacceptable for one country to develop while others do not, or for some countries to advance while others are left behind" (Xi 2015c). This underscores that the outcomes of global governance should be fairly and equitably shared among all participants of extensive consultation and joint contribution, ensuring win–win cooperation and common development. This concept is at the core of China's vision of extensive consultation, joint contribution, and shared benefits.

The principle of shared benefits serves both as an incentive for countries to actively engage in extensive consultation and joint contribution and as a crucial safeguard for advancing global governance under this framework. Only by ensuring that all nations have equal rights, equal opportunities, and equal access to governance outcomes can mutual trust between countries be strengthened, the coalition for joint contribution expanded, globalization stabilized, and global development made more balanced. Ultimately, this will allow the achievements of governance to be distributed more equitably among peoples worldwide, fostering the prosperity of humanity as a whole.

5.6.3 Practicing Genuine Multilateralism

Multilateralism is an effective pathway to maintaining peace and promoting development. Its essence lies in the principle that international affairs should be handled through collective consultation and that the future and destiny of the world should be jointly determined by all nations. For a long time, China has upheld the banner of multilateralism, actively participating in multilateral activities centered on the

United Nations and engaging in a wide range of multilateral treaties and international conventions. Through these efforts, China has made significant contributions to safeguarding world peace and advancing common development. The world today is undergoing profound changes unseen in a century.

To practice genuine multilateralism, it is essential to uphold the vision of building a human community with a shared future and remain committed to the common values of humanity—peace, development, fairness, justice, democracy, and freedom. This requires transcending ideological biases and maximizing the openness and inclusiveness of cooperation mechanisms, concepts, and policies to jointly safeguard global peace and stability. A peaceful and developing world must accommodate diverse civilizations and respect multiple paths to modernization.

Secondly, to practice genuine multilateralism, it is necessary to uphold international law as the foundation, and effectively safeguard the fair and just systems, orders, and rules. The international community should be governed by rules and consensus reached collectively by all countries, rather than being dictated by one or a few countries. There is only one international system—the international system with the United Nations at its core. There is only one international order—the international order with international law as its foundation. There is only one set of rules—the basic norms of international relations based on the purposes and principles of the UN Charter.

Thirdly, to practice genuine multilateralism requires the opposition of "pseudo-multilateralism". "Pseudo-multilateralism" superficially flies the flag of multilateralism, but in essence, it aims to create "small circles" and blocs politics, and even to divide the world by ideological alignment and camp selection, disrupting the international order and creating confrontation and division. Genuine multilateralism moves in the same direction as the democratization and legalization of international relations, advocating equality among nations regardless of size, and handling state-to-state relations through cooperation, negotiation, and consultation rather than power, force, and coercion.

Fourth, to practice genuine multilateralism requires the joint support and maintenance of members of the international community, and even more so, the contribution and demonstration of major countries. The world's major countries should become models for upholding the purposes and principles of the UN Charter, leaders in following international rules, and pioneers in providing necessary international public goods for global well-being. What is particularly important is that the world's major countries should lead the international community in firmly establishing the concept of building a human community with a shared future, upholding the banner of openness, inclusiveness, cooperation, and win–win results, promoting the common values of peace, development, fairness, justice, democracy, and freedom for all humanity, and further deepening and expanding the connotation and extension of multilateralism.

5.6.4 Promoting the Building of a Human Community with a Shared Future

Standing at a new historical starting point in building a human community with a shared future, Xi Jinping has clearly articulated the common values of humanity, emphasizing the need to "promote the common values of peace, development, fairness, justice, democracy and freedom for all humanity" (Xi 2021b: 16). The proposal of these common values aligns with the historical trend of human civilization's progress and guides the evolution of the global rule of law civilization.

In his report to the 19th National Congress of the CPC, Xi Jinping explicitly called for all peoples around the world to work together in building a human community with a shared future, creating a world that enjoys lasting peace, universal security, common prosperity, openness and inclusiveness, and cleanliness and beauty. On December 1st, 2017, in his keynote speech at the CPC in Dialogue with World Political Parties High-level Meeting, Xi Jinping provided a clear definition of the concept of "*Ren Lei Ming Yun Gong Tong Ti*" (人类命运共同体) (a human community with a shared future):

> As the name suggests, it means that the future and destiny of every nation and every country are closely interconnected. We should stand together through thick and thin, sharing both honor and disgrace, and strive to turn our planet—the place where we were born and raised—into a harmonious global family, transforming the aspirations of people around the world for a better life into reality. (Xi 2018: 510)

In response to the profound question of our times—"What is happening to the world, and what should we do?"—Xi Jinping has creatively put forward the major strategic vision of building a human community with a shared future. He emphasizes the following key principles:

1. We must insist on dialogue and consultation to build a world of lasting peace. Promoting fair and just global governance and advancing the democratization of international relations are essential for maintaining global stability.
2. We must adhere to joint contribution and shared benefits to build a universally secure world. This requires strengthening the rule of law in international relations, upholding the authority of international law, and opposing any actions that, under the guise of "rule of law", undermine the legitimate rights of other countries or disrupt national peace and stability. No country should arbitrarily initiate war or violate the international rule of law. Instead, all nations should work together to achieve common, cooperative, and sustainable security.
3. We must pursue cooperation and mutual benefits to build a world of common prosperity. Promoting a more equitable global order requires enhancing the role and influence of developing countries in global governance and fostering an open, inclusive, balanced, and win–win form of economic globalization. The "Belt and Road Initiative" exemplifies this commitment to the vision of a shared future.
4. We must embrace exchanges and mutual learning to build an open and inclusive world. All civilizations are equal in value; while humans only differ in skin

color and language, civilizations only vary in their diversity and richness, not in superiority or inferiority.

5. We must strive to build a clean and beautiful world by protecting our one and only planet. This entails working together to establish a harmonious relationship between humanity and nature, fostering a shared life community between people and the environment.

The groundbreaking vision of building a human community with a shared future embodies the outstanding achievements of Chinese civilization and the universal values pursued by all humanity. It reflects the historic transformation of China's relationship with the world in the new era. Since its inception, this vision has resonated strongly on a global scale, becoming part of multiple UN agreements, as well as declarations and outcome documents within international multilateral mechanisms. It has received positive responses at the national, regional, and global levels across key areas of global governance, gaining increasing recognition and support from the global community. Demonstrating significant international influence, this vision is steadily transitioning from concept to action, advancing toward the realization of a human community with a shared future.

5.7 Conclusion

The Chinese modernization of rule of law is a new path that aligns with the country's specific national conditions, reflects its socialist nature, and embodies the objective laws governing the modernization of legal systems in civilized societies. It is a path that both conforms to China's realities and draws upon the achievements of global rule of law civilization.

To advance this path effectively, we must accurately understand its essence and characteristics while facilitating its integration with the broader development of global rule of law civilization. The significance of the Chinese modernization of rule of law lies not only in the fact that it is the right and necessary course for China to realize the modernization of rule of law, but also in its role as a pioneering model for developing countries pursuing rule of law modernization. It provides valuable and dynamic experiences for other developing nations in addressing the challenges of law-based governance and advancing smoothly toward rule of law modernization.

References

Aristotle. 1885. *The Politics of Aristotle*. Translated by Jowett, B. Oxford: Clarendon Press.

Chen, H. 2019. Explorations and Contributions of China's Path to Rule of Law Civilization. *Southeast Academic Research* 6: 20–28.

Deng, X. 1994. *Selected Works of Deng Xiaoping (Volume II)*. Beijing: People's Publishing House.

Luo, S. 2021. Evaluation Criteria and Elements for Good Laws and Good Governance in China. *Tribune of Study* 5: 130–136.
People's Daily. 2018. Xi Jinping, Li Keqiang, Li Zhanshu, Wang Yang, Wang Huning, Zhao Leji, and Han Zheng Respectively Participate in the Deliberations of Some Delegations at the National People's Congress Meeting (1). March 8.
Wang, A. 1974. *Collected Works of Wang Wen Gong*. Shanghai: Shanghai People's Publishing House.
Wang, X., Li, X. and Ma, Y. 2021. The country is the people, and the people are the country: A summary of General Secretary Xi Jinping's important discourses on the people-oriented development concept. *People's Daily* (1), June 28.
Xi, J. 2007. *Zhejiang, China: A New Vision for Development*. Hangzhou: Zhejiang People's Publishing House.
Xi, J. 2012. Study, Promote and Implement the Spirit of the 18th CPC National Congress by Focusing on Adherence to and Development of Socialism with Chinese Characteristics. *Qiushi*. Available at http://www.qstheory.cn/dukan/2020-06/04/c_1126073278.htm. Accessed January 15, 2025.
Xi, J. 2014a. *Speech at the Celebration of the 60th Anniversary of the Founding of the National People's Congress*. Beijing: People's Publishing House.
Xi, J. 2014b. *Xi Jinping: The Governance of China (Volume I)*. Beijing: Foreign Languages Press.
Xi, J. 2015a. Accelerating the Construction of a Socialist Rule of Law Country. *Qiushi* 1.
Xi, J. 2015b. Speech at the Seminar for Provincial and Ministerial-Level Main Leaders on Studying and Implementing the Spirit of the Fourth Plenary Session of the 18th Party Congress and Comprehensively Advancing the Rule of Law. In *Excerpts from Xi Jinping's Discourses on Comprehensive Law-Based Governance*, edited by Central Compilation and Translation Bureau. Beijing: Central Literature Press.
Xi, J. 2015c. Towards a Mutually Beneficial Partnership for Sustainable Development—Speech at the UN Sustainable Development Summit. *People's Daily* (2), September 27.
Xi, J. 2017a. *Excerpts from Xi Jinping's Discourses on Socialist Political Construction*. Beijing: Central Party Literature Press.
Xi, J. 2017b. *Secure a Decisive Victory in Building a Moderately Prosperous Society in All Respects and Strive for the Great Success of Socialism with Chinese Characteristics for a New Era*. Beijing: People's Publishing House.
Xi, J. 2018. *On Building a Human Community with a Shared Future*. Beijing: Central Party Literature Press.
Xi, J. 2019a. Speech at the Central Conference on the Work of the Chines People's Political Consultative Conference and the Celebration of the 70th Anniversary of the Founding of the CPPCC. *Qiushi*. September 20. Available at http://www.qstheory.cn/yaowen/2019-09/20/c_1125020990.htm.
Xi, J. 2019b. Strengthening the Party's Leadership over Comprehensive Law-based Governance. *Qiushi*. February 15. Available at http://www.qstheory.cn/dukan/qs/2019-02/15/c_1124114454.htm.
Xi, J. 2020a. *On Adhering to Comprehensive Law-Based Governance*. Beijing: Central Party Literature Press.
Xi, J. 2020b. *The Governance of China (Volume III)*. Beijing: Foreign Language Press.
Xi, J. 2021a. Resolutely Follow the Path of Socialist Rule of Law with Chinese Characteristics to Provide Strong Legal Guarantees for the Comprehensive Construction of a Socialist Modernized Country. *Qiushi* 5: 4–15.
Xi, J. 2021b. *Speech at the Celebration of the 100th Anniversary of the Founding of the Communist Party of China*. Beijing: People's Publishing House.
Xi, J. 2022. Speech at the Central Conference on Work Related to the People's Congress. *Qiushi*. Februart 28. Available at http://www.qstheory.cn/dukan/qs/2022-02/28/c_1128420137.htm.
Yu, Z. 2021. The Theme of the Rule of Law Mission in Xi Jinping Thought on the Rule of Law. *Journal of Shandong University (Philosophy and Social Sciences)* 3: 10–17.

Zhang, W. 2021. Achieving the Unity of Law-based Governance of the Country and Rule-based Governance of the Party. *Political Science and Law* 5: 10–11.
Zhou, S. 2021. Adhere to the People-Centered Thought on the Rule of Law. *Law Science Magazine* 1: 19–25.

Chapter 6
Overall Goals of Chinese Modernization of Rule of Law

The Chinese modernization of rule of law must follow the right path and establish clear objectives to rally collective efforts and achieve long-term effectiveness. The overall goals of the new path for the Chinese modernization of rule of law provide a correct direction for advancing comprehensive law-based governance in the new era. With well-defined goals, we must remain unwavering in upholding the nature and direction of this path and firmly adhere to the socialist rule of law with Chinese characteristics. The formulation of these overall goals should be based on a profound summary of successful experiences and historical achievements in rule of law development, leading to a more systematic and innovative scientific articulation of its guiding principles.

Since the 18th National Congress of the Communist Party of China, the Party Central Committee, with Xi Jinping at its core, has approached the rule of law from a strategic perspective concerning the future of the Party and the nation. It has systematically planned and implemented rule of law reforms, integrating comprehensive law-based governance into the broader vision of national rejuvenation—the Chinese Dream. This approach has been embedded within major national frameworks, including the "Five-Sphere Integrated Plan" and the "Four-Pronged Comprehensive Strategy", as well as the modernization of the national governance system and capacity.

Focusing on critical questions such as why and how to advance law-based governance, the Party has carried out extensive and effective theoretical and practical explorations that connect historical and contemporary contexts, integrate domestic and international perspectives, and combine theory with practice. These efforts have led to significant achievements in rule of law development. A deep and comprehensive understanding of the overall goals of the Chinese modernization of rule of law not only ensures a clear and correct direction for the strategic framework of this new path but also underscores the need to view and plan its development from the broader perspective of the Party and the country's overall progress, continuously advancing the Chinese modernization of rule of law.

X. Dong and Y. Li, *Chinese Legal Family and Chinese Modernization of Rule of Law*,
https://doi.org/10.1007/978-981-96-7529-6_6

6.1 The Construction of a Socialist Rule of Law System

Within the overall goals of the Chinese modernization of rule of law, the construction of a socialist rule of law system with Chinese characteristics holds a fundamental position.

The socialist rule of law system with Chinese characteristics serves as the overall approach for advancing comprehensive law-based governance. At the National Conference on Comprehensive Law-Based Governance, Xi Jinping emphasized the importance of developing this rule of law system, calling for the acceleration of efforts to establish a well-developed system of legal norms, an efficient system for implementing the rule of law, a rigorous system for supervising the rule of law, a robust system for safeguarding the rule of law, and a comprehensive system of intra-Party regulations.

6.1.1 Establishing a Well-Developed System of Legal Norms and an Efficient System for Implementing the Rule of Law

Establishing a well-developed system of legal norms requires adhering to a legislative-first approach, upholding the principle of legislation for the people, and incorporating socialist core values. Every piece of legislation must align with the spirit of the Constitution, reflect the will of the people, and gain their support. The principles of fairness, justice, and transparency must be upheld throughout the legislative process. Additionally, the legislative framework must be improved through a balanced approach of enactment, revision, repeal, and interpretation, ensuring that laws and regulations remain timely, systematic, targeted, and effective (CCCPC 2014: 8).

To achieve this, two key aspects must be addressed. First, legislative efforts must be accelerated in key areas. As governance in various sectors is brought under the rule of law, particular focus should be placed on strengthening legislation in critical fields such as national security and advancing legislative work in emerging areas like the digital economy. A well-developed legal framework is essential for national governance and for meeting the people's growing needs for a better life. Furthermore, rule-based governance of the Party must be leveraged as a political safeguard for the Party and the country's development, ensuring that state laws and Party regulations complement and reinforce each other (Xi 2022).

Second, the legislative procedures for improving the legal system must be refined. It is crucial to address inconsistencies and lack of coordination among different branches of law, rectify gaps in the existing legal framework—especially those arising from changing socioeconomic conditions—and enhance the systematic coherence of laws and regulations. Additionally, efforts should be made to improve the scientific rigor of legislation, ensuring that laws and regulations are more operable and applicable in practice.

6.1.2 Establishing a Rigorous System for Supervising the Rule of Law and a Robust System for Safeguarding the Rule of Law

Law-based governance requires the establishment of a rigorous system for supervising the rule of law. This system must regulate and constrain public power while protecting citizens' rights through multiple channels, including intra-Party supervision, social supervision, public opinion supervision, administrative supervision, judicial supervision, and audit supervision. This enables the genuine implementation of the rule of law.

Strict law enforcement and impartial administration of justice cannot be achieved without robust supervision over legal implementation. Strengthening legal supervision is essential to prevent and correct arbitrary decision-making that overrides the law, abuses of power, and corruption. It also helps curb noncompliance with laws and lax enforcement. Only through rigorous supervision can a culture of legal compliance be cultivated across society, thereby enhancing the authority and vitality of the socialist rule of law.

The system for safeguarding the rule of law generally comprises political, ideological, organizational, and operational safeguards. The leadership of the CPC serves as the political safeguard for the socialist rule of law. The ideological safeguard lies in promoting socialist rule of law theory and strengthening rule of law awareness among all members of society. The organizational safeguard involves building a capable and professional rule of law workforce. Meanwhile, the operational safeguard requires establishing a scientific system of rule of law indicators and assessment standards to ensure effective implementation (Zhang 2014).

A strong safeguard system is essential for advancing the rule of law in China. It serves as a crucial mechanism for promoting social fairness and justice, enhancing public well-being, and ensuring the effective implementation of constitutional and legal provisions. Only when the safeguard system is well-structured, mechanisms are sound, and resources are sufficient can strict law enforcement and impartial administration of justice be guaranteed, thereby laying the foundation for the unified and correct implementation of the Constitution and laws.

6.1.3 Establishing a Comprehensive System of Intra-Party Regulations

A comprehensive system of intra-Party regulations is both a necessity for advancing the Chinese modernization of rule of law and an inherent requirement for strengthening the Party building and enhancing its governance capacity. As the ruling party, the Communist Party of China must standardize and systematize intra-Party regulations while adhering to scientific, democratic, and law-based governance within the framework of the Constitution. This is a crucial means of strengthening the Party building and maintaining its vitality and advanced nature.

A comprehensive system of intra-Party regulations should be coordinated and aligned with the national legal system, forming a complementary and mutually reinforcing relationship. The establishment of intra-Party regulations must adapt to the evolving times and the Party's strategic guidelines. It requires timely adjustments, revisions, and streamlining of existing norms, regulations, and provisions to build a comprehensive system of intra-Party regulations. This ensures the full and effective implementation of the law-based governance and law-based exercise of state power.

6.2 The Modernization of the National Governance System and Governance Capacity

The modernization of the national governance system and governance capacity is to institutionalize, scientize, standardize, and proceduralize the national governance system, thereby transforming the institutional strengths of all aspects of socialism with Chinese characteristics into the effectiveness of national governance.

6.2.1 Basic Elements of the Modernization of the National Governance System and Governance Capacity

Generally speaking, the basic elements of the modernization of the national governance system and governance capacity include the following aspects:

1. Institutionalization. Institutional development is the foundation of the modernization of the national governance system and governance capacity. The socialist system with Chinese characteristics is a scientific system formed by the Party and the people through long-term practice and exploration. All work and activities of national governance in our country are carried out in accordance with the socialist system with Chinese characteristics. The national governance system and governance capacity of our country are the concentrated embodiment of the

socialist system with Chinese characteristics and its implementation capacity (Xia 2019).
2. Participation or Democratization. A modernized national governance system is no doubt a democratic one. The generation and operation of its public power must follow democratic rules, so that all sectors of society and the public can participate in national governance and social governance through institutional arrangements and space. In this way, national governance can adhere to a people-oriented approach and ensure that the people are the masters of the country.
3. Multiple Governance. The national governance system is not a simple adjustment model. It requires the joint promotion of multiple governance models and methods such as politics, law, morality, religion, and culture. Among various adjustment methods, law-based governance, as the main line, plays fundamental and protective roles.
4. Supervision. The supervision system of national governance and social governance can effectively prevent various irregularities and unlawful behaviors, ensure the institutionalization and standardization of the operation of public power, and maintain a series of systems and procedures for the operation of social power and public order.
5. Efficiency. A modernized national governance system should be scientific, strategic, systematic, and effective, which is conducive to improving administrative efficiency and economic benefits, thereby effectively maintaining social stability and social order.
6. Rule of Law. The rule of law is an important support and guarantee for the national governance system and governance capacity. The basic mode of national governance and social governance is the rule of law, and the modernization of national governance and social governance depends on the rule of law development in various fields. It is necessary to use the advantages of the predictability and operability of the rule of law to build social consensus during the transition period, enable different stakeholders to pursue and maximize their own interests according to law, and realize the modernization of the national governance system and governance capacity on the track of the rule of law.

6.2.2 The Modernization of the National Governance System and Governance Capacity and the Rule of Law

Promoting the modernization of the national governance system and governance capacity requires the advancement of comprehensive law-based governance. The rule of law is the basic way to regulate social interests, the concentrated embodiment of social fairness and justice, and the most important foundation for the construction of the socialist system with Chinese characteristics.

First, the rule of law is an inherent requirement for the modernization of the national governance system and governance capacity. In contemporary China, the basic socio-economic conditions for national governance and social governance are the socialist market economy, and the market economy requires the market mechanism to scientifically and rationally allocate resources. The operation and development of the socialist market economy cannot be separated from the rule of law. In a sense, the market economy is essentially a rule of law economy.

Secondly, promoting the modernization of the national governance system and governance capacity is a systematic project that cannot be separated from the path of the rule of law. In the process of modernizing the national governance system and governance capacity, it is necessary to face all kinds of social contradictions and conflicts, and to take multi-faceted and multi-level reform measures. The CPC Central Committee has realized,

> As reform enters a critical period and a deep-water zone, and the international situation is complex and volatile, the tasks of reform, development, and maintaining stability faced by our Party are unprecedentedly heavy, and the contradictions, risks, and challenges are unprecedentedly numerous. The rule of law plays an increasingly prominent and important role in the overall work of the Party and the country. (CCCPC 2014: 2)

Thirdly, promoting the rule of law in national governance is both a beneficial guarantee and goal for the development of the socialist path with Chinese characteristics, and a major measure to realize the modernization of the national governance system and governance capacity. The realization of the modernization of national governance inevitably requires the full intervention of the rule of law. The new path for the Chinese modernization of rule of law is an important way to realize the modernization of national governance. Promoting the modernization of the national governance system and governance capacity is to promote and realize the rule of law, democratization, scientification, and informatization of the national governance system and governance capacity, with a primary focus on the rule of law.

6.2.3 *The Modernization of the National Governance System and Governance Capacity and the Party's Governance Capacity and Level*

The modernization of the national governance system and governance capacity encompasses not only "national governance" in a narrow sense, but also the Party's governance capacity and level. The modernization of the national governance system and governance capacity cannot be separated from the improvement of the Party's governance capacity and level.

The Party's governance capacity is the Party's ability to lead the state power, economic and cultural undertakings, and social affairs, which is specifically unfolded through its governing system, ways, and methods. The Fourth Plenary Session of the 16th Central Committee of the CPC put forward the concept of "scientific, democratic, and law-based governance". Scientific governance emphasizes the science-based governance, using scientific ideas, systems, and methods to allocate and use power and govern the country; democratic governance means that the Party should persist in governing for the people, ensure that the people are the masters of the country, and exercise power and manage the country through democratic systems and procedures; law-based governance serves as the guarantee for the Party's governance capacity.

In the context of the Chinese modernization of rule of law, improving the Party's governance capacity needs to be unfolded through "law-based governance". Law-based governance is the institutional requirement for building socialism with Chinese characteristics, and also the practical requirement for realizing the great rejuvenation of the Chinese nation. Law-based governance needs to adapt to the rule of law trend in socio-economic development, actively use legal means to control social development and adjust various interest relations, and be good at solving various contradictions and problems within the framework of the rule of law. Through law-based governance, the Party's will, line, guidelines, and policies are implemented in all aspects of economic, political, cultural, social, and ecological civilization construction, so as to enhance the Party's ability to respond to challenges and resist risks. Maintaining the authority of the Constitution and laws is the basic requirement of law-based governance. The Party's governance should conform to the spirit and principles of the rule of law, as well as legal norms, using the Constitution and laws to govern the country and society.

6.3 The Great Rejuvenation of the Chinese Nation

Realizing the great rejuvenation of the Chinese nation is the Party and the country's political declaration for the future. It focuses on upholding and developing socialism with Chinese characteristics, reflecting the CPC's high sense of historical responsibility and mission pursuit. The realistic foundation for realizing the national rejuvenation is to achieve the "two centenary goals".

In 2021, marking the 100th anniversary of the founding of the Communist Party of China, the first centenary goal—building a moderately prosperous society in all respects—was successfully achieved as planned. We are now striving toward the second centenary goal: to build China into a modern socialist country that is prosperous, strong, democratic, culturally advanced and harmonious by the 100th anniversary of the founding of the People's Republic of China. The "two centenary goals" are actually the embodiment of the great rejuvenation of the Chinese nation in the new era. The historic endeavor of China's national rejuvenation has been driven by generations of dedicated patriots and remains a profound commitment uniting all Chinese people.

6.3.1 The Dream of the Great Rejuvenation and the "Four Greats"

To realize the great rejuvenation of the Chinese nation, firstly, we must seek national independence and the people's liberation, and secondly, we must realize national prosperity and strength and common prosperity of the people. The "*Si Ge Wei Da*" (四个伟大) (Four Greats) are major decisions on governing the country put forward by Comrade Xi Jinping in his report to the 19th National Congress of the CPC. The "*Wei Da Dou Zheng*" (伟大斗争) (great struggle), "*Wei Da Gong Cheng*" (伟大工程) (great project), "*Wei Da Shi Ye*" (伟大事业) (great cause), and "*Wei Da Meng Xiang*" (伟大梦想) (great dream) are closely interconnected, mutually reinforcing and interactive (Xi 2019: 16). To realize the "great dream"—the Chinese dream of the great rejuvenation of the Chinese nation, it must be carried out together with the practice of carrying out the great struggle, building the great project, and advancing the great cause.

To realize the great dream, we must carry out the great struggle. To achieve national rejuvenation, we must carry out a great struggle with many new historical characteristics by effectively responding to major challenges, resisting major risks, overcoming major obstacles, and solving major contradictions. Any thoughts and behaviors of seeking pleasure, being passive and slack, and avoiding contradictions are wrong. To this end, we must more consciously uphold the Party's leadership and adhere to the socialist system with Chinese characteristics, resolutely oppose all words and deeds that weaken, distort, or deny the Party's leadership and our country's socialist system, and oppose all acts that harm the interests of the people; firmly safeguard national security and development interests, and oppose all acts that split the motherland, undermine national unity, and social harmony and stability. It it also essential to firmly promote the spirit of struggle, improve the ability to struggle, and constantly achieve new victories in the great struggle.

To realize the great dream, we must build a great project. This great project refers to the Party building that is being promoted in depth. History has and will continue to prove that without the leadership of the Communist Party of China, national rejuvenation will inevitably be a fantasy. As the vanguard of the times and the backbone of the nation, the Communist Party of China, as a Marxist ruling party, will surely dare to face problems, eliminate all factors that damage the Party's advanced nature and purity, continuously enhance the Party's political leadership, ideological leadership, organization capabilities, and social appeal, and ensure the smooth development of the new great project of Party building.

To realize the great dream, we must advance the great cause. Socialism with Chinese characteristics is a great cause that benefits all Chinese people. Socialism with Chinese characteristics is the theme of all the Party's theories and practices since the reform and opening-up, and is the product of the integration of the basic principles of Marxism with China's actual conditions and characteristics of the times. Since the reform and opening-up, we have always upheld the great banner of socialism with Chinese characteristics, continuously promoted the all-round development of people, and the people's sense of gain, happiness, and security has been increasing day by day. To this end, in the new era, we need to consciously enhance our confidence in the path, theory, system, and culture of socialism with Chinese characteristics. Besides, we must adhere to the principle of practical efforts in revitalizing the country, and always uphold and develop socialism with Chinese characteristics, so as to promote common prosperity and social justice.

6.3.2 *Inseparable from the Realization of the Overall Goals of the Chinese Modernization of Rule of Law*

Realizing the great rejuvenation of the Chinese nation has significant strategic significance for the modernization of the national governance system and governance capacity, and for the comprehensive improvement of the Party's governance capacity and level. At the same time, building a socialist rule of law system with Chinese characteristics, which is the overall goal of advancing comprehensive law-based governance, is also one of the major strategic goals of realizing the great rejuvenation of the Chinese nation. The great rejuvenation of the Chinese nation cannot be separated from the dream of the rule of law, while to realize the great rejuvenation we must advance comprehensive law-based governance (CCCPC 2014: 2).

First, the realization of the great rejuvenation of the Chinese nation requires the scientific decision-making of Party and government institutions, the effective protection of the people's rights and interests, and the long-term stability of the national and social order, all of which can only be realized under the system and order of rule of law. We must raise the Chinese modernization of rule of law to a new height in the overall development strategy of realizing the great rejuvenation of the Chinese nation; incorporate the promotion of rule of law spirit and the cultivation of rule of law culture into the realization of the great rejuvenation. We must further promote the standardization and institutionalization of various undertakings and projects through rule of law means; further strengthen the legitimacy basis for the construction of various undertakings and mechanisms; and further ensure and safeguard the legitimate rights of various social subjects in realizing the great dream through rule of law means, so as to provide comprehensive institutional guarantees for the realization of a socialist modernized country.

Secondly, the international and domestic situation shows that there are various opportunities and challenges in the path towards realizing the great rejuvenation of the Chinese nation. New problems and new contradictions indicate that the new path is still bumpy and arduous. To carry out the great struggle, build the great project, and advance the great cause, we urgently need the guarantee of the rule of law system. The Report of the 19th National Congress of the CPC clearly put forward the major judgment that "socialism with Chinese characteristics has entered a new era, and the principal contradiction facing Chinese society in the new era is the contradiction between the people's ever-growing needs for a better life and unbalanced and inadequate development". This major judgment not only points out a new direction for the economic, political, cultural, social, and ecological civilization construction in the new era, but also provides a decision-making basis and theoretical support for realizing the great dream. The realization of the great rejuvenation of the Chinese nation has entered a critical stage. On the road to rejuvenation, the Party and the country still face multiple tasks and many contradictions, risks, and challenges. To consolidate the governing foundation and protect the basic rights of the people,

> There is an increasing expectation that the Party and the country will, through implementing the basic strategy of advancing comprehensive law-based governance, further deepen reforms in the field of rule of law and improve the rule of law system for promoting common prosperity and social justice, in order to effectively respond to the new rule of law needs of the people. (Gong 2022)

The Chinese modernization of rule of law is not only important contents and internal goals for realizing the great rejuvenation of the Chinese nation, but also the institutional driving force and action guarantee. As President Xi Jinping emphasized,

> When the rule of law thrives, the nation thrives; when the rule of law is strong, the country is strong. At present, our country is at a critical stage of realizing the great rejuvenation of the Chinese nation, the world is undergoing profound changes unseen in a century, the tasks of reform, development, and maintaining stability are arduous and heavy, and opening up to the outside world is being deepened. We need to better play the role of the rule of law in consolidating the foundation, stabilizing expectations, and ensuring long-term benefits. (Xi 2022)

To realize the great rejuvenation of the Chinese nation, we must elevate the advancement of comprehensive law-based governance to a more prominent and critical position of overarching, foundational, and strategic significance.

6.3.3 *Requiring Adherence to the Basic Principles of the Chinese Modernization of Rule of Law*

Realizing the great rejuvenation of the Chinese nation cannot be separated from the realization of the overall goals of the Chinese modernization of rule of law. Therefore, it is essential to adhere to the basic principles of the Chinese modernization of rule of law, including always upholding the Party's leadership, adopting a people-oriented approach, adhering to the principle of equality for all before the law, integrating the law-based governance and moral governance, and proceeding from China's national conditions.

To realize the great rejuvenation of the Chinese nation and the Chinese modernization of rule of law, we must uphold the Party's leadership. The leadership of the Communist Party of China is determined by history and chosen by the people. It is the foundation and lifeline of the Party and the country, directly relating to the interest and destiny of all Chinese people. The Party's leadership is the most essential feature of socialism with Chinese characteristics, the most fundamental guarantee of the socialist rule of law, and the greatest advantage of the socialist system with Chinese characteristics. We must implement the Party's leadership throughout the new path for the Chinese modernization of rule of law.

To realize the great rejuvenation of the Chinese nation and the Chinese modernization of rule of law, we must always adopt a people-oriented approach. The people's status as masters of the country is the essence and core requirement of the socialist rule of law. The establishment of the socialist market economy system has built a socio-economic soil for the elaboration of the people-oriented concept of respecting the people and caring for the people's livelihood. In this context, the CPC Central Committee put forward the strategic concept of "*Yi Ren Wei Ben*" (以人为本) (people-orientedness) and "*Guan Zhu Min Sheng*" (关注民生) (caring for the people's livelihood); the Fourth Plenary Session of the 18th Central Committee of the Party took "people-oriented concept" as the core concept and goal for the construction of rule of law; and the National Conference on Comprehensive Law-Based Governance emphasized that comprehensive law-based governance must always "adhere to a people-oriented approach". The basic task of the Chinese modernization of rule of law is to confirm and protect the people's rights, especially the right to be the masters of the country and manage the country.

To realize the great rejuvenation of the Chinese nation and the Chinese modernization of rule of law, we must adhere to the principle of equality for all before the law. Equality is the basic attribute of socialist law. The principle of equality for all before the law emphasizes that all citizens and organizations are in an equal position in enjoying rights and assuming obligations, and does not allow anyone to have privileges above the law. To adhere to the principle of equality for all before the law, we must ensure that all citizens and organizations enjoy the rights stipulated by the Constitution and laws equally, and also perform the obligations stipulated by the Constitution and laws equally; at the same time, the legitimate rights and interests of citizens and organizations are equally protected, and illegal acts are investigated according to law; before the law, no citizen or organization is allowed to enjoy privileges other than the law. The Chinese modernization of rule of law must adhere to the principle of equality for all before the law and safeguard social fairness and justice.

To realize the great rejuvenation of the Chinese nation and the Chinese modernization of rule of law, we must uphold the integration of law-based governance and moral governance. The governance of the country and society requires the joint functioning of law and morality: morality serves as the foundation while law is the guarantee. To uphold the integration of law-based governance and moral governance, it is essential to advance both the rule of law and rule of virtue simultaneously. This requires not only emphasizing the regulatory function of law but also the educative function of morality, ensuring that law and morality complement each other and that law-based governance and moral governance reinforce each other. Moreover, integrating law-based governance with moral governance necessitates aligning socialist rule of law with the promotion of socialist morality, which involves fostering a socialist rule of law culture, strengthening rule of law publicity and education and moral education, guiding the public to develop a strong sense of rule of law, creating a social atmosphere where the whole people abide by the law, advancing law-based governance across multiple levels and fields, and promoting the socialist core values.

To realize the great rejuvenation of the Chinese nation and the Chinese modernization of rule of law, we must proceed from China's national conditions. The socialist path, theory, and system with Chinese characteristics are China's most basic national conditions. Proceeding from our country's national conditions, we need to summarize and apply the successful experiences of the Party in leading the people to implement the rule of law, focus on major theoretical and practical issues in the construction of the socialist rule of law, absorb the essence of Chinese legal culture, learn from the beneficial experience of foreign rule of law, and develop socialist rule of law theories that conform to China's actual conditions, have Chinese characteristics, and reflect the laws of social development, so as to provide theoretical guidance and academic support for the Chinese modernization of rule of law.

6.4 The Basic Establishment of a Law-Based Country, Government, and Society

The 19th National Congress of the Communist Party of China scientifically proposed a two-stage strategy for building the rule of law in China. The first stage, from 2020 to 2035, aims to build on the achievement of a moderately prosperous society and, through fifteen years of further efforts, basically realize socialist modernization. By that time, a law-based country, government, and society will be basically established. The second stage, from 2035 to the mid-twenty-first century, will involve another fifteen years of effort to build China into a modern socialist country that is prosperous, strong, democratic, culturally advanced and harmonious. By then, the country will see comprehensive progress in material, political, spiritual, social, and ecological civilization, achieving the modernization of the national governance system and governance capacity (Xi 2019: 22–23).

The basic establishment of a law-based country, government, and society is the most visible and representative goal in the basic realization of the Chinese modernization of rule of law. The process of forging a new path for the Chinese modernization of rule of law is in essence a profound rule of law revolution. "In this process, the law-based country, government, and society are interconnected, forming an organic whole for the rule of law in China" (Gong 2018: 42). A law-based country is the goal of building a law-based government and a law-based society, while the construction of the latter two must align with and serve the development of the former. A law-based government is the primary subject and focus of a law-based country and serves as the precursor and model for a law-based society. A law-based society, in turn, is the foundation and support for the law-based country and law-based government, and their construction must be rooted in the solid development of a law-based society (Yuan 2020).

6.4.1 *Strategic Framework of the Basic Establishment of a Law-Based Country, Government, and Society*

1. **Advancing sound lawmaking, strict law enforcement, impartial administration of justice, and the observance of law by all**

The basic establishment of a law-based country, government, and society requires comprehensive advancement in sound lawmaking, strict law enforcement, impartial administration of justice, and the observance of law by all.

Sound lawmaking ensures that every law aligns with the spirit of the Constitution, reflects the will of the people, and gains their support. This requires the improvement of the socialist legal system with Chinese characteristics centered on the Constitution, reinforcing its status as the fundamental law within the legal framework. It also necessitates the clear definition of legislative priorities in the new era, particularly by focusing on property rights protection, contract enforcement, market unification, fair exchange, equitable competition, and effective regulation, so as to protect the rights and interests of participants in the socialist market economy, maintain market order, and promote economic development. Additionally, sound lawmaking also requires the enhancement of lawmakers' rule of law awareness, especially the principles of the "people-oriented approach" and "legislation for the people".

Strict law enforcement requires that governments at all levels innovate law enforcement mechanisms under the Party's leadership and within the framework of the rule of law. This entails improving law enforcement procedures, advancing integrated law enforcement, reinforcing law enforcement accountability, and establishing a law-based administrative system characterized by unified power and responsibility with strong authority and high efficiency. Efforts should be made to accelerate the development of a law-based government that is scientifically structured, with clearly defined powers and responsibilities, strict law enforcement, transparency, fairness, integrity, efficiency, adherence to the law, and honesty (CCCPC 2014: 15). Strict law enforcement also necessitates the establishment and refinement of mechanisms for decision-making in accordance with the law, fully performing governmental functions within legal boundaries, and implementing lifetime accountability for major decisions alongside retrospective accountability mechanisms. Reforms in administrative law enforcement must be deepened, administrative organization and procedural legal frameworks improved, and legal codification of institutions, functions, powers, procedures, and responsibilities promoted. Law enforcement should adhere to the principles of legality, standardization, fairness, and civility, ensuring that all statutory duties are fulfilled and that actions beyond legal authorization are prohibited. Additionally, mechanisms should be strengthened to constrain and supervise administrative enforcement powers, with rigorous internal legality reviews for major governmental decisions and efforts to standardize and legalize administrative authority at all levels (Xi 2015b: 133).

Impartial administration of justice requires improving judicial management systems and mechanisms for the exercise of judicial power, regulating judicial conduct, and strengthening supervision over judicial activities to ensure that every case delivers fairness and justice. The independence and fairness of adjudication and prosecution must be safeguarded by clearly defining hierarchical judicial authority and establishing robust internal supervision and restraint mechanisms. Judicial reforms must be deepened to optimize the allocation of judicial power, regulate judicial conduct, and build a fair, efficient, and authoritative socialist judicial system. Furthermore, legal frameworks must be established to ensure that fact-finding aligns with objective truth, case outcomes meet substantive justice, and judicial processes uphold procedural fairness (CCCPC 2014: 20–23). Public participation in the judicial process should be enhanced, and judicial safeguards for human rights strengthened, ensuring that fairness and justice are perceptible in people's daily lives. "Publicity should be used to promote justice and build credibility, establishing an open, dynamic, transparent, and convenient judicial system that eliminates secretive operations and resolutely curbs judicial corruption" (Xi 2015a).

The observance of law by all means that the spirit of socialist rule of law must be promoted, and a socialist legal culture must be cultivated to encourage proactive and voluntary compliance with the law across society. A societal atmosphere where law-abiding behavior is honored and law-breaking is shamed must be fostered, so that all citizens become devoted advocates, conscientious observers, and resolute defenders of socialist rule of law (CCCPC 2014: 26). The awareness of socialist rule of law embodies the organic unity of the Party's leadership, the people's status as masters of the country, and the law-based governance, and the advancement of comprehensive law-based governance requires the cultivation of such awareness. To this end, we must view the efforts to spread basic legal knowledge among the people and to encourage them to abide by the law as long-term, fundamental tasks of the law-based governance, promoting extensive rule of law publicity and education campaigns, and guiding the public to consciously abide by the law, seek legal solutions when disputes arise, and rely on legal frameworks to resolve problems.

2. **Advancing law-based governance, law-based exercise of state power, and law-based administration in a coordinated manner**

At the National Conference on Comprehensive Law-Based Governance, Xi Jinping emphasized the need to advance law-based governance, law-based exercise of state power, and law-based administration in a coordinated manner, and to promote the integrated construction of a law-based country, government, and society. Comprehensive law-based governance is a systematic endeavor that requires holistic planning with greater emphasis on systematization, integration, and coordination (Xi 2021).

Law-based governance, law-based exercise of state power, and law-based administration are closely interconnected and mutually reinforcing. Law-based governance pertains to national and social governance, law-based exercise of state power concerns the Party's governance and leadership approach, and law-based administration is a fundamental requirement for government self-improvement. Advancing these three dimensions in a coordinated manner aligns with the principles of the Chinese modernization of rule of law. All national and social affairs are interrelated and cannot be viewed in isolation. The rule of law at the national level necessitates law-based governance, which involves building a law-based country and a law-based society. The Party's adherence to the rule of law requires law-based exercise of state power. The government's commitment to the rule of law demands law-based administration, which entails the construction of a law-based government (Ma 2019).

3. **Promoting the integrated construction of a law-based country, government, and society**

The 19th National Congress of the Communist Party of China established the basic establishment of a law-based country, government, and society as a key objective in achieving socialist modernization by 2035. This marked the beginning of a new era of comprehensive law-based governance in China. In the first phase of the Chinese modernization of rule of law from 2020 to 2035, the integrated construction and basic establishment of a law-based country, government, and society reflect the fundamental direction of the Chinese modernization of rule of law, which will undoubtedly signify the basic establishment of the rule of law in China (Gong 2018: 43).

A law-based country, government, and society are interconnected and inherently unified, forming the three pillars of rule of law construction. Achieving the basic establishment of these three elements requires synchronized planning, implementation, and construction.

Adhering to an "integrated approach" is an intrinsic requirement of the coordinated advancement of the "*Si Ge Quan Mian*" (四个全面) (Four Comprehensives) strategic layout. This layout, established by the CPC Central Committee with comrade Xi Jinping at its core, is a major governance strategy. Comprehensive law-based governance is both a key component and a vital safeguard of this strategic layout. An "integrated approach" better meets the growing public demand for democracy, rule of law, fairness, and justice. Only by adhering to this approach can people genuinely experience fairness and justice, achieving a stronger sense of gain, happiness, and security.

An "integrated approach" is also a necessary requirement for comprehensively deepening reform. Reforms should be advanced within the framework of the rule of law, and the rule of law should be improved through reform. Only by following an "integrated approach" and advancing reform through rule of law thinking and methods, can the rule of law effectively guide, standardize, and safeguard reform. This ensures timely confirmation and consolidation of reform achievements while keeping all aspects of reform on the track of the rule of law. The Chinese modernization of rule of law is a vast and complex system that demands holistic planning and balanced coordination. An "integrated approach" allows for the mobilization of various forces to establish a complete and effective institutional system at the national, governmental, and societal levels, thus advancing the building of the rule of law in China.

A law-based country, government, and society complement each other: a law-based country is the ultimate goal, a law-based government is the primary subject, and a law-based society is the foundation. A law-based country is the goal of building a law-based government and a law-based society, while the construction of the latter two must be centered around this goal by innovating institutions, improving mechanisms, and defining responsibilities. A law-based government is the core focus of building a law-based country. While the "integrated approach" requires systematic advancement, it must also emphasize key priorities, particularly strengthening the construction of a law-based government.

6.4.2 *Organizational and Talent Guarantee for the Basic Establishment of a Law-Based Country, Government, and Society*

The development of a professional rule of law workforce is a crucial organizational and talent guarantee for the Chinese modernization of rule of law. To advance comprehensive law-based governance, it is essential to "significantly enhance the political and ideological quality, professional competence, and ethical standards of the rule of law workforce, building a socialist rule of law team that is loyal to the Party, the country, the people, and the law" (CCCPC 2014: 30). Strengthening the construction of the rule of law workforce is essential for fulfilling various tasks of the Chinese modernization of rule of law. The effective implementation of the fundamental strategy of law-based governance, the coordinated advancement of law-based governance, law-based exercise of state power, and law-based administration, and the integrated construction of a law-based country, government, and society, cannot be achieved without a high-caliber rule of law workforce.

To build a high-caliber rule of law workforce, the political development must be placed at the forefront. Strengthening education on ideals and beliefs, socialist core values, and socialist rule of law principles is essential to cultivating a socialist rule of law workforce that remains loyal to the Party, the country, the people, and the law. Secondly, it is necessary to standardize, professionalize, and institutionalize rule of law workforce by improving the legal professional admission system. A mechanism should be established to recruit legislative personnel, judges, and prosecutors from qualified lawyers and legal scholars. A streamlined and well-regulated system for recruiting graduates of political and legal studies should also be implemented, along with enhanced career security measures. Lastly, strengthening the legal services workforce will reinforce the commitment of legal professionals to the path of socialist rule of law with Chinese characteristics. A well-structured, complementary legal service system should be built, integrating social lawyers, public lawyers, and corporate lawyers into a balanced and effective lawyer community.

The new path for the Chinese modernization of rule of law not only sets the direction for developing rule of law workforce, but also imposes new demands on legal education and the training of rule of law talents. Innovating the cultivation mechanisms for rule of law talents and producing high-quality legal professionals are fundamental objectives of workforce development and key pillars of the Chinese modernization of rule of law. To achieve this, Marxist rule of law theory and Chinese Rule of Law Philosophy must guide legal education, reinforcing confidence in the path and theories of socialism with Chinese characteristics. As President Xi emphasized,

> The Chinese Rule of Law Philosophy for the New Era must be incorporated into legal textbooks, classrooms, and minds. Promoting nationwide legal awareness should be treated as a foundational project, with officials at all levels acting as models of respecting, learning, observing and applying the law. We should better present the rule of law in China to the world, enhancing the international influence and discourse power of China's rule of law system and rule of law theories. (Xi 2022)

6.5 Conclusion

Since the 18th National Congress of the Communist Party of China, the CPC Central Committee, with Comrade Xi Jinping at its core, has elevated the advancement of comprehensive law-based governance to a strategic priority concerning the future of the Party and the country. By integrating it into the realization of the Chinese Dream of national rejuvenation, the Party has pioneered a grand, comprehensive, and far-reaching new path for the Chinese modernization of rule of law.

The realization of the great rejuvenation of the Chinese nation is inseparable from achieving the overall goals of this new path and requires adherence to its basic principles. Promoting the Chinese modernization of rule of law must not only fulfill the overarching goal of comprehensive law-based governance, namely, establishing a socialist rule of law system with Chinese characteristics, but also serve as a key component in the modernization of the national governance system and governance capacity. By aligning the modernization of governance with the rule of law, China ensures that the modernization of the national governance system and governance capacity is realized on the track of the rule of law.

References

CCCPC. 2014. *Decision of the Central Committee of the Communist Party of China on Major Issues Concerning Advancing Comprehensive Law-Based Governance*. Beijing: People's Publishing House.

Gong, P. 2018. Strategic Arrangements for the Chinese Modernization of Rule of Law in the New Era. *China Legal Science* 3: 27–50.

Gong, P. 2022. Common Prosperity and Social Justice: Important Features of the New path for the Chinese Modernization of Rule of Law. *Democray & Legal System*. January 3. Available at http://e.mzyfz.com/mag/paper_47179_24304.html.

Ma, H. 2019. Advance Law-Based Governance, Law-Based Exercise of State Power, and Law-Based Administration in a Coordinated Manner, and Promote the Integrated Construction of a Law-Based Country, Government, and Society. *Legal Daily* (1), May 20.

Xi, J. 2015a. Accelerating the Construction of a Socialist Rule of Law Country. *Qiushi* 1.

Xi, J. 2015b. *Xi Jinping on Strengthening Party Conduct, Integrity, and the Fight Against Corruption: Selected Discourses*. Beijing: Central Party Literature Press, China Fangzheng Press.

Xi, J. 2019. *Xi Jinping on Staying True to the Party's Original Aspiration and Founding Mission: Selected Important Discourses*. Beijing: Central Party Literature Press, Party Building Publications Press.

Xi, J. 2021. Resolutely Follow the Path of Socialist Rule of Law with Chinese Characteristics to Provide Strong Legal Guarantees for the Comprehensive Construction of a Socialist Modernized Country. *Qiushi* 5: 4-15.

Xi, J. 2022. Unswervingly Pursue the Path of Socialist Rule of Law with Chinese Characteristics, and Better Promote of the Construction of a Socialist Rule of Law System with Chinese Characteristics. *Qiushi*. February 15. Available at http://www.qstheory.cn/dukan/qs/2022-02/15/c_1128367893.htm.

Xia, J. 2019. China's Exploration of the Modernization of the National Governance System and Governance Capacity. *Guang Ming Daily* (6), December 19.

Yuan, S. 2020. Adhering to the Integrated Construction of a Law-Based Country, Government, and Society. *People's Daily* (9), April 21.

Zhang, W. 2014. Vigorously Strengthening the Rule of Law Workforce. *People's Court Daily* (5), November 19.

Part III
The Inheritance and Development of the Chinese Legal Family in Chinese Modernization of Rule of Law

From a historical and cultural perspective, the inheritance and development of the Chinese Legal Family in the new era have laid the historical foundation and cultural bedrock for constructing the Chinese modernization of rule of law.

The Report of the 19th National Congress of the Communist Party of China emphasized the need to deeply explore the ideological concepts, humanistic spirit, and moral norms embedded in China's outstanding traditional culture, and to integrate them with contemporary demands through inheritance and innovation, allowing Chinese culture to exhibit enduring charm and contemporary vitality. The profound legal culture within the Chinese Legal Family is an essential component of traditional culture. Advancing the Chinese modernization of rule of law requires not only drawing upon and learning from Western experiences in the development of rule of law but, more importantly, proceeding from China's own realities. It must connect with tradition, extract the essence of traditional legal culture, and integrate external experiences with indigenous resources.

Chapter 7
Transformation and Innovation of Excellent Traditional Chinese Legal Thoughts

The Chinese modernization of rule of law is deeply rooted in the country's excellent traditional legal culture. It represents a unique Chinese path to the modernization of rule of law, built upon the creative transformation and innovative development of outstanding traditional legal thoughts.

President Xi Jinping has emphasized, only by being adept at inheritance can we achieve better innovation. He further pointed out, we have our own history and culture, our own systems and mechanisms, and our own national conditions. The governance of our country involves unparalleled complexities and unique characteristics, as well as the advantages and experiences we have accumulated over time. We must neither undervalue ourselves nor forget our roots. In other words, in advancing the rule of law and improving national governance in the new era, we must remain grounded in China's realities, draw lessons from the past, engage with the present, and look toward the future.

As the "source of water" and the "root of the tree" (Hu and Dong 2018) for the rule of law in China, the traditional legal culture represented by the Chinese Legal Family has played an irreplaceable role in nurturing and enriching modern legal development. To endow the Chinese Legal Family with contemporary significance and to revitalize China's rule of law wisdom in the new era, it is essential to extract its essence to address the current challenges in China's development through creative transformation and innovative development. As the theoretical guide for advancing the Chinese modernization of rule of law, contemporary Chinese Rule of Law Philosophy inherits and develops many outstanding legal resources from the Chinese Legal Family.

X. Dong and Y. Li, *Chinese Legal Family and Chinese Modernization of Rule of Law*,
https://doi.org/10.1007/978-981-96-7529-6_7

7.1 Upholding the Law and Strengthening the Country Through Law

7.1.1 The Authority of Law in Traditional Legal Thought

Throughout history, China has stood majestically in the East, continuously growing and strengthening. It is unimaginable that such a feat could have been achieved without a legal system for governance, state stability, and social order. Law represents the will of the ruling class in control of state power. As a political measure and policy, it serves as the objective foundation and standard for governing the country.

Ancient Chinese thinkers consistently emphasized that law is fundamental to state governance. The Chinese people's understanding of the function of law was ahead of its time in global political civilization, and its practical application has been passed down and refined through generations. Looking back at the evolution of the Chinese Legal Family, "the earliest and most systematic discussions of law were articulated by Legalist scholars, whose core principle was '*Yi Fa Wei Feng*' (以法爲奉) (upholding the law)" (Zhang 2021: 21). As early as the Warring States period, Legalist scholars recognized the significance of the rule of law in state governance and national strength. Han Fei asserted, "A nation is neither inherently strong nor weak. If those who uphold the law are strong, the nation is strong; if those who uphold the law are weak, the nation is weak" (from *Han Feizi* 《韓非子》), systematically explaining the relationship between legal governance and national prosperity. Shang Yang stated, "Law is the lifeblood of the people and the foundation of governance" (from *Book of the Lord Shang* 《商君書》), emphasizing that the rule of law is essential for social stability and effective governance. Guan Zhong further elaborated, "Only when rulers and subjects, the noble and the humble, all abide by the law can the great governance be achieved" (from *Guanzi* 《管子》), highlighting the necessity of legal compliance across all levels of society to ensure long-term stability.

Confucianism, which had a profound and lasting influence on the Chinese Legal Family, also recognized the authority of law. While Confucius advocated "*Wei Zheng Yi De*" (爲政以德) (governing with virtue) (from *Analects* 《論語》), he also warned that "If punishments are not applied fairly, the people will be at a loss as to what to do" (from *Analects* 《論語》). He called for the integration of law and morality in governance, striving to prevent wrongdoing before it occurs and promoting a legal system that aims to eliminate the need for punishment altogether. Mencius expanded on Confucius' ideas, emphasizing the necessity of law in governance: "When those in high position do not adhere to moral principles, and those below disregard laws; when the government does not uphold the Way, and officials do not respect regulations; when the noble violate righteousness, and the common people breach the laws—the survival of such a state is merely a matter of luck" (from *Mencius* 《孟子》). Relying solely on personal will or emotions without a consistent legal framework would lead to disastrous consequences.

Thus, throughout history, successive rulers emphasized the role of law as a means to maintain and develop the economy, ensure the functioning of the state apparatus, enhance government efficiency, and ultimately achieve social stability, effective governance, and long-term national security.

7.1.2 "Strengthening the Country Through Law" in the Chinese Modernization of Rule of Law

The Chinese Rule of Law Philosophy in the new era, grounded in the reflection on the rise and fall of human societies over millennia, reveals the historical law that "When the rule of law thrives, the nation thrives; when the rule of law is strong, the country is strong" (Xi 2020b: 225). By inheriting the governance wisdom that "If those who uphold the law are strong, the nation is strong; if those who uphold the law are weak, the nation is weak" (from *Han Feizi* 《韓非子》), it advances the new concept of "*Feng Fa Qiang Guo*" (奉法强国) (strengthening the country through law), and points out a new path for the Chinese modernization of rule of law.

The firm conviction in "strengthening the country through law" stems from the fundamental grasp of the historical rules of rule of law development in the Chinese Rule of Law Philosophy. While the meaning of the "rule of law" has evolved over time, the enduring spirit of "upholding the law" remains consistent. As Xun Kuang stated, "Law is the foundation of governance" (from *Xunzi* 《荀子》), and Shen Dao emphasized, "Decisions must be made according to the law—this is the great Way of the state" (from *Shenzi* 《慎子》). Chinese Rule of Law Philosophy continues to affirm the supreme status of law in national governance, emphasizing that "the law is an important tool for governing the country, and the rule of law is an important support for the national governance system and governance capacity" (Xi 2020b: 92). Legal institutions serve as the starting point for governance, national governance cannot function without a legal system, and the rule of law is an indispensable means of governance. Law-based governance is the core content of China's socialist rule of law and the fundamental strategy for the Party to lead the people in national governance. At present, it is imperative to place comprehensive law-based governance in an even more prominent position, relying on the law as the highest and most fundamental rule for governance and law-based governance as the most reliable and stable means of administration. As Xi Jinping emphasized,

> We must place Party and state affairs on the track of the rule of law, coordinate social forces, balance social interests, regulate social relations, and standardize social behavior within the framework of the rule of law, and rely on the rule of law to resolve various social conflicts and issues. (Xi 2020b: 104)

The concept of "strengthening the country through law" is also reflected in the systematic exposition of the function and value of rule of law in the Chinese Rule of Law Philosophy. Xi Jinping, with a strategic and holistic perspective, pointed out,

> On the new journey of comprehensively building a modern socialist country while coordinately advancing the great struggle, the great project, the great cause, and the great dream, we must place greater emphasis on the rule of law, rigorously enforce the rule of law, and better leverage its role in consolidating the foundation, stabilizing expectations, and ensuring long-term benefits. (Xi 2020b: 227)

"*Gu Gen Ben*" (固根本) (consolidating the foundation) refers to reinforcing the foundation for the long-term governance of the Communist Party of China, maintaining the fundamental structure of the people's democratic dictatorship and the system of people's congresses, upholding Marxism's guiding position in the ideological field, and preserving the basic political and economic systems of socialism, so as to ensure national security, social stability, and long-term political continuity. "*Wen Yu Qi*" (稳预期) (stabilizing expectations) means placing economic, political, cultural, social, ecological, and cyberspace affairs within the framework of rule of law, forming a stable, reliable, and enduring rule of law order that helps stabilize the expectations for economic growth, political integrity, cultural prosperity, social justice, environmental sustainability, and a well-regulated cyberspace. In this way, it ensures the realization of common prosperity, an improved quality of life for all, and the ultimate expectation of building a modern socialist country and achieving national rejuvenation. "*Li Chang Yuan*" (利长远) (ensuring long-term benefits) underscores the importance of preserving fundamental and far-reaching strategies through legal mechanisms, making the rule of law a pillar for the future. As Xi Jinping stated, "Our commitment to advancing comprehensive law-based governance and unwavering enforcement of the rule of law is driven by the long-term interest of future generations and sustainable development" (Xi 2015: 12–13). The profound legal philosophy condensed in these three phrases—"consolidating the foundation, stabilizing expectations, and ensuring long-term benefits"—encapsulates the necessity of building a modern socialist country on the track of the rule of law. It also fully demonstrates that the idea of "strengthening the country through law" in the Chinese Rule of Law Philosophy is a philosophical extraction of China's experience in the development of rule of law.

The new concepts and strategies of "strengthening the country through law" reinforce the entire Party and the whole people's firm commitment to upholding the rule of law while opposing the rule by man. This vision guides the Party and the people in accelerating the building of rule of law in China on the new journey toward building a modern socialist country. Through the power of law, political stability, economic development, cultural prosperity, social harmony, ecological sustainability, national unity, public well-being, and national security can be effectively safeguarded.

7.1.3 Governance and Exercise of State Power Complied with the Constitution

The principles of "*Yi Xian Zhi Guo, Yi Xian Zhi Zheng*" (依宪治国、依宪执政) (governance complied with the Constitution, and exercise of state power complied with the Constitution) represent the practical implementation of the Chinese modernization of rule of law in advancing the concept of "strengthening the country through law". In the new era, President Xi Jinping, recognizing China's new historical positioning and the necessity of comprehensive law-based governance, has explicitly stated: "To uphold law-based governance, we must first uphold the governance complied with the Constitution; to uphold law-based administration, we must first uphold the exercise of state power complied with the Constitution" (Xi 2020b: 126).

Xi Jinping has emphasized: "The Constitution is the fundamental law of our country, the overarching charter for national governance, and the concentrated expression of the will of the Party and the people. It holds the highest legal status, legal authority, and legal effect" (Xi 2020b: 126). He further stated that "the Constitution is the fundamental basis for comprehensive law-based governance" (Xi 2020b: 201) and "the fundamental legal basis for our Party's long-term governance" (Xi 2020b: 201). The Party has always attached great importance to the role of the Constitution in governance, as reflected in Xi Jinping's remark: "The Party and the law, the Party's leadership and law-based governance, are highly unified. We must unwaveringly uphold the governance and exercise of state power complied with the Constitution of the People's Republic of China" (Xi 2015: 37). These important expositions have creatively developed Marxist constitutional theory and elevated the Party's understanding of "governance and exercise of state power complied with the Constitution" to a new level.

The Constitution of the People's Republic of China, as the fundamental law of our country, formally establishes the great struggle and achievements of the CPC in leading the people through revolution, construction, and reform. It enshrines the national system of people's democratic dictatorship led by the working class and based on the alliance of workers and farmers, as well as the political system of people's congresses. It affirms the guiding role of Marxism in the ideological sphere and lays out the fundamental national tasks, guiding principles, core leadership, development path, and national objectives. Furthermore, it provides the institutional foundation for the system of multiparty cooperation and political consultation under the leadership of the CPC, the system of regional ethnic autonomy, and the system of community-level self-governance. It codifies the principles of socialist rule of law, democratic centralism, and respecting and safeguarding human rights. The Constitution also outlines China's fundamental policies, including the implementation of a socialist market economy and the coordinated development of material, political, spiritual, social, and ecological civilization. These provisions reflect the socialist nature of the Constitution, encapsulate the collective will and fundamental interests of the Chinese people of all ethnic groups, and serve as the legal foundation ensuring China's continued progress along the path of socialism with Chinese characteristics despite challenges and risks. In the Constitution, we read "*Zhong Guo zhi Lu*" (中国之路) (the path of China), comprehend "*Zhong Guo zhi Li*" (中国之理) (the principles of China), and derive confidence in China's historical, present, and future trajectory—forming the basis of China's constitutional confidence (Zhang 2022b: 11).

A retrospective view of the 43-year history of the current Constitution, 71-year history of the PRC's Constitution, and even the near-centennial development of the Constitution under the Party's leadership, unequivocally demonstrates that "the Constitution is inextricably linked to the country's future and the people's destiny" (Xi 2020b: 9). The principles of governance and exercise of state power complied with the Constitution lie at the core of Chinese Rule of Law Philosophy, functioning as the foremost task in advancing comprehensive law-based governance and building a socialist rule of law system with Chinese characteristics.

7.2 Codified Legal Civilization and Good Governance Through Good Laws

7.2.1 The Tradition of Codified Laws in Imperial China

The enduring and profound nature of Chinese civilization is largely attributed to its well-structured and insightful classical texts. Among these, the extensive legal codes passed down through generations embody a sophisticated codified legal civilization that encapsulates profound legal thought and governance wisdom. The ancient Chinese people placed great emphasis on the rule of law, and successive rulers recorded their legal and regulatory principles in written form to maintain legal stability and uphold the regulatory function of codified law. Consequently, the Chinese Legal Family is distinctly characterized by "*Fa Dian Wen Ming*" (法典文明) (a codified legal civilization). As one scholar notes, "According to existing records, from the *Jiu Zhang Lü* (《九章律》) (the *Nine Chapters Law*) to the *Da Qing Lü Li* (《大清律例》) (the *Great Qing Legal Code*), approximately 160 legal codes were promulgated (Hou, Zhang and Jia 1997: 56).

The *Zuo Zhuan* (《左傳》) (*The Commentary of Zuo*) records: "During the Xia, when rebellions arose, the *Yu Xing* (《禹刑》) (the *Penal Code of Yu*) was established to restore order; when the Shang dynasty encountered political disorder, the *Tang Xing* (《湯刑》) (the *Penal Code of Tang*) was enacted; when the Zhou dynasty faced political disorder, the *Jiu Xing* (《九刑》) (the *Code Nine Penalties*) was instituted". While this account is not sufficient enough to confirm the existence of such written codes as *Yu Xing* and *Tang Xing* in the slave society of ancient China, it does illustrate that from the dawn of Chinese civilization, rulers recognized the importance of legislation in social governance. During the Warring States period, against the backdrop of "*Li Beng Yue Huai*" (禮崩樂壞) (the decline of the ritual and music system) and "*Bai Jia Zheng Ming*" (百家爭鳴) (the flourishing of diverse schools of thought), Li Kui synthesized the reform experiences of different states and compiled China's first feudal legal code—the *Fa Jing* (《法經》) (the *Canon of Laws*). With the unification of China under the Qin dynasty, a systematic and comprehensive *Qin Lü* (《秦律》) (*Qin Code*) was established based on the Legalist reforms of Shang Yang, achieving the principle that "the governance system operates smoothly, various affairs are handled appropriately, and all are governed by law" (from *Records of the Grand Historian* 《史記》). The Han dynasty, continuing the Qin's legal framework, saw Xiao He revise and refine the Qin laws into the *Jiu Zhang Lü*, laying the foundation for over four centuries of Han's legal tradition. Despite political fragmentation and turmoil during the Three Kingdoms period, Wei, Jin, Northern and Southern dynasties, remarkable feudal legal codes such as the *Tai Shi Lü* (《泰始律》) (*Taishi Code*), the *Bei Wei Lü* (《北魏律》) (the *Northern Wei Code*), and the *Bei Qi Lü* (《北齊律》) (the *Northern Qi Code*) emerged. The Sui and Tang dynasties, building upon this tradition, witnessed the pinnacle of Chinese codified law with the compilation of the *Tang Lü Shu Yi* (《唐律疏議》) (the *Tang Code with Commentaries*) under Zhangsun Wuji and others, synthesizing both ancient legal wisdom and contemporary judicial practice.

The legal tradition continued through the Song, Yuan, Ming, and Qing dynasties, exemplifying the enduring principle: "Drawing from past legal traditions to establish lasting laws for posterity" (from *Complete Books of the Four Repositories* 《四庫全書》). In the early twentieth century, under the influence of Western legal traditions, the Chinese Legal Family gradually "disintegrated". However, the historical legacy and profound impact of codified legal civilization endured, shaping the modern lawmaking, judicial practices, and legal education.

As the ancient saying goes, "people with petty shrewdness attend to trivial matters, while people with vision establish laws". In traditional Chinese legal culture, large-scale state legislation has long been regarded as a symbol of national unity, social stability, and good governance. Periods of flourishing governance were typically accompanied by a well-developed legal system. President Xi Jinping affirms the critical role of codified law in sustaining national unity and social stability, noting:

> Emperor Taizong of Tang emphasized the importance of upholding the law for governance, and the *Zhen Guan Lü* (《貞觀律》) (*Zhenguan Code*) contributed to the flourishing era known as the "*Zhen Guan zhi Zhi*" (貞觀之治) (Zhenguan Prosperity); the *Tang Lü* (《唐律》) (the *Tang Code*) revised from the *Zhen Guan Lü* laid the legal foundation for the flourishing of the Tang Dynasty. (Xi 2020b: 226)

7.2.2 The Inheritance of Codification Spirit in the Chinese Modernization of Rule of Law

The Chinese modernization of rule of law has inherited and developed the legal tradition of "codified legal civilization". In the contemporary development of rule of law, great emphasis is placed on legislative quality and the codification of laws, aligning with the principle that "good laws are the prerequisite for good governance" (Xi 2020b: 233). The construction of a socialist rule of law system with Chinese characteristics must adhere to the principle of legislation first.

The compilation of the "Civil Code" serves as the most representative example in this respect. Following the founding of the People's Republic of China, attempts were made respectively in the 1950s and 1960s to draft a Civil Code, but historical circumstances prevented the completion. The compilation of a comprehensive Civil

Code thus became a longstanding aspiration of generations of civil law scholars and legal reformers. Since the reform and opening-up, the National People's Congress successively enacted individual civil laws such as the *Law of Succession* in 1985, the *General Principles of Civil Law* in 1986, and the *Guarantee Law* in 1995, which "laid a solid institutional, practical, theoretical, and public opinion foundation for compiling the Civil Code" (Zhang 2020: 7).

As the first law titled "Code" in the history of the PRC, the Civil Code holds a pivotal position within the socialist rule of law system. Since the 18th National Congress of the CPC, President Xi Jinping has prioritized the compilation of the Civil Code as part of his commitment to comprehensive law-based governance. In October 2014, the Fourth Plenary Session of the 18th CPC Central Committee made a strategic decision to "compile the Civil Code", and the Standing Committee of the NPC actively advanced the codification process. On March 15th, 2017, the *General Provisions of Civil Law* was adopted at the Fifth Session of the 12th NPC, marking a solid first step toward compiling the Civil Code. Finally, on May 28th, 2020, the Third Session of the 13th NPC overwhelmingly passed the *Civil Code of the People's Republic of China*, fulfilling the century-long dream of a comprehensive Civil Code for the Chinese people.

Throughout the codification process, President Xi Jinping personally chaired three meetings of the Standing Committee of the Political Bureau of the Central Committee, reviewing the draft versions of the Civil Code. His important instructions and guidance provided a clear roadmap for its development, making it the longest legislative and codification process in the history of the PRC. Xi Jinping emphasized:

> The Civil Code systematically integrates civil legal norms developed through more than 70 years of practice since the founding of the PRC, draws from the 5,000-year-old legal traditions of the Chinese nation, and incorporates beneficial achievements of global rule of law civilization. It is a Civil Code that embodies the socialist nature of our country, aligns with the interests and aspirations of the people, and responds to the demands of the times. It is a Civil Code that equally protects various rights, including life and health, property security, transaction convenience, personal happiness, and human dignity. It is a Civil Code that carries distinct Chinese characteristics, practical relevance, and contemporary significance. (Xi 2020a: 7)

The compilation and implementation of the Civil Code is a vivid embodiment of the Chinese Rule of Law Philosophy in the new era.

7.2.3 Building the Rule of Law in China Characterized by Good Laws and Good Governance

The strategic goal of the Chinese modernization of rule of law is to build the rule of law in China characterized by good laws and good governance, an endeavor that both inherits and innovates upon the traditional Chinese legal philosophy of "codified legal civilization".

Traditional Chinese legal culture holds that "a law devoid of benevolence cannot be called a law" (from *Mozi* 《墨子》) and that "if good laws are established under heaven, the world will be well governed; if good laws are established in a country, the country will be well governed" (by Wang Anshi). This philosophy underscores the role of good laws in fostering development and ensuring good governance, embodying the wisdom of ancient Chinese statecraft. The Chinese modernization of rule of law follows this principle, striving to enact "good laws" through sound lawmaking in the new era.

President Xi Jinping has cited Han Fei's statement that "laws should evolve with the times to ensure good governance, and governance should adapt to societal changes to achieve success" (from *Han Feizi* 《韓非子》). He emphasizes the need to formulate laws that respond to the evolving needs of the times, driving institutional innovation, resolving social conflicts, and promoting societal progress. He also underscores that the formulation of "good laws" must adhere to the principle of lawful legislation, requiring legislative bodies at all levels to strictly follow due process and jurisdictional limits. This approach helps prevent unauthorized, redundant, or arbitrary legislation while mitigating the influence of departmental interests and local protectionism.

Focusing on the emerging challenges and contradictions of the new era, Xi Jinping has particularly highlighted the need to accelerate legislation in key areas such as national security, technological innovation, public health, cultural education, ethnic and religious affairs, biosecurity, ecological civilization, risk prevention, antitrust regulation, and foreign-related legal affairs. He has also called for timely research and legal frameworks to address issues related to the digital economy, internet finance, artificial intelligence, big data, and cloud computing. In response to pressing concerns of the people, legal measures have been strengthened to tackle telecom fraud, new types of drug-related crimes, and problems in the entertainment industry, such as cult-like fandoms, fan culture chaos, and fraudulent "yin-yang contracts". These efforts aim to close regulatory loopholes and ensure the healthy development of the Chinese modernization of rule of law through good laws and good governance.

At its core, the law-based governance is about governing effectively through good laws. Good laws represent the value standard and rational pursuit of the rule of law, while good governance serves as its operational model and mode of realization. The organic integration of "good laws" and "good governance" encapsulates the essence of socialist rule of law, providing a strong institutional foundation for the Chinese modernization of rule of law.

7.3 The People as the Foundation of the State

7.3.1 The Historical Evolution and Cultural Connotation of People-Centered Thought

President Xi Jinping stated, "In China, the ideas of people-centered thought and the rule of law have existed since ancient times. As early as several thousand years ago, there was the saying, 'The people are the foundation of a state, and a state can enjoy peace only when the foundation is firm'" (*People's Daily* 2015). This people-centered philosophy fostered a legal system that, as noted by Bodde and Morris (1967: 41), was in some respects "more humane and intelligent than its Western counterpart".

The concept of "*Min Ben Si Xiang*" (民本思想) (people-centered thought) in ancient China originated during the transition between the Shang and Zhou dynasties and was later developed by Confucianism, becoming a defining feature of Chinese political thought and one of the most progressive elements of traditional Chinese political culture. The people, as the primary force of social production, the main source of military power, and the backbone of state taxation, not only created material civilization and ensured the survival and development of the state but also contributed to the flourishing of spiritual civilization (Zhang 2022a: 123). The people are the source of sovereign authority, the decisive factor in political stability, the implementers of production activities, and the defenders of national security" (Dong and Zhang 2023).

Traditional Chinese civilization has long emphasized a people-centered approach to governance. During the Shang and Zhou periods, although a systematic theory of people-centered thought had yet to take shape, historical developments already demonstrated the crucial role of ordinary people in determining a state's rise and fall. As the *Shang Shu* (《尚書》) (the *Book of Documents*) states, "The people should be drawn close, not suppressed. The people are the foundation of a state, and a state can enjoy peace only when the foundation is firm".

Originating in the pre-Qin period, this emphasis on the people was later refined by Confucianism into a comprehensive theory of people-centered thought, profoundly influencing national governance for generations. The people-centered thought of Confucius was expressed through his philosophy of "*Ren*" (仁) (benevolence), advocating governance through virtue, ensuring the people's welfare, and respecting their will. Mencius further developed this into the doctrine of "*Ren Zheng*" (仁政) (benevolent governance), asserting that "The essence of a state is the people, followed by the god of land and the god of grain (which stand for state power), and lastly the ruler," highlighting that the people form the foundation of the state—without the people, there is no state, and without the state, there is no ruler. Xunzi expanded on this idea, stating, "The ruler is like a boat, while the common people are like water; water can carry a boat, but it can also capsize it," illustrating that effective governance is inseparable from the power of the people.

In the Han dynasty, Confucianism became the orthodox ideology, marking the beginning of the Confucianization of Chinese legal traditions. During the Tang dynasty, economic prosperity elevated people-centered thought to new heights, making it a core ideology. By the Ming and Qing dynasties, the concept had become even more refined. Throughout history, the continuous rise and fall of dynasties have proven the enduring truth: "He who wins the hearts of the people wins the world, while he who loses the hearts of the people loses the world."

7.3.2 The People-Oriented Development Concept in the Chinese Modernization of Rule of Law

The fundamental value orientation of the Chinese modernization of rule of law requires the advancement of comprehensive law-based governance and the building of rule of law in China, with adherence to a people-oriented approach that effectively upholds and promotes social fairness and justice. The Chinese Rule of Law Philosophy in the New Era inherits the core values of ancient people-centered thought, such as "closeness to and care for the people" and the principle that "among all affairs, the people's livelihood is paramount". At the same time, it enriches these values with new connotations in response to the evolving times, demonstrating a distinct emphasis on the people-oriented nature.

On the one hand, Chinese Rule of Law Philosophy establishes the people's status as masters of the country from the legal perspective and is committed to improving the institutional system that ensures their principal position. This is not only a scientific inheritance and cultural continuation of traditional people-centered thought but also an expansion of its meaning in the modern era. Traditional Chinese legal culture emphasized the authority and supremacy of the monarch, and its people-centered thought often carried strong imprints of feudal autocracy, relying heavily on enlightened rulers and virtuous ministers to implement policies from the top down, thus exhibiting certain historical limitations (Zhang 2022a). In contrast, contemporary Chinese Rule of Law Philosophy stresses the principal position of the people, respecting their will and aspirations while ensuring the protection of their legitimate rights and interests. President Xi Jinping has emphasized, "the most extensive and profound foundation for comprehensive law-based governance is the people, and we must uphold the principle of governing for the people and relying on the people" (Xi 2022: 288). He also stated, "The country is the people, and the people are the country" (Xi 2022: 9). The people are the fundamental driving force behind national and social development, as well as the primary subject and source of power in law-based governance. Therefore, in all aspects—lawmaking, law enforcement, administration of justice, and the observance of law—the people's principal position must always be upheld.

On the other hand, Chinese Rule of Law Philosophy emphasizes that the rule of law should serve the well-being of the people. In ancient times, *Huainanzi* (《淮南子》) stated, "Governance has its constants, and benefiting the people is fundamental". In the new era, President Xi Jinping similarly affirmed that "the fundamental purpose of advancing comprehensive law-based governance is to protect the rights and interests of the people by law... ensuring that they can live and work in peace and contentment" (Xi 2021b). Governing must start from the people and ultimately aim to benefit them. Only by addressing the people's pressing difficulties and safeguarding their fundamental interests can our country gather the strength needed for its construction and national rejuvenation.

The Chinese modernization of rule of law establishes the people-oriented development concept as the fundamental stance in building the rule of law China, answering the essential question of whom the rule of law serves and upon whom it depends. The rule of law in China must align with the people's aspirations and expectations, safeguard their fundamental interests, and be driven by the broadest and deepest foundation—the people themselves.

7.3.3 Implementation Path to the People-Oriented Development Concept

The people-oriented nature is the essence of contemporary Chinese Rule of Law Philosophy, which has solid practical value. The implementation path is mainly carried out under the guidance of sound lawmaking, strict law enforcement, impartial administration of justice, and the observance of law by everyone.

1. **Committing to the people-oriented approach in sound lawmaking**

Legislation is the primary link of the rule of law, so paying attention to legislation means paying attention to the source.

The Fourth Plenary Session of the 18th CPC Central Committee stressed the necessity to pay attention to legislative work, achieve the combination of democracy and science in the specific legislative process, reflect the people's substantive demands, and gain the people's support and belief. Strengthening democratic legislation is the internal requirement and the important aspect of promoting the construction of socialist rule of law by developing people's democracy in the whole process. "Only when the law is the conscious expression of the people's will and is made with the people's will and created by the people's will, can a definite grasp be ensured" (Xi 2020b: 204).

Firstly, speed up and improve the communication mechanism. In the construction of socialist rule of law with Chinese characteristics, strengthening democratic legislation as well as enhancing legislative democracy and public participation will help fully absorb the will of the people, promote the construction of a complete legal system, and lay a solid legislative foundation for building the rule of law China characterized by good laws and good governance. To this end, efforts should be made to improve the mechanism for soliciting opinions on legislation, expand the coverage and representativeness of public participation, and enhance the transparency of legislation. Explanations should be given to those relatively concentrated opinions that have not been adopted (CCCPC 2021b).

Secondly, improve the platform and the carrier of democratic public opinion expression of the National People's Congress. It is highly recommended that new media and new technologies be used actively to expand the channels of public participation in legislation, and improve the mechanism of legislative hearing and public opinion survey (CCCPC 2021a), the working mechanism of absorbing public opinion be improved, the wisdom of the people be taken advantage of, and the social situation and public opinion of all aspects based on the fundamental interests of the overwhelming majority of the people be integrated.

Thirdly, give full play to the role of deputies to the National People's Congress. Deputies to the National People's Congress are the "spokesmen" of the people. In the process of long-term practice and exploration, many effective forms for deputies to the National People's Congress to participate in legislation have been formed gradually. At the same time, it is necessary to innovate and improve the mechanism for deputies to the National People's Congress at all levels to participate in legislation, and give more play to the role of deputies to the National People's Congress in drafting and amending laws.

2. **Serving the people in strict law enforcement**

Strictness is the premise and foundation for the orderly operation of society and the guarantee of authority and credibility. Strict law enforcement is to strictly abide by the rules within the framework of the Constitution and laws, so as to be fair and strict.

Firstly, law enforcers must establish the concept of law enforcement for the people. Law enforcers are the staff of state organs and the representatives of public power, but their power is given by the people and should naturally serve the people. The rights of the people matter most, so strict law enforcement requires law enforcers to put the vital interests of the people first, consciously safeguard the rights and interests of the people, and create a good legal environment for the people.

Secondly, professional ethics should be observed strictly. Law enforcers should establish correct professional ideals, act according to industry norms, listen to the opinions of the people, understand the needs of the people, and truly enforce the law for the people.

Thirdly, law enforcers are the executors and enforcers of the law. A good way of thinking on the rule of law should be developed to improve the level of law enforcement, improve the credibility of national law enforcement organs, and make law enforcers and law enforcement departments the most reliable dependence of the broad masses of the people.

3. **Putting the people first in impartial administration of justice**

Justice is an important means to safeguard national security, public security, and social order and good customs. It is the last line of defense and relief mechanism to protect human rights (Liu 2021: 9). To achieve impartial administration of justice and ensure that judicial work in China can uphold the people as the core, the specific implementation path of impartial justice can be started from the following three aspects.

Firstly, ensure that the judiciary exercises its power independently and impartially and meet the expectations of the people. For one thing, the administration and localization of judicial power must be removed, which requires all provinces in China to strengthen the full integration of various resources of judicial organs, especially in the aspect of judicial funds. For another, the relationship between fair justice and the public should be effectively coordinated. It is the starting point of the work of judicial organs to fully understand the needs and wishes of the broad masses of the people, increase the depth of the broad masses of the people's participation in judicial work, and protect the broad masses of the people's enthusiasm for judicial work.

Secondly, deepen the reform of the judicial responsibility system and safeguard the rights and interests of the people. For one thing, the profound relationship between the Party's leadership and the reform of the judicial responsibility system should be understood. Judicial work should accept the Party's leadership, and the people's court must strengthen the reform and implementation of the judicial responsibility system. For another, the relationship between decentralization and supervision should be handled correctly. To make justice public is to let the broad masses of the people know relevant information.

Thirdly, a complete restriction and supervision system should be built. Internal supervision should be conducted through three stages: Pre-event focuses on reshaping regulatory concepts and clearly defining responsibilities; In-event involves full process supervision, with strict oversight of the judicial power exercised by various administrative departments; Post-event emphasizes strengthening accountability, forming a closed-loop regulatory cycle of pre-event, in-event, and post-event. On the other hand, external supervision mainly depends on the active participation of the broad masses of the people and the broadened channels and methods of supervision.

4. **Enhancing the concept of equality in the observance of law by everyone**

The Party and the government's strategy of comprehensive law-based governance must fully reflect the principal position of the people. To guide the participation of the broad masses of the people, it is necessary to create a good law enforcement and law-abiding social atmosphere. This fully shows that only when the law is revered and respected by the people can it exert its maximum force.

The specific implementation path of the observance of law by everyone can be started from the following aspects. Firstly, implement the work of popularizing the law among the whole people and establish the concept of equality. In the process of promoting law popularization, excellent deeds and models should be discovered to encourage the people to keep up with these models. At the same time, the participation mechanism in law popularization should be broadened to enrich law popularization resources and expand the scope of law popularization. Meanwhile, on the basis of traditional news communication carriers, new forms should be explored to make full use of the communication role of mobile phones, the Internet, television and other media.

Secondly, implement the punishment and reward system to enhance public awareness of the rule of law. A mechanism for dishonest behavior has been established to severely punish the seriously dishonest behavior of market subjects, and to improve personal credit records. The major theoretical viewpoints on the issues of the relationship between morality and law, the basis of major reform in the law and the legalization of social governance in the Chinese Rule of Law Philosophy have been comprehensively implemented into the process of the construction of the social credit system to promote the legalization of the social credit system, and then serve the improvement of social governance standard system and the modernization of social governance (Tan and Liu 2021: 7).

7.4 Complementary Roles of Morality and Law in Governance

7.4.1 The Roles of Morality and Law in Imperial China

Throughout the time-honored development of Chinese Legal Family, the interplay between the Legalist school and Confucianism has been a constant. The fusion of the Legalist principle of "*Yi Fa Wei Feng*" (以法爲奉) (upholding the law) and the Confucian emphasis on "*De Zhu Xing Fu*" (德主刑輔) (Virtue as the primary principle and punishment as a secondary means) thus constitutes the successful governance experience of "*De Fa Xiang Ji*" (德法相濟) (integrating morality and law) in China's traditional legal culture. It reflects the distinct views on morality and law in imperial China, and highlights China's unique legal tradition.

"Virtue" is a unique spiritual gene that runs through China's five thousand years of civilization and a basic legislative guiding ideology in the process of legal development. In the social changes and reforms in imperial China, the game between Confucian "governing with virtue" and Legalist "governing with law" is generally shown. If "governing with law" outweighs "governing with virtue", that is, ignoring the role of morality in society, it may lead to tyranny and cruel punishment. If "governing with virtue" outweighs "governing with law", it may lead to "rule by man". Therefore, "joint governance of virtue and law" is a compromise and balance between the flexibility of "governing with virtue" and the rigidity of "governing with law".

The governance approach of integrating morality and law can be traced back to Gao Yao (皋陶), a leader of the Huaxia (華夏) tribes in prehistorical China. More than 4000 years ago, he proposed the idea that the people should have a clear understanding of the "*Wu Xing*" (五刑) (Five Punishments), which in turn supports the "*Wu Jiao*" (五教) (Five Teachings). The Five Teachings refer to virtues such as father's righteousness, mother's kindness, elder brother's friendliness, younger brother's respect, and son's filial piety, thus representing morality. Gao Yao insisted on clarifying the Five Punishments to assist the Five Teachings, so as to achieve good governance in the country. The correct application of punishments ultimately led to the effect of "no punishment", and the society was harmonious and orderly.

Later Confucius stated, "If you govern the people through administrative decrees and regulate them through punishments, they may avoid wrongdoing but will lack a sense of shame. If you guide them through virtue and unify them through rites, they will cultivate a sense of shame and self-discipline" (from *Analects*《論語》). From the Western Zhou's concept of "*Ming De Shen Fa*" (明德慎罰) (the promotion of virtue and the imposition of penalty with prudence), to the idea of "*De Zhu Xing Fu*" proposed by the Western Han scholar-official Dong Zhongshu, and finally to the explicit proclamation in the *Tang Code* that "Virtue and rites are the foundation for governance, while punishment serves as its support", the governance strategy of integrating morality and law underwent a long historical process. Dynasties that successfully complemented morality and law in governance were often marked by prosperity and stability.

7.4.2 *Integrating Law-Based Governance and Moral Governance in the Chinese Modernization of Rule of Law*

Drawing on historical experience, Chinese Rule of Law Philosophy in the new era has embraced this principle, emphasizing the complementary and unified relationship between morality and law. It advocates a governance strategy that integrates law-based governance and moral governance, calling for a close integration of legal and moral development, as well as external regulation and self-discipline, to ensure that law and morality complement and reinforce each other.

President Xi Jinping has stated: "Law brings stability to the nation, while morality nurtures the people's hearts" (Xi 2020b: 165), and "law is codified morality, while morality is law internalized in the heart; both serve to regulate social behavior and maintain social order" (Xi 2020b: 109). This perspective not only underscores the regulatory and binding function of law but also highlights the guiding and educative role of morality, organically integrating the two to form a distinct socialist rule of law philosophy with Chinese characteristics. While law is coercive, morality exerts an intangible educative influence. "Governing a country and society requires both law-based governance and moral governance, ensuring their mutual reinforcement and complementarity" (Xi 2021a: 114). Law and morality are inseparable and must function in coordination to achieve effective national governance.

Building on past achievements and looking toward the future, Chinese Rule of Law Philosophy in the new era has endowed this governance approach with new meanings. The moral principles emphasized by Chinese Rule of Law Philosophy align with the socialist core values and serve as ethical standards for the practice of socialism with Chinese characteristics. The laws it refers to reflect the collective will of the Chinese people and provide legal guarantees for the great practice of socialism with Chinese characteristics. Furthermore, a key contribution of Chinese Rule of Law Philosophy lies in expanding the application of this integrated approach. It particularly emphasizes applying the concept of integrating morality and law to the Party building, the cultivation of rule of law talents, and rural governance, thereby proposing new implementation paths and requirements for the practical application of this integrated approach. Finally, Chinese Rule of Law Philosophy further develops the dialectical relationship between law-based governance and moral governance. Traditional legal culture has, to some extent, regarded the "governing with virtue and rites" as superior to the "governing with law and punishments". In contrast, Chinese Rule of Law Philosophy underscores the principal position of the rule of law, highlighting the coordinated advancement of law-based governance, law-based exercise of state power, and law-based administration. It positions the rule of law as a critical component in advancing the Chinese path to modernization.

7.4.3 The Contemporary Significance of Morality and Law in Governance

The complementary roles of morality and law in governance has a long history in China. It represents a successful experience of national governance in imperial China and embodies the essence of traditional Chinese legal culture, fully demonstrating the political and legal wisdom of the Chinese nation. The functions of morality and law are inherently unified, both serving the goal of achieving "good governance" in a socialist country with Chinese characteristics. The integration of law-based governance and moral governance holds significant practical value for advancing the Chinese modernization of rule of law.

First, integrating law-based governance and moral governance contributes to the comprehensive law-based governance. Specifically, in lawmaking, "good laws" must align with human nature and reflect public opinion, drawing nourishment from morality in the process of formulating legal norms. In law enforcement and administration of justice, law enforcers and judges must act impartially, possessing not only strong legal expertise but also a sense of morality and responsibility to ensure that each case is handled in a manner that is lawful, reasonable, and fair. In the observance of law, legal rules can impose mandatory behavioral constraints, while moral education can deepen individuals' understanding and internalization of the law. In sum, in lawmaking, law enforcement, administration of justice, and the observance of law, morality and law must work in a coordinated manner to enhance the level of comprehensive law-based governance and better achieve its goals.

Second, the integrated approach of law-based governance and moral governance facilitates the cultivation of socialist core values. The Report of the 19th National Congress of the CPC states that cultural confidence is a more fundamental, deeper, and more enduring force in the development of a country and a nation. The integration of morality and law is a unique and outstanding tradition in Chinese culture, deeply rooted in China's history and well suited to the demands of the present era. In the new era, emphasizing the integration of law-based governance and moral governance constitutes a crucial aspect of contemporary Chinese Rule of Law Philosophy. The role of "governing with virtue" in imperial China, which maintained social order through moral education, remains relevant today in fostering a sense of community, adherence to social norms, harmonious social relations, and shared social values. Creatively transforming and innovatively developing the cultural legacy of "joint governance of virtue and law" in alignment with contemporary realities will help establish a shared moral and ideological foundation in society. This, in turn, will promote the cultivation of socialist core values and consolidate the collective strength of the Chinese nation in unity and progress.

Third, the integration of law-based governance and moral governance contributes to the great rejuvenation of the Chinese nation. At the level of national prosperity, "rule of law" serves as a safeguard for political and economic development, while "rule of virtue" plays a crucial role in enhancing economic vitality and promoting social progress. At the level of national rejuvenation, the Chinese nation, having experienced both historical glories and hardships, aspires to revival more than ever before. The "rule of law" provides steadfast protection on this path, helping to overcome challenges. At the same time, the process of national rejuvenation requires unwavering efforts to absorb the intellectual essence and contemporary significance of China's rich traditional culture, guiding people toward a correct understanding of history, nationality, and culture, strengthening the Chinese people's cultural confidence, and enabling the country to present a dignified and confident image on the world stage. At the level of people's well-being, the essence of integrating law-based governance and moral governance lies in a people-oriented approach that safeguards the interests of the people and enhances individual well-being. As members of the nation, individuals should, on the one hand, abide by laws and internalize legal norms into their daily behavior, and on the other hand, cultivate moral character by upholding values such as benevolence, righteousness, propriety, wisdom, and trustworthiness. This will contribute to fostering a positive social atmosphere and building a harmonious and prosperous society.

7.5 The Key to Governance Lies in Selecting the Right People

7.5.1 The Administration of Officials in Imperial China

As intermediaries between rulers and the people, officials were pivotal in implementing governance and upholding order. This understanding led imperial China to develop rigorous systems for official administration. Rulers in imperial China without exception attached great importance to the careful selection, management and assessment of officials.

Traditional Chinese legal culture has always placed great emphasis on the selection of talents and the appointment of officials, upholding the principle of "*Xuan Xian Ren Neng*" (選賢任能) (selecting the virtuous and employing the capable). As a result, a number of exemplary officials known for their unwavering commitment to justice—such as Wei Zheng (魏征), Bao Zheng (包拯), Hai Rui (海瑞), and Yu Chenglong (于成龍)—emerged throughout history. These figures have become enduring symbols of justice in the minds of modern Chinese people and are regarded as "living embodiment of the spirit of the Chinese Legal Family" (Hou, Zhang and Jia 1997: 59). In the political philosophy of Confucius, the "*Ju Xian Cai*" (舉賢才) (selection of worthy individuals) was a key principle: "If virtuous officials are elevated above corrupt ones, the people will be loyal. But if corrupt officials are placed above the virtuous, the people will lose trust in authority" (from *Analects* 《論語》). Similarly, Mozi stated that "honoring the worthy is the foundation of governance" (from *Mozi* 《墨子》), advocating for an equitable and merit-based system for appointing officials. During the Han dynasty, starting with Emperor Wu, the system of "*Ju Xiao Lian*" (舉孝廉) (selecting the filial and incorrupt) was established, whereby local authorities recommended individuals known for their filial devotion and upright conduct for government service. Emperor Taizong of the Tang dynasty, when discussing official appointments, remarked that "benevolent governance depends on virtuous talent" and that "it is not necessary to fill all official positions, only to find the right people".

In traditional society, rulers primarily governed through officials and laws, with the enforcement and implementation of laws also relying on the officials themselves. Consequently, from its inception, the Chinese Legal Family placed great importance on maintaining the integrity of the bureaucracy. Among the bamboo slips excavated in the Shuihudi Qin Tomb, "*Wei Li zhi Dao*" (《爲吏之道》) (*The Way of Being an Official*) set forth the duties, behavioral norms, and reward-and-punishment mechanisms for officials. Besides, legal codes such as the "*Zhi Li Lü*" (《置吏律》) (*Regulations on the Appointment of Officials*), "*Nei Shi Za*" (《内史雜》) (*Regulations on the Ministry of the Interior*), "*Wei Za*" (《尉雜》) (*Regulations on Military Affairs*), and "*Xiao Lü*" (《效律》) (*Efficiency Laws*) functioned similarly to modern administrative regulations. The Han dynasty's "*Shang Ji Lü*" (《上計律》) (*Laws on Annual Reports*), based on Qin's legal traditions, introduced further refinements. During the Wei, Jin, and Northern and Southern dynasties, an annual official evaluation system was implemented, determining promotions, demotions, dismissals, and punishments based on performance. The Sui dynasty established a bureaucratic system composed of the "*San Sheng*" (三省) (Three Departments), "*Liu Bu*" (六部) (Six Ministries), and "*Er Shi Si Si*" (二十四司) (Twenty-Four Commissions), streamlining local governance. It also mandated that local officials of the ninth rank and above be appointed and dismissed directly by the central "*Li Bu*" (吏部) (Ministry of Personnel), with annual performance reviews and a mandatory reporting visit to the central government. Provincial governors and county magistrates served fixed three-year terms without reappointment, and local officials were prohibited from serving in their home regions to prevent nepotism and collusion with local elites. These institutional and legal measures laid the foundation for later dynasties and had a lasting positive impact.

Beyond legal regulations, traditional Chinese governance also sought to improve administrative competence and reinforce officials' moral self-discipline through non-legal norms. Among these, "*Guan Zhen*" (官箴) (official admonitions) played a crucial role. According to *Shuo Wen Jie Zi* (《说文解字》) (a Chinese dictionary compiled c. 100 CE during the Eastern Han dynasty), the character for "Zhen", "箴", originally referred to a tool used for sewing clothes, from which its meaning evolved to signify admonition and moral exhortation. Thus, *Guan Zhen* refers to admonitory texts that serve as warnings, exhortations, and guidelines for officials. This tradition in Chinese history traces back to the pre-Qin period, with some of the earliest records found in classical texts. One notable example is the "*Yu Ren zhi Zhen*" (《虞人之箴》) (*The Admonition of the Supervisor of Forestry and Hunting*), documented in *Zuo Zhuan* (《左傳》) (*The Commentary of Zuo*). During the Han dynasty, Yang Xiong authored "Shi Er Zhou Zhen" (《十二州箴》) (*The Admonition for the Twelve Zhous*), and in the Tang dynasty, both Emperor Taizong's "*Di Fan*" (《帝範》) (*The Norms of the Emperor*) and Empress Wu Zetian's "*Chen Gui*" (《臣軌》) (*The Code for Ministers*) provided ethical guidance for officials. By the Ming and Qing dynasties, "*Guan Zhen*" culture had reached its peak, with both state-sponsored and privately authored admonitory texts proliferating. This body of literature emphasized the duty of officials to care for the people's well-being while also advocating for the restraint and prudent exercise of power.

7.5.2 Talent Guarantee for the Chinese Modernization of Rule of Law

Entering the new era, President Xi Jinping has emphasized that advancing comprehensive law-based governance requires the establishment of a high-caliber rule of law workforce that possesses both integrity and professional competence. He has cited the historical insight of Hai Rui that "if the right people are chosen but the right laws are not in place, affairs will not succeed; if the right laws are in place but the right people are not chosen, the laws will be ineffective. Only when both people and laws are in harmony can governance be achieved" (from the *Treatise on Governing the People* 《治黎策》). This quotation profoundly underscores the necessity of selecting the right personnel as a fundamental requirement for building a socialist rule of law country.

As China advances its modernization of rule of law, a comprehensive legal framework has gradually taken shape. However, to ensure its effective implementation, there is an urgent need for a highly competent legal workforce that adheres strictly to the law, enforces it rigorously, and ensures that violations are met with accountability. Compared to the past, China now places even greater emphasis on talent cultivation, and the systems for selecting and training legal professionals have been continuously refined and improved.

In response to China's specific national conditions, Chinese Rule of Law Philosophy in the new era provides an innovative interpretation of the selection and cultivation of rule of law talents. It offers a profound answer to questions regarding the composition and standards of the contemporary rule of law workforce, and explicitly calls for enhancing the political and ideological quality, professional competence, and ethical standards of this workforce. The goal is to build a strong contingent of judicial, procuratorial and public security officers that is loyal to the Party, the country, the people, and the law, ensuring that they have firm political beliefs, strong professional expertise, a good sense of responsibility and discipline, and good moral character. A well-trained rule of law workforce—including both specialized legal professionals and legal service providers—serves as the foundation for improving the quality and efficiency of legislation, law enforcement, and judicial processes. It also provides the necessary talent guarantee for implementing rule of law practices and advancing the Chinese modernization of rule of law.

7.5.3 The Cultivation of Rule of Law Talents

To achieve the talent guarantee for the Chinese modernization of rule of law, firstly, we must "research and arrange the long-term plan for cultivating rule of law talents in the new era, and innovate the mechanism for talent cultivation" (Xi 2020b: 274). President Xi pointed out, "Advancing comprehensive law-based governance is a systematic project, and the cultivation of rule of law talents is a key component. If the cultivation of rule of law talents does not improve and talents cannot emerge in this field, it is impossible to do a good job in the advancement of comprehensive law-based governance" (Xi 2020b: 174). Consequently, it is imperative that we "strive to cultivate a large number of high-quality rule of law talents and reserve forces" (Xi 2020b: 231). On the basis of the current legal education and talent cultivation system, we need to further rationalize the disciplinary structure, improve the legal discipline system and curriculum system, promote the interdisciplinary integration of legal disciplines with other disciplines, and "adhere to what should be adhered to, improve what should be improved, adjust what should be adjusted, and innovate what should be innovated" (Xi 2020b: 175), so as to provide a strong talent guarantee for advancing the comprehensive law-based governance and building the rule of law in China.

Secondly, we must focus on a small number of key officials, do a good job in the construction of leading bodies at all levels of legislative, law enforcement, and judicial organs, and select personnel who are good at using rule of law thinking and methods to leadership positions. We should select talents based on their abilities, implement the system of key Party and government leaders fulfilling the primary responsibility for advancing the law-based governance. These key officials should serve as important organizers, promoters, and practitioners of the law-based governance, and implement the major decisions and deployments on the rule of law. At the same time, they should play a leading role and act as models of respecting, learning, observing and applying the law, thereby fostering the favorable social ethos of respecting, learning, observing, applying and protecting the law.

7.6 Conclusion

President Xi Jinping has emphasized:

> History and reality tell us that only by inheriting the excellent traditional Chinese legal culture, exploring a rule of law path suitable for our own country from the practice of our revolution, construction, and reform, and drawing on the beneficial achievements of foreign legal systems, can we solidify the rule of law foundation in the building of a socialist modernized country in all respects and the great rejuvenation of the Chinese nation. (Xi 2021b)

Chinese Rule of Law Philosophy in the new era creatively inherits the country's outstanding traditional legal ideas and institutions while developing them innovatively based on the realities of contemporary China. This has established the historical and cultural foundations for the Chinese modernization of rule of law. Through a critical inheritance and modern revitalization of the Chinese Legal Family, it has endowed China's traditional legal civilization with new contemporary meaning. In the process of reshaping the former brilliance of the Chinese Legal Family, it has also provided a robust rule of law foundation for modernizing national governance. At the same time, it comprehensively showcases China's rule of law image in the new era and contributes Chinese wisdom and strength to global governance.

References

Bodde, D., and Morris, C. 1967. *Law in Imperial China.* Cambridge: Harvard University Press.

CCCPC. 2021a. Implementation Outline of the Construction of a Law-Based Government (2021–2025). *People's Daily* (1), August 12.

CCCPC. 2021b. The Plan for Building the Rule of Law in China (2022–2025). *People's Daily* (1), January 11.

Dong, X., and Zhang, Y. 2023. The Translation and Dissemination of "Guanzi": Bringing Chinese Governance Wisdom to the World. November 16. Available at https://www.cssn.cn/skgz/bwyc/202311/t20231116_5697047.shtml.

Hou, W., Zhang L. and Jia G. 1997. A Brief Discussion on the Characteristics and Values of the Chinese Legal Family. *Journal of the Northeast Normal University* 3: 57–61.

Hu, B., and Dong, X. 2018. Drawing on the Essence of Traditional Legal Culture to Build a Socialist Law-Based Country. December 12. Available at http://sscp.cssn.cn/xkpd/fx_20156/201812/t20181212_4792036.html.

Liu, H. 2021. Xi Jinping Thought on the Rule of Law and the Construction of Human Rights Protection System. *Chinese Journal of Human Rights* 1: 1–12.

People's Daily. 2015. Xi Jinping Delivered a Speech in the British Parliament (1). October 21.

Tan, B., and Liu, Z. 2021. Theoretical Support and Guidance of Xi Jinping Thought on the Rule of Law on Social Credit System. *Journal of Henan University of Economics and Law* 3: 7–16.

Xi, J. 2015. *Excerpts from Xi Jinping's Discourses on Comprehensive Law-Based Governance.* Beijing: Central Literature Press.

Xi, J. 2020a. Fully Recognizing the Significance of the Promulgation and Implementation of the Civil Code: Ensuring Better Legal Protection of People's Lawful Rights and Interests. *The People's Congress of China* 12: 6–9.

Xi, J. 2020b. *On Adhering to Comprehensive Law-Based Governance*. Beijing: Central Party Literature Press.

Xi, J. 2021a. *On Upholding People's Status as Masters of the Country*. Beijing: Central Party Literature Press.

Xi, J. 2021b. Resolutely Follow the Path of Socialist Rule of Law with Chinese Characteristics to Provide Strong Legal Guarantees for the Comprehensive Construction of a Socialist Modernized Country. *Qiushi* 5: 4–15.

Xi, J. 2022. *The Governance of China (Volume IV)*. Beijing: Foreign Language Press.

Zhang, W. 2020. The Chinese Story and Legal Principle of the Civil Code. *Law and Social Development* 5: 5–20.

Zhang, Q. 2021. The Theoretical Origins, Basic Characteristics, and Significance of Xi Jinping's Thought on the Rule of Law. *Studies in Ideological Education* 1: 20–25.

Zhang, J. 2022a. On the People-Centered Thought in Ancient China. *China Legal Science* 5: 122–142.

Zhang, W. 2022b. Profoundly Grasping the Historical Logic, Theoretical Logic and Practical Logic of the Governance Complied with the Constitution and the Exercise of State Power Complied with the Constitution. *Modern Law Science* 5: 3–24.

Chapter 8
Value and Significance of Revitalizing the Chinese Legal Family in the New Era

Abstract The Chinese people's great pursuit of the rule of law has never ceased, nor has the development and evolution of the Chinese Legal Family. The Chinese modernization of rule of law represents a new stage in the development of the Chinese Legal Family, while the rich traditional legal culture within the Chinese Legal Family has contributed to the achievements of the Chinese modernization of rule of law. The great revitalization of the Chinese Legal Family in the new era holds profound significance and value.

The Chinese Legal Family represents a significant achievement in the Chinese nation's exploration of self-governance and an integral part of its original civilization. The Chinese people's great pursuit of the rule of law has never ceased, nor has the development and evolution of the Chinese Legal Family. The progression of the Chinese Legal Family and the Chinese modernization of rule of law are not two entirely separate processes, nor are they merely sequential or even substitutive. Rather, the Chinese modernization of rule of law emerges as a continuation of the concrete evolution of the Chinese Legal Family, undergoing continuous refinement and ultimately shaping itself into a systematic mechanism of innovation.

The Chinese modernization of rule of law is grounded in a deep confidence in indigenous legal cultures such as Confucian and Legalist traditions. It builds upon the legal and political theories developed under the leadership of the Communist Party of China, as well as a century of experience in advancing the rule of law. At the same time, it remains future-oriented, focusing on cutting-edge issues related to the rule of law, so as to enhance the discourse and global influence of China's rule of law. In other words, the Chinese modernization of rule of law represents a new stage in the development of the Chinese Legal Family, while the rich traditional legal culture within the Chinese Legal Family has contributed to the achievements of the Chinese modernization of rule of law. The great revitalization of the Chinese Legal Family in the new era holds profound significance and value.

X. Dong and Y. Li, *Chinese Legal Family and Chinese Modernization of Rule of Law*,
https://doi.org/10.1007/978-981-96-7529-6_8

8.1 Promoting the Creative Transformation and Innovative Development of Excellent Traditional Chinese Legal Culture

To revitalize the Chinese Legal Family in the new era, is to creatively transform and innovatively develop the excellent traditional Chinese legal culture. It is by no means a mechanical inheritance of tradition, but the addition of innovative elements on the basis of inheriting its essence, making it more adaptable to the development needs of modern society. In other words, the Chinese modernization of rule of law is not just a simple replacement of traditional legal practices, but a more complex integration and innovation of culture and systems. It needs to draw on the essence of legal wisdom spanning thousands of years, and also introduce the principles and practices of modern rule of law, endowing excellent traditional Chinese legal culture with new connotations for the new era.

The Chinese modernization of rule of law is actually an effective integration of excellent traditional Chinese legal thoughts and modern rule of law concepts, and based on this, a series of new ideas and strategies for governing the country with both traditional heritage and modern ideas have emerged, which are reflected in all aspects of building the rule of law in contemporary China.

8.1.1 Improving Sound Lawmaking

Improving sound lawmaking is one of the key tasks in advancing the comprehensive law-based governance and the Chinese modernization of rule of law.

Chinese Rule of Law Philosophy in the new era inherits and develops such excellent legal resources of the Chinese Legal Family as "upholding the law and strengthening the country through law" and "codified legal civilization and good governance through good laws", highly affirming the supreme position of law in national governance and striving to promote sound lawmaking. Since the 18th National Congress of the Communist Party of China, the CPC Central Committee with Comrade Xi Jinping at its core has attached great importance to legislative work, continuously improving the quality of legislation and enhancing the socialist rule of law with Chinese characteristics with the Constitution as its core. The scientificity of sound lawmaking lies in the scientificity of the legislative system, which is embodied in the timeliness, systematicness, pertinence, and effectiveness of laws and regulations, as well as in their enforceability and operability, thereby formulating "good laws" through scientific legislation. "Not every law can govern the country, and not every law can govern the country well; the more we emphasize the rule of law, the more we need to improve the quality of legislation" (Xi 2020: 20). Therefore, while maintaining the authority of the Constitution, efforts should also be made to strengthen legislation in key areas, emerging areas, and foreign-related areas, constructing a complete system of laws and regulations to provide a legal basis and guarantee for "good laws and good governance".

Sound lawmaking in the new era is also influenced by the excellent traditional Chinese legal thought of "the people as the foundation of the state", deeply promoting democratic legislation. The people are the broadest and deepest foundation for law-based governance. Therefore, to carry out legislative work and improve the legal system, it is necessary to always uphold the principal position of the people. One concrete practice of democratic legislation is the establishment of "*Ji Ceng Li Fa Lian Xi Dian*" (基层立法联系点) (local legislative outreach offices), which is a microcosm of developing the whole-process people's democracy. These outreach offices connect the highest organ of state power at one end and the local citizens at the other, expanding the channels, forms, and contents of public participation in legislation. They are beneficial explorations in developing democratic legislation and innovative mechanisms for complying with and expressing the will of the people. Regarding the people-oriented nature of the rule of law in legislation, President Xi Jinping believes that "The people's expectations for legislation are no longer about whether there are laws, but whether the laws are good, effective, and capable of solving practical problems" (Xi 2020: 20). To ensure that laws benefit the people, the Party and the state are committed to strengthening legal amendments in the field of the people's livelihood, so that more reform achievements can fairly benefit all members of society.

8.1.2 Promoting Strict Law Enforcement

In his speech at the celebration of the 60th anniversary of the founding of the National People's Congress, President Xi Jinping quoted an ancient saying: "A state does not enjoy permanent order nor suffer permanent chaos. When laws are strictly enforced, the nation thrives; when they are lax, it descends into chaos" (from *Comments of a Recluse* 《潜夫論》), so as to emphasize that the vitality of law lies in its enforcement; its authority stems from the same (Gu 2023). Laws that are not strictly enforced will have their vitality and authority severely damaged, directly undermining the foundation of law-based governance. In other words, the effectiveness of law depends on its implementation, and the means of implementation lies in law enforcement. Therefore, vigorously promoting strict law enforcement is also one of the key tasks in advancing the comprehensive law-based governance and the Chinese modernization of rule of law.

"The focus of promoting strict law enforcement lies in addressing prominent issues such as non-standard, non-strict, non-transparent, and uncivilized law enforcement, as well as inaction and arbitrary action" (Xi 2020: 114). Regarding these issues, building a law-based government serves as the mainstay of contemporary China's efforts to develop the rule of law. This endeavor is conducive to urging the government to practice law-based administration and urging state personnel to enhance their awareness and ability to handle affairs according to law. In line with the excellent tradition of the Chinese Legal Family that emphasizes "the key to governance lies in selecting the right people", it is imperative to build a high-caliber workforce for law enforcement within administrative organs. At the forefront of administrative law enforcement work, administrative law enforcers must adhere to the principle of loyalty to the law and defending the law, externalize the spirit and belief of the rule of law into the norms of administrative law enforcement, and adhere to the use of rule of law thinking and methods to strictly enforce the law and dare to take responsibility. In particular, key Party and government leaders must, in fulfilling the primary responsibility for advancing the law-based governance, take the lead in respecting, learning, observing and applying the law, strictly make decisions in accordance with laws and regulations, and adhere to the employment orientation that values legal literacy and competence, so as to place various administrative law enforcement work in their jurisdictions on the track of the rule of law.

8.1.3 Ensuring Impartial Administration of Justice

Justice is the lifeline of the rule of law, and the administration of justice serves as the last line of defense for social fairness and justice. Impartial administration of justice plays a crucial role in advancing the rule of law and is also a longstanding tradition in Chinese Legal Family.

As early as the Warring States period, Han Fei asserted that "The law does not favor those in power, just as a measuring line does not bend towards curves" (from *Han Feizi*《韓非子》), emphasizing that the law should be fair, impartial, and equally applied to all. To ensure judicial fairness, imperial China developed a tradition of joint trials for major cases, with the "*San Si Hui Shen*" (三司會審) (Three-Judicial-Office Joint Trial) as a representative practice. The "*San Si*" (三司) (Three Judicial Offices) were central judicial bodies in imperial China, and the idea of "joint trial" traces its roots to "*Shang Jun Shu*" (《商君書》) (the *Book of Lord Shang*), in which Shang Yang proposed appointing three judicial officials: one stationed at the palace, one under the *Yu Shi Tai* (禦史台) (the Censorate), and one designated by the *Cheng Xiang* (丞相) (Counselor-in-chief). During the Han Dynasty, this arrangement evolved into the offices of *Ting Wei* (廷尉) (Chamberlain for Law Enforcement), *Yu Shi Zhong Cheng* (禦史中丞) (Palace Censor), and *Si Li Xiao Wei* (司隸校尉) (Metropolitan Commandant), which jointly adjudicated significant cases. By the Tang Dynasty, the process further matured into "*San Si Tui Shi*" (三司推事) (Judgment by the Three Judicial Offices), referring to *Xing Bu* (刑部) (Ministry of Justice), *Yu Shi Tai*, and *Da Li Si* (大理寺) (Court of Judicial Review). It was not until the Ming Dynasty that the term "*San Si Hui Shen*" officially appeared. During the Ming and Qing dynasties, *Xing Bu*, *Da Li Si*, and *Du Cha Yuan* (都察院) (Court of Censors) were confirmed as the "*San Si*". They collaboratively presided over critical, complex, and contentious cases, significantly enhancing the rigor of trial procedures and ensuring that major cases were handled in a standardized and just manner. This institutional arrangement played a vital role in safeguarding fairness and justice within the judicial process.

Drawing lessons from this tradition, President Xi Jinping has emphasized the need to ensure that the people experience fairness and justice in every judicial case. He advocates for the establishment of an open, dynamic, transparent, and convenient judicial system, resolutely curbing judicial corruption, and upholding the principle of equality before the law. This reflects the judiciary's role in safeguarding the interests, aspirations, and rights of the people, embodying the legal tradition of "the people as the foundation of the state". To achieve this, the tradition of "the key to governance lies in selecting the right people" in the Chinese Legal Family should be further implemented in the recruitment and development of judicial personnel. Judicial officers must uphold a firm belief in the law, remain impartial and incorruptible, and steadfastly adhere to the impartial administration of justice.

8.1.4 Guiding the Observance of Law by All

The prestige of the law is rooted in the internal recognition and belief of the people. To advance comprehensive law-based governance, it is essential to actively guide the observance of law by all.

To cultivate the rule of law concept of the whole people, it is necessary to adhere to moral governance while advancing law-based governance, thereby encouraging self-reflection, self-discipline, and self-restraint among the people. Drawing on the historical experience of "joint governance of virtue and law" in imperial China, the Chinese Rule of Law Philosophy in the new era emphasizes the synthesized force of law and morality, and requires that law-based governance and moral governance be grasped with both hands and both hands must be hard. It is necessary to nourish the spirit of the rule of law with morality, highlight the connotation of the rule of law in moral education, and guide the whole people to consciously fulfill their legal obligations, social responsibilities, and family responsibilities. Therefore, in advancing the Chinese modernization of rule of law, it is imperative to actively promote socialist core values, inherit traditional Chinese virtues, and cultivate social morality, professional ethics, family virtues, and personal integrity. Strengthening the ideological and moral construction of the whole people helps to enhance their awareness and recognition of national identity, thereby constructing a more civilized socialist rule of law with Chinese characteristics.

Guiding the observance of law by all also requires efforts to enhance the whole people's concept of the rule of law, which is also a manifestation of the tradition "the key to governance lies in selecting the right people" on a national scale. Therefore, China must view the efforts to spread basic legal knowledge among the people and to encourage them to abide by the law as long-term, fundamental tasks of the law-based governance. Legal education should start with children, and at the same time, it should improve the reward mechanism for law-abiding integrity and the punishment mechanism for illegal and dishonest behavior, creating a social atmosphere in which all citizens respect and abide by the law.

8.1.5 Strengthening National Confidence

In the new era of China's advancement of comprehensive law-based governance, the awareness of legal subjectivity has been increasingly strengthened in China (Hu and Dong 2020). The era of measuring Chinese law by Western civilized standards has become history. As China rises on the global stage, breaking the Western dominance in the rule of law discourse and constructing China's own narrative has become an urgent task in building the rule of law in China. This process constitutes both a rectification of origins and purification of foundations, as well as a reinforcement of cultural confidence and cohesion within the Chinese nation.

The inheritance and innovation of the Chinese Legal Family in the Chinese Rule of Law Philosophy in the new era exemplify the promotion of socialist rule of law culture. This modernization of the Chinese Legal Family profoundly demonstrates the Chinese people's cultural and national confidence in "*Zhong Guo zhi Zhi*" (中国之治) (the Chinese Governance). It also highlights the unique Chinese characteristics of the Chinese modernization of rule of law, contributing Chinese wisdom to the global development of rule of law civilization. By drawing upon the essence of excellent traditional Chinese legal culture, the revitalized Chinese Legal Family in the new era provides continuous momentum for the building of rule of law in China. With its rich connotations, scientific system, and robust theoretical foundation, it serves as a powerful tool to break free from the constraints of the "Western-centric" legal narrative, demonstrating the institutional advantages of China's legal system in a time of profound global changes unseen in a century, and providing strong support for China's increasingly significant role on the international stage.

8.2 Highlighting the Chinese Characteristics of the Modernization of Rule of Law

In the report of the 20th National Congress of the CPC, President Xi Jinping emphasized, "the Chinese path to modernization is a socialist modernization under the leadership of the CPC, sharing common characteristics with modernization in other countries but with features rooted in its own national conditions" (Xi 2023: 22). Similarly, while adhering to common features of the modernization of rule of law—such as the supremacy of the Constitution, respect for and protection of human rights, checks and balances on public power, and the safeguarding of fairness and justice—the Chinese modernization of rule of law distinctly embodies Chinese characteristics.

In his speech at the celebration of the 100th anniversary of the founding of the CPC, Xi Jinping proposed the important concept of "*Liang Ge Jie He*" (两个结合) (the two integrations), namely: adhering to the integration of the basic tenets of Marxism with China's specific realities, and with China's excellent traditional culture. Therefore, it is crucial to recognize that the Chinese modernization of rule of law is not a mere replica of the Western modernization model. Instead, it represents an institutional and practical innovation with distinct Chinese characteristics, achieved under the leadership of the CPC on the path of socialism with Chinese characteristics. It reflects the creative transformation and innovative development of excellent traditional Chinese legal culture and embodies the great revitalization of the Chinese Legal Family in the new era.

8.2.1 Under the Leadership of the Communist Party of China

The Chinese path to modernization is a modernization led by the Communist Party of China, and accordingly, the Chinese modernization of rule of law must also be carried out under the leadership of the CPC. This is the first and most defining feature of the "Chinese characteristics" of the modernization of rule of law.

A review of history reveals that upholding the leadership of the CPC is the most valuable experience in China's legal development. During the period of the New Democratic Revolution, in the Central Soviet Area, the CPC led the formulation of multiple legal documents, including the *Outline of the Constitution of the Chinese Soviet Republic*, the *Land Law of the Chinese Soviet Republic*, the *Labor Law of the Chinese Soviet Republic*, and the *Marriage Law of the Chinese Soviet Republic*. In the Shaanxi-Gansu-Ningxia Border Region, with Yan'an as the center, the CPC formulated constitutional and legal documents such as the *Program of Governance for the Shaanxi-Gansu-Ningxia Border Region* and the *Principles of the Constitution of the Shaanxi-Gansu-Ningxia Border Region*. These New Democratic constitutional documents fully embodied the unity of the Party's principles and the will of the people, playing a crucial role in rallying public support, consolidating revolutionary bases, and advancing the struggle for national independence and the people's liberation under the Party's leadership.

In 1948, amid continuous victories in the War of Liberation and the expansion of CPC-led liberated areas, the *North China People's Government Policy Program* was adopted at the Provisional People's Congress of North China under the Party's leadership. This was the first New Democratic constitutional document formulated by a people's congress with legislative authority. It laid the ideological and institutional groundwork for establishing the constitutional system of the People's Republic of China, creating the nationwide system of the people's congresses, forming the central government, and advancing the CPC's governance and exercise of state power complied with the Constitution. On the eve of the PRC's founding, the Party led the Chinese People's Political Consultative Conference in drafting the *Common Program*, which served as a provisional constitution. In 1954, under the strong leadership of the CPC Central Committee with Comrade Mao Zedong at its core, the First Session of the First National People's Congress adopted the *Constitution of the People's Republic of China*.

Since the advent of the new era of upholding and developing socialism with Chinese characteristics, President Xi Jinping has placed even greater emphasis on strengthening the Party's comprehensive leadership over legal development. The establishment of the Central Committee for Comprehensive Law-Based Governance has further reinforced the centralized and unified leadership of the Party over the comprehensive rule of law.

The Party's leadership in legal development manifests not only in political leadership, which includes the Party's leadership in legislation, its guarantee of law enforcement, its support for judicial justice, and its rigorous observation of law, but also in ideological leadership. On the path to the modernization of rule of law, the CPC has consistently upheld Marxist theory on the rule of law, with special attention to its guidance for contemporary China, and has explicitly established the Chinese Rule of Law Philosophy in the new era as the fundamental guiding ideology for building the rule of law China. This new philosophy has emerged from the great practice of advancing comprehensive law-based governance and promoting the modernization of rule of law. It systematically summarizes China's historical achievements and rich experience in legal development, creatively transforms and innovatively develops excellent traditional Chinese legal culture, and critically inherits and selectively draws upon the achievements of human rule of law civilization. By deeply revealing the intrinsic logic of the rule of law and modernization, as well as the universal laws of legal modernization, it serves as both the fundamental guiding principle for China's legal development in the new era and a beacon illuminating the future of the Chinese modernization of rule of law.

8.2.2 *The Modernization of a Major Developing Country*

Building the rule of law in China characterized by good laws and good governance within a major developing country of over 1.4 billion people, vast territory, and unbalanced regional development presents unprecedented significance, difficulty, and complexity, inevitably requiring a unique path and approach.

On one hand, grounded in China's national conditions, we must unswervingly adhere to the path of socialist rule of law with Chinese characteristics, follow the objective laws of rule of law modernization, and integrate the general principles of human society's rule of law development with the specific rules of China's rule of law development. We must combine evolutionary and constructivist models, endogenous and exogenous paths, and bottom-up evolution with top-down promotion to forge a new path for the Chinese modernization of rule of law, showcasing the grand vision of China's rule of law. We must adopt a scientific approach and working policy of seeking progress while maintaining stability, advancing step by step, and ensuring continuous progress. We must proceed from reality, avoiding both disregard for national conditions and overstepping stages, as well as clinging to old ways and being bound by conventions. The rule of law in a major country, in particular, must avoid "great leaps" and "reckless actions", and preclude any catastrophic errors.

On the other hand, the rule of law in a major country requires a global perspective and vision. While managing our own affairs well, we must actively respond to the common concerns of all countries in the field of the rule of law, contributing Chinese wisdom and strength to the global rule of law modernization. This marks a major distinction between the Chinese modernization of rule of law and the Western model in terms of development paths and patterns.

Achieving the modernization of rule of law in a major country like China carries extraordinary significance. President Xi Jinping pointed out, "With a population of over 1.4 billion, China's entry into a modernized society as a whole, surpassing the combined scale of all the existing developed countries, will fundamentally reshaping the global landscape of modernization and be profoundly influential in human history" (Xi 2022). The promotion and realization of the Chinese modernization of rule of law will inevitably transform the Western-centric landscape of the rule of law, unveiling a completely new vision of the global rule of law civilization.

8.2.3 A Continuation of the Chinese Legal Family

The Chinese nation has a history of human existence spanning millions of years, a cultural history of ten thousand years, and a civilization history of over five thousand years. Legal civilization is an integral part of the Chinese civilization, and the Chinese Legal Family is a significant hallmark of China's legal civilization. Since ancient times, China has developed this unique legal system in world legal history. Originating in the Qin Dynasty, the Chinese Legal Family gradually matured during the Sui and Tang dynasties, with its codified legal system persisting until the Ming and Qing dynasties. Even today, its jurisprudential vitality remains vibrant. President Xi Jinping has pointed out: "China's ancient legal system contains a wealth of wisdom and resources… We must study the traditions, successes, and failures of China's ancient legal system, extract and inherit the essence of Chinese legal culture, absorb its nutrients, and use them wisely" (Xi 2015).

Excellent traditional Chinese legal culture integrates the Confucian ideals of "*Ren Yi Li Zhi Xin*" (仁義禮智信) (benevolence, righteousness, propriety, wisdom, and trustworthiness); the Daoist principles of harmony between humans and nature; and the Legalist doctrines of strict laws, clear rewards and punishments. These diverse philosophical influences have shaped a distinctive legal philosophy and governance model. Even today, foundational legal principles from the Chinese Legal Family—such as the governance strategy of integrating rites and law, the people-centered thought, the value pursuit of harmony and no litigation, the principle of "*De Zhu Xing Fu*" (德主刑輔) (Virtue as the primary principle and punishment as a secondary means), the concept of equality before the law, and the humanitarian principle of leniency—continue to hold unique value and modern significance. These Chinese legal principles form an essential intellectual and cultural foundation for the Chinese modernization of rule of law. Additionally, China's legal heritage, including classical texts such as *Fa Jing* (《法經》) (the *Canon of Laws*), *Zhen Guan Lü* (《貞觀律》) (*Zhenguan Code*), and *Tang Lü Shu Yi* (《唐律疏議》) (the *Tang Code with*

Commentaries), has laid the legal groundwork for the country's modernization of rule of law.

Throughout the process of advancing the Chinese modernization of rule of law, we have consistently upheld historical confidence in the Chinese Legal Family and its legal civilization. By excavating and transmitting the essence of Chinese legal culture, we continue to revitalize the Chinese Legal Family, promoting its creative transformation, innovative development, and modern adaptation. Compared to the Western modernization of rule of law, the continuation of China's profound legal civilization represents a defining characteristic and unique advantage of the Chinese modernization of rule of law.

The integration of excellent traditional Chinese legal culture with the Chinese modernization of rule of law represents both a cross-temporal cultural dialogue and a profound institutional reform. Legal principles from the Chinese Legal Family, such as upholding the law and strengthening the country through law, codified legal civilization and good governance through good laws, the people as the foundation of the state, complementary roles of morality and law in governance, and the key to governance lying in selecting the right people, have been creatively transformed and innovatively developed through their integration with modern legal ideas. This fusion has given rise to new governance concepts and strategies that are deeply rooted in tradition while embracing modern legal principles. In this process, we witness the convergence and integration of China's ancient legal wisdom with contemporary rule of law ideals, constructing a bridge between history and the future, tradition and innovation. It also demonstrates the unique Chinese path to the modernization of rule of law—one that both respects and revitalizes the essence of ancient legal culture while boldly incorporating and assimilating the advanced ideas of modern legal systems.

8.2.4 The Modernization of Comprehensive Law-Based Governance

In the history of Western legal thought, the modern thinker Immanuel Kant first proposed the concept of "Rechtsstaat" (a state governed by the rule of law). The so-called "Rechtsstaat" means to govern the state by law and form a political state based on the rule of law. Building on the excellent traditional Chinese legal thoughts and systems, the Chinese modernization of rule of law is not merely a "Rechtsstaat" in the Western context, but a comprehensive law-based governance and the building of the rule of law in China in the Chinese context.

Comprehensive law-based governance requires the Communist Party of China, as the leading and governing party, to exercise state power in accordance with the law, practice national governance complied with the Constitution, laws, and Party regulations, take the lead in respecting and upholding the law, operate within the framework of constitutional and legal provisions, and support and ensure that the people's congresses, governments at all levels, the Chinese People's Political Consultative Conference, supervisory organs, judicial organs, and procuratorial organs perform their functions and carry out their work in accordance with the law and their respective charters, thereby forming a strong synergy in governance. Under the leadership of the Party, the whole people manages national and social affairs, as well as economic and cultural undertakings, in accordance with the law, while lawfully exercising their rights to be informed, to participate, to express their views, and to supervise governance. The people also lawfully practice democratic elections, democratic consultation, democratic decision-making, democratic management, and democratic supervision, effectively engaging in the country's political life. Governments at all levels must adhere to law-based administration and strict law enforcement, accelerating the development of a government that is scientifically structured, clearly defined in terms of powers and responsibilities, strict in law enforcement, open and just, intelligent and efficient, clean and honest, and ultimately satisfactory to the people. Judicial authorities at all levels must independently and impartially exercise their judicial and procuratorial powers, thereby establishing a fair, efficient, and authoritative socialist judicial system. Meanwhile, the entire society must respect, learn, observe, apply, and safeguard the law, ensuring that the people exercise their legal rights, fulfill their legal obligations, and assume legal responsibilities in accordance with the law.

The comprehensive law-based governance is a systematic project that requires adherence to a systematic perspective and thinking, integrating the law-based governance and moral governance, integrating law-based governance of the country and rule-based governance of the Party, and balancing domestic and foreign-related rule of law efforts. It necessitates the coordinated advancement of law-based governance, law-based exercise of state power, and law-based administration, as well as the integrated construction of a law-based country, government, and society. In this process, it is essential to correctly handle the relationships between politics and the rule of law, reform and the rule of law, security and development, order and vitality, law-based governance and moral governance, and law-based governance of the country and rule-based governance of the Party.

Ultimately, while the Western modernization of rule of law centers on building a "Rechtsstaat", China not only seeks to establish a law-based country but also a law-based society, economy, and culture. Furthermore, beyond constructing a socialist rule of law country, China aims to promote the rule of law in international relations and contribute to a fairer, more just, equitable, and inclusive global governance system and human societal order. This represents a continuation of Chinese Legal Family in the new era and marks a fundamental strategic distinction between the Chinese modernization of rule of law and the Western model.

8.3 Contributing to the Construction of an Independent Chinese Legal Knowledge System

President Xi Jinping profoundly pointed out, "The developmental level of a country hinges equally on the advancement of natural sciences and the progress of philosophy and social sciences. A country cannot be at the forefront of the world without thriving natural sciences, nor can it attain preeminence in the world without flourishing philosophy and social sciences" (Xi 2016: 2). He further emphasized, "Accelerating the development of a philosophy and social sciences system with Chinese characteristics ultimately comes down to building China's independent knowledge system" (People's Daily 2022).

As a key discipline within philosophy and social sciences, jurisprudence is a profound academic field essential for governance and social well-being. The great revitalization of the Chinese Legal Family in the new era represents a significant step toward building an independent Chinese legal knowledge system and a critical endeavor for advancing socialist rule of law in China. By deeply studying and carrying forward excellent traditional Chinese legal thought and systems, China can better integrate these elements with the practice of socialism with Chinese characteristics, ultimately shaping a legal theoretical system and discourse system that embody distinct Chinese characteristics, style, and ethos.

8.3.1 A Key Initiative for Strengthening Confidence in the Theory, System, and Culture of Socialism with Chinese Characteristics

Building an independent Chinese legal knowledge system represents a fundamental transformation in the field of legal studies. Constructing an independent knowledge system is the foundation for a country to establish confidence in its theory, system, and culture.

By promoting the development of an independent Chinese legal knowledge system—rooted in the great revitalization of the Chinese Legal Family in the new era and benefiting from the practical experience of socialism with Chinese characteristics under the leadership of the CPC—Chinese legal studies will undergo a fundamental shift from merely adopting Western theories to creating China's own legal scholarship and contributing to the global legal academia. It will mark a historic transformation from being a "follower" to a "peer" and ultimately a "leader" in the global legal field. The deep exploration and inheritance of the rich legacy of the Chinese Legal Family combined with the realities of contemporary China will be a groundbreaking development not only in the history of socialist rule of law and Chinese legal studies but also in the global legal academia. The significance of this development is fundamentally reflected in the dialectical relationship between "socialism" and "Chinese characteristics".

"Socialism" is the essential attribute, political orientation, and theoretical foundation of Chinese legal studies. Chinese legal studies must uphold the Marxist stance, viewpoints, and methodology, reflect the essence of socialism, focus on socialist objectives, serve the practical needs of socialist modernization, advance contemporary socialist theories, expand the path for the Chinese modernization of rule of law, and contribute to new forms of human rule of law civilization. "Chinese characteristics", on the other hand, define the fundamental specifications, cultural origins, and scientific nature of Chinese legal studies. Chinese legal studies must be grounded in China's national conditions and current practices, inherit the legacy of Chinese legal civilization, cultivate a legal consciousness rooted in national traditions, and effectively utilize indigenous legal resources. It must also embody the spirit of the times and shape the distinctive qualities of the Chinese nation.

The dialectical unity of "socialism" and "Chinese characteristics" determines the correct path for developing Chinese legal studies. Without "socialism", Chinese legal studies would inevitably lose its proper direction and goals. Without "Chinese characteristics", it would become rigid and dogmatic, failing to contribute meaningfully to the global legal academia.

8.3.2 The Urgent Need to Cultivate High-Quality Rule of Law Talents with Both Integrity and Competence

The 20th National Congress of the CPC proposed the goals of "further improving the socialist rule of law system with Chinese characteristics", "adhering to comprehensive law-based governance and building the rule of law in China", "comprehensively advancing the rule of law across all aspects of the country's work" and "building a modernized socialist country in all respects under the rule of law". These strategic ideas and objectives set higher standards and requirements for the cultivation of rule of law talents.

The key to cultivating high-quality rule of law talents with both integrity and competence lies in educating law students with a legal knowledge system that is independently developed by China, rather than one imported from foreign countries. We must position legal education and promote its reform and development in accordance with the strategic thinking of building a modernized socialist country in all respects and promoting the great rejuvenation of the Chinese nation on the track of the rule of law, in order to cultivate more rule of law talents who are both ethical and proficient. We should educate and mentor students by employing an independent Chinese legal knowledge system that integrates Chinese Rule of Law Philosophy in the new era as its essence, is rooted in the practice of socialist rule of law with Chinese characteristics, promotes excellent traditional Chinese legal culture, and embodies the common values of all humanity. Through imparting knowledge and values, we aim to cultivate generation after generation of steadfast believers, dedicated builders, and resolute defenders of socialist rule of law with Chinese characteristics.

8.3.3 The Inevitable Requirement for Promoting the Chinese Modernization of Rule of Law

There exists no ready-made formula for promoting the modernization of rule of law in China—a developing country with a population of over 1.4 billion, the world's second-largest economy, and a socialist country upholding Chinese characteristics. We cannot simply continue the template of our traditional legal culture, nor can we simply apply the template of foreign modernization of rule of law, let alone find a ready-made "textbook" or invite a wise "teacher".

We can only respond to the "questions posed by China" and "questions of our times" regarding the modernization of rule of law through self-developed theoretical innovations. Our self-initiated and groundbreaking practices must be guided by self-developed and original theories. As President Xi Jinping profoundly stated, "Upholding and developing socialism with Chinese characteristics requires continuous exploration in both practice and theory, where evolving theories guide evolving practices" (Xi 2016: 2).

8.4 Conclusion

As an integral part of Chinese civilization, the Chinese Legal Family has never perished and will never perish. On the contrary, the great revitalization of the Chinese Legal Family should be a landmark achievement of the great rejuvenation of the Chinese nation in the field of the rule of law.

The great revitalization of the Chinese Legal Family in the new era spans three dimensions: history, reality, and future. It integrates the creative transformation and innovative development of excellent traditional Chinese legal culture, highlights the Chinese characteristics of the modernization of rule of law in the integration with modern rule of law concepts, helps to build an independent Chinese legal knowledge system, thereby contributing Chinese wisdom and strength to global governance.

References

Gu, H. 2023. On the Inheritance and Innovation of China's Outstanding Traditional Legal Culture in Xi Jinping's Thought on the Rule of Law—From the Perspective of the 20th CPC National Congress Report on Law-Based Governance. *Journal of Chongqing University (Social Science Edition)*. April 6. Available at https://kns.cnki.net/kcms/detail/50.1023.C.20230405.0956.004.html.

Hu, B., and Dong, X. 2020. From "Being Told by Others" to "Telling Others": On the Overseas Publicity of China's Legal Image in the Nineteenth Century from the Perspective of Orientalism. *Law and Modernization* 6: 91-106.

People's Daily. 2022. Xi Jinping Emphasizes During His Visit to Renmin University of China: Inheriting the Revolutionary Legacy under the Party's Leadership and Rooted in China, and

Pioneering a New Path to Building World-class Universities with Chinese Characteristics (1). April 26.

Xi, J. 2015. Accelerating the Construction of a Socialist Rule of Law Country. *Qiushi* 1.

Xi, J. 2016. *Speech at the Symposium on Philosophy and Social Sciences*. Beijing: People's Publishing House.

Xi, J. 2020. *On Adhering to Comprehensive Law-Based Governance*. Beijing: Central Party Literature Press.

Xi, J. 2022. Implementing the New Development Philosophy in the New Stage of Development Inevitably Requires the Establishment of a New Development Pattern. *Qiushi*. August 31. Available at http://www.qstheory.cn/dukan/qs/2022-08/31/c_1128960034.htm.

Xi, J. 2023. *Selected Readings from the Works of Xi Jinping (Volume I)*. Beijing: People Press.

Part IV
Conclusion

Chapter 9
Chinese Rule of Law Civilization in the New Era

Abstract Today, as the entire nation vigorously advances the "Chinese modernization of rule of law", the concept of the Chinese Legal Family has regained contemporary significance. The Chinese Legal Family in the new era has entered a new phase, wherein the Communist Party of China leads the Chinese people in addressing the strategic context of the great rejuvenation of the Chinese nation and the momentous global changes unseen in a century, and developing through the grand practice of comprehensive law-based governance. The excellent traditional Chinese legal culture is a historical and cultural resource for the construction of the socialist rule of law with Chinese characteristics, while the system of the socialist rule of law with Chinese characteristics represents the new phase of the Chinese Legal Family. Accordingly, the path for the Chinese modernization of rule of law is the only path towards the revitalization of the Chinese rule of law civilization in the new era. The great exploration of the Chinese nation on the path to building the rule of law has never ceased, nor has the development and evolution of the Chinese Legal Family.

9.1 Introduction

The Chinese people take pride in their long-standing institutional and cultural traditions. According to Liang Qichao, the principle of "governing the country by law" proposed by the early Legalist school during the Spring and Autumn period is in essence the Eastern origin of "rule of law" (Liang 1991: 1269). The Chinese Legal Family, which represents the overall achievements of the legal system construction in imperial China, is considered the pinnacle of China's indigenous "rule of law" system, and has been recognized worldwide as a treasure that embodies the progress of human society and institutional civilization.

Today, as the entire nation vigorously advances the "Chinese modernization of rule of law", the concept of the Chinese Legal Family has regained contemporary significance. The Chinese Legal Family in the new era has entered a new phase, wherein the Communist Party of China leads the Chinese people in addressing the

X. Dong and Y. Li, *Chinese Legal Family and Chinese Modernization of Rule of Law*,
https://doi.org/10.1007/978-981-96-7529-6_9

strategic context of the great rejuvenation of the Chinese nation and the momentous global changes unseen in a century, and developing through the grand practice of comprehensive law-based governance. The excellent traditional Chinese legal culture is a historical and cultural resource for the construction of the socialist rule of law with Chinese characteristics, while the system of the socialist rule of law with Chinese characteristics represents the new phase of the Chinese Legal Family. Accordingly, the path for the Chinese modernization of rule of law is the only path towards the revitalization of the Chinese rule of law civilization in the new era. The great exploration of the Chinese nation on the path to building the rule of law has never ceased, nor has the development and evolution of the Chinese Legal Family. The great revitalization of the Chinese Legal Family in the new era is the cultural mission of contemporary legal professionals.

9.2 The Chinese Modernization of Rule of Law Marks a New Phase of the Chinese Legal Family

By the Tang dynasty, the Chinese legal family reached a peak in its development, forming a sustained influence that radiated throughout East Asia. Then by the late Qing dynasty, the development of Chinese rule of law experienced a fierce collision between "tradition" and "modernity". This collision is, of course, just one specific aspect of the broader historical process of "ancient versus modern" changes in China. It is generally believed that the Chinese legal family "disintegrated" at that time, and the modernization process of Chinese rule of law was suddenly initiated under the dominance of external driving forces. This raises a very important question: Does the initiation of the modernization process, accompanied by the "disintegration" of the Chinese Legal Family, mean that the "continuity" of the Chinese rule of law civilization was interrupted? If so, it would imply that China's modernization of rule of law was forcibly driven by external forces, which is clearly untenable.

As one scholar sharply pointed out, "The influence of the Chinese Legal Family gradually waned after the late Qing dynasty" (Xi 2022: 289–290). This statement is extremely precise: it is the influence of the Chinese Legal Family that declined, not the Chinese Legal Family itself. The Chinese Legal Family itself did not "disintegrate" nor "terminate", but rather continued to exist with difficulty and kept its exploration. When speaking of the late Qing dynasty, President Xi Jinping summarized,

> After the Opium War of 1840, China gradually became a semi-colonial and semi-feudal society. At that time, in order to save the nation from peril and achieve national rejuvenation, the Chinese people and countless patriots tirelessly struggled to seek a political system suitable for the national conditions. Before the Xinhai Revolution, movements such as the Taiping Heavenly Kingdom, the Self-Strengthening Movement, the Hundred Days' Reform, the Boxer Rebellion, and the Late Qing reforms all failed. After the Xinhai Revolution, China tried various forms such as constitutional monarchy, imperial restoration, parliamentary system, multi-party system, and presidential system. Various political forces and their representatives emerged, but none found the correct answer. China remained fragmented,

> impoverished, and weak, with foreign powers still rampant, plundering interests, and the Chinese people still living in suffering and humiliation. (Xi 2020: 68)

There is no universally applicable model of the rule of law in the world, nor is there a one-size-fits-all path of the rule of law for all countries. The rule of law model and path suitable for China are not pointed out by others nor copied from others, but can only come from the arduous exploration of the Chinese nation, based on its traditions and actual conditions.

In terms of historical development, "change" is the norm. However, the continuity, consistency, and regularity exhibited by the changes therein are aspects we need to pay attention to. "From the perspective of the ancient-modern continuity of the quality of being 'Chinese', the reason why Chinese history has always remained Chinese is that it maintains its Chinese characteristics while adapting to the circumstances, keeping pace with the times, establishing itself through change, and sustaining its resilience" (Ren 2021: 59). "Constancy" refers to the constant way, which is the cultural accumulation in the historical process that has lasted for thousands of years, the rational condensation of understanding and experience during the long formation and development of the Chinese Legal Family, and the spiritual core that connects tradition with the future. It contains the direction and path for the development of Chinese rule of law. On the other hand, "Change" refers to transformation, which is the generational replacement, renewal, and development of the legal system, legal framework, ideas, and culture during the formation and development of the Chinese Legal Family. The excellent traditional Chinese legal culture contained in the Chinese Legal Family can be integrated with modern legal concepts through creative transformation and innovative development. As a historical and cultural foundation, it has facilitated the new development of the rule of law for the Chinese nation in the new era. The unity of "constancy" and "change" constitutes its quality of being "Chinese" for the development of Chinese rule of law.

Therefore, the process of Chinese modernization of rule of law is unified with the development and evolution of the Chinese Legal Family within the inherent logic of the development of Chinese rule of law. The Chinese modernization of rule of law represents a new phase in the development of the Chinese Legal Family, and a new stage in the Chinese nation's exploration of self-governance.

9.3 The Revitalized Chinese Legal Family Constitutes a Concrete Manifestation of the Chinese Modernization of Rule of Law

"The worldwide onset of modernization began with the rise of European capitalism, while China's modernization started during the late Qing dynasty and early Republic of China. The modernization of rule of law was also awakened in that unique historical wave" (Zhang 2022: 6). The initiation of Chinese modernization of rule of law is not simply the result of external drives but has profound internal roots. The path for the Chinese modernization of rule of law has no model to imitate and no predefined pattern to follow. Instead, it is a new journey for the Chinese nation to explore self-governance, a new achievement of the Chinese civilization of rule of law, and the concrete manifestation of the Chinese modernization of rule of law.

The Chinese modernization of rule of law has offered the Chinese Legal Family, with new issues, new paths, and new contributions. Since modern times, the unprecedented internal and external challenges faced by the Chinese nation are akin to what Li Hongzhang described in his memorial to the throne: "We are faced with a momentous change unseen in more than three thousand years" (Li 2008: 107). But we can find no ready-made answers from the development model of Western countries. "Since modern times, many have attempted to replicate Western models of governance in China, but all have ultimately failed" (Xi 2022: 290). "The great social transformations in contemporary China are not simply continuations of our country's historical and cultural templates, nor are they mere applications of templates envisioned by classical Marxist authors, nor are they reprints of other countries' socialist practices, nor are they replicas of foreign modernization" (People's Daily 2021). Despite facing setbacks and hardships, the Chinese nation's determined pursuit of the rule of law has culminated in a unique path, harmonizing historical legal traditions with contemporary practices, and forging a model tailored to China's specific context. As President Xi Jinping summarized,

> History and reality tell us that only by inheriting the excellent traditional Chinese legal culture, exploring a rule of law path suitable for our own country from the practice of our revolution, construction, and reform, and drawing on the beneficial achievements of foreign legal systems, can we solidify the rule of law foundation in the building of a socialist modernized country in all respects and the great rejuvenation of the Chinese nation. (Xi 2021)

The new path chosen by the Chinese nation in response to new challenges will also provide new solutions and make new contributions to the civilization of rule of law and the path of modernization for all humanity.

9.4 Summary and Prospects

The Chinese Legal Family is profound in its foundation, rich in content, far-reaching in its influence, and significant in its meaning. It is a major achievement of the Chinese nation's exploration of self-governance, a crystallization of the Chinese rule of law wisdom and spirit, and a brilliant pearl in the history of global civilization of rule of law. The splendor and glory of the Chinese Legal Family lie not only in its creation of remarkable achievements that have attracted worldwide attention. The institutional values, thinking methods, and spiritual qualities embodied in the Chinese Legal Family are invaluable intellectual resources for the Chinese modernization of rule of law. Only by striving to find the convergence point between historical legal traditions and contemporary legal practices, and discovering the right direction of rule of law development, can we truly transcend the technical levels of legislation and adjudication, and deeply understand the unique characteristics of the Chinese Legal Family from the perspective of national governance and civilization construction. "As an important part of Chinese civilization, the Chinese Legal Family has never perished, cannot perish, and will not perish" (Wei 2023: 15). Through the inheritance, transformation, and integration of the excellent components of the Chinese Legal Family, the system of socialist rule of law with Chinese characteristics will undoubtedly display a new outlook.

Since modern times, the Chinese nation has undergone arduous exploration on the path of rule of law development and has finally found a suitable path under the leadership of the Communist Party of China. "Specifically, regarding the achievements of our rule of law construction, we can list dozens or even scores of accomplishments. However, they all boil down to the establishment of the path of socialist rule of law with Chinese characteristics" (Xi 2020: 105). "The path of socialist rule of law with Chinese characteristics is a concentrated embodiment of the achievements and experiences of socialist rule of law construction and is the only correct path for building a socialist rule of law country" (Xi 2020: 93). This is the path of rule of law most suitable for China's national conditions, as well as the only correct path to realizing the great rejuvenation of the Chinese nation.

The great rejuvenation of the Chinese nation is inseparable from the revitalization of the Chinese civilization of rule of law, which on the other hand means that in China's development of rule of law, the Chinese Legal Family, with its unique characteristics and global significance, has returned to the center stage of global rule of law development. The Chinese modernization of rule of law is a form of modernization with Chinese characteristics, and marks a new stage in the development of the Chinese Legal Family. This determines that the revitalization of the Chinese rule of law civilization must be based on the practice of socialist rule of law with Chinese characteristics, "to view from the perspective of China and of the times, to base on China's reality and solve China's problems, and to continuously promote the creative transformation and innovative development of excellent traditional Chinese culture" (*People's Daily* 2022). At the same time, the revitalization of the Chinese rule of law civilization also requires the broad absorption and reference to the world's excellent achievements in the rule of law.

Currently, "as the momentous global changes unseen in a century accelerate and the world enters a new period of turbulence and transformation, there is an urgent need to address such issues of the era as 'What is happening to the world?' and 'Where is humanity heading?'" (*People's Daily* 2022). The revitalized Chinese Legal Family, under the leadership of the Communist Party of China, synthesizes the practice of socialist rule of law with Chinese characteristics, the heritage of traditional Chinese legal culture, and the best of global rule of law achievements. This new phase represents a significant achievement in combining Marxist theory on the rule of law with the actual practice of Chinese rule of law, and with the excellent traditional Chinese legal culture. It will help advance the development of Chinese civilization of rule of law, promote the great rejuvenation of the Chinese nation, and provide unique Chinese wisdom for global governance. In this way, the Chinese Legal Family in the new era makes significant original contributions to the civilization of rule of law for all humanities, creating new forms of rule of law civilization.

References

Li, H. 2008. Discussing the Inadvisability of Dismantling Shipbuilding Plans. In *Complete Works of Li Hongzhang, Volume 5*, edited by Gu, T. and Dai, Y. Hefei: Anhui Education Publishing House.

Liang, Q. 1991. On the Development of Chinese Jurisprudence. In *Complete Works of Liang Qichao, Volume 5*. Beijing: Beijing Publishing House.

People's Daily. 2021. Resolution of the Central Committee of the CPC on the Major Achievements and Historical Experience of the Party's Century-Long Struggle (1). November 17.

People's Daily. 2022. Xi Jinping emphasizes during his visit to Renmin University of China: Inheriting the Revolutionary Legacy under the Party's Leadership and Rooted in China, and Pioneering a New Path to Building World-Class Universities with Chinese Characteristics (1). April 26.

Ren, J. 2021. Constancy and Change: Reconstructing the Grand Narrative of Chinese History through Five Major Changes. *Chinese Culture* 2: 37-64.

Wei, Z. 2023. On the Evolutionary Direction of the Chinese Legal Family. *Eastern Jurisprudence* 5: 4–15.

Xi, J. 2020. *On Adhering to Comprehensive Law-Based Governance*. Beijing: Central Party Literature Press.

Xi, J. 2021. Resolutely Follow the Path of Socialist Rule of Law with Chinese Characteristics to Provide Strong Legal Guarantees for the Comprehensive Construction of a Socialist Modernized Country. *Qiushi* 5: 4-15.

Xi, J. 2022. *The Governance of China (Volume IV)*. Beijing: Foreign Language Press.

Zhang, W. 2022. On the New Path of Chinese Modernization of Rule of Law. *Chinese Law*, 1: 5-31.

The manufacturer's authorised representative in the EU is Springer Nature Customer Service Centre GmbH, Europaplatz 3, 69115 Heidelberg, Germany. If you have any concerns regarding our products, please contact ProductSafety@springernature.com

Printed and bound by CPI Group (UK) Ltd, Croydon, CR0 4YY
01/10/2026
02225925-0002